D0841742

# Conscience First,
# Tradition Second

*SUNY Series in Religion, Culture, and Society*

Wade Clark Roof, Editor

# Conscience First, Tradition Second

## A Study of Young American Catholics

*Patrick H. McNamara*

STATE UNIVERSITY OF NEW YORK PRESS

Published by
State University of New York Press, Albany

© 1992 State University of New York

All rights reserved

Printed in the United States of America

No part of this book may be used or reproduced
in any manner whatsoever without written permission
except in the case of brief quotations embodied in
critical articles and reviews.

For information, address State University of New York
Press, State University Plaza, Albany, N.Y., 12246

**Library of Congress Cataloging-in-Publication Data**

McNamara, Patrick H.
    Conscience first, tradition second : a study of young American
Catholics / Patrick H. McNamara.
        p.      cm. — (SUNY series in religion, culture, and society)
    Includes bibliographical references and index.
    ISBN 0-7914-0813-2. — ISBN 0-7914-0814-0 (pbk.)
    1. Catholic high school students—United States—Religious life.
    2. Catholic high school students—United States—Attitudes.
    3. Catholic high school students—United States—Longitudinal
    studies.    4. Christian education of young people—United States-
    —Case studies. 5. Catholic high schools—United States—Case
    studies.    I. Title.    II. Series.
    BX932.M36      1992
    282'.73'0835—dc20                                                90-22768
                                                                      CIP

10   9   8   7   6   5   4   3   2   1

LIBRARY
ALMA COLLEGE
ALMA, MICHIGAN

## *Dedication*

To the graduating seniors of St. Martin's High School from 1977 to 1989 and to their teachers, principals, and assistant principals whose generous cooperation made possible this study. No words can capture my special debt to Primo Contreras whose encouragement, insights, and sense of humor lightened up the many months of writing. A special thanks to my family who deserve their medals for sheer patience.

LIBRARY
ALMA COLLEGE
ALMA, MICHIGAN

# Contents

# List of Figures

# List of Tables

# *Foreword*

Parents and teachers who are likely to read this book are also likely to be personally concerned about the behavior and beliefs of youngsters in the current generation of high school students. They want these students to retain the best of the Catholic traditions, even while participating in the postVatican II revitalization of church and society. The task of education has always been to hand down the values of the culture, and the task of the teacher (and parent) has always been to demonstrate how these values should be interpreted by the individual conscience.

We like to think that moral values are perennially applicable, that the Ten Commandments of our grandparents' days remain the Ten Commandments of our grandchildren. What is at question in this survey study is not the eternal validity of Christian morality, but the motivation for accepting it intellectually and conforming to it behaviorally. The assumption of this discourse is that American Catholics had been accustomed to practice a kind of rote religion and morality, adhering to the traditional patterns because they have always been there. Since the Second Vatican Council, however, the further assumption has been that motivation comes from conscious rather than from long habit.

Motivation is very difficult to measure, and we have to accept the answers of people who tell us why they behave the way they do. Ready explanations of delinquency, for example, are provided by school administrators and teachers. First, parents are not exerting the positive influence expected of them in the home environment. Second is "peer pressure," because apparently all the other kids are guilty of dissolute behavior. The third excuse seems to be biological, or glandular. It is just "natural" for a teenager to loosen up on personal morality. In other words, you can't blame the school for failing to accomplish what the school brochure says it will do.

One of the perennial frustrations of educators in the Catholic secondary school system is the realization that the religious beliefs and practices of their students decline from the freshman year to the senior year. As they move toward graduation they attend Mass less frequently and pray less often. Their attitudes become more liberal on divorce and birth control. On the other hand, most students make measurable progress in the learning of language and history, of mathematics and science. With competent instructors of religion they do increase their knowledge of the Church and its teachings concerning ethics and morality. There is no question that the content of religion courses, and the teaching methods of instructors, have been modernized in the better Catholic high schools like St. Martin's.

When we look at the postgraduate behavior of St. Martin's students we see a reflection of what has been happening in the larger Catholic population. From 1977 to 1989, weekly Mass attendance went down, from 80 to 50 percent. The minority who are still willing to say that premarital sex is immoral declined from 29 to 20 percent. It is safe to say that all the measurable norms of devotional Catholicism have shown a downward curve since the Second Vatican Council. Traditional teachings about premarital and extramarital sex relations, birth control, and abortion are being more and more questioned. The changes found in the general Catholic population over the decades are showing up now in surveys of Catholic high school students.

There can be no question that the American Catholic population is now quite different from its progenitors of a generation or two ago. Obviously, the educational institution that interlocks with the other Catholic institutions has also changed along with them. Furthermore, these Catholic people and their institutions have continued to be part of the total American culture. To what extent can we compare and identify organized Catholicism in ways that differ markedly from the secular culture of this society? The general notion among Catholics and other commentators is that Catholics have become "Americanized." They have "made it" now in the American system, successful in business and the professions and in higher education and politics.

In one respect, the Catholic educational enterprise is willing to "go it alone." The whole American network of Catholic secondary schools—diocesan, parochial, and private—has been maintained by the voluntary support of the Catholic laity, with no subsidies from public monies. The casual observer may suggest that this educational system has "peaked out" and has passed its prime. In the thirteen years from 1977 to 1989 covered by the statistics on St. Martin's high school, there has been a national loss of 15 percent in the number of Catholic secondary schools and a 26 percent decline in the number of students attending these schools. Several "causes" may help to explain this shrinkage: *financial* in the high cost of facilities that replace vowed religious personnel; *demographic* in the smaller cohorts of teenage Catholics: *credible* in the weaker confidence that parents have in such religious education.

Conservative clergy and laity decry the "decline" of Catholic secondary schooling, not in terms of demography or expense or credibility, but in the uneasy feeling that the schools have failed to live up to their advertised goals. It is the persistent assumption that the Catholic high school is intended to provide excellent moral and spiritual guidance. The religious aim of the school is to make good Catholics of the students, citizens with a strong sense of social justice and personal morality. Serious research of the "outcomes" of these high schools, however, has found that many of the graduates are more secular than religious.

This generalization allows for exceptions, but it would be an error to extrapolate the findings from a successful school like St. Martin's to all secondary Catholic schools, nor does the author attempt to do so. Indeed, the personal accounts by the graduates reveal large differences among the students themselves, and sharp contrast with their parents. The theology teachers were said to be "liberal," which seems to have left a wide latitude in the students' interpretation of perennial Catholic values. The concept of "selective" Catholicism allows for a range, from the nuclear to the marginal Catholic, verging even on the dormant.

One need not claim the gift of prophecy to say that today's youth presage the future of American Catholicism. We have enough data to foretell that these young people are likely to replicate the flexible categories of believers who now call themselves Catholics. The schools are producing both "devotional" and "selective" Catholics who will identify themselves somewhere along the spectrum of traditionalists at one end and progressives at the other.

It is not always easy to avoid the stereotypes that are readily attributed to religious believers, because conservative, even fundamentalist, Catholics are willing to identify themselves. They are likely to promote pilgrimages to Medjugorje, subscribe to *The Wanderer,* praise the tenets of Opus Dei, and insist that every parish should schedule at least one Latin Mass every Sunday. They are far right, both in their politics and in their economic practices. For the most part, they are either unaffected by the Council, or think it was a mistake.

Out of the same Catholic system of secondary education there emerge Catholics who laud liberation, lean to the left in politics, and promote programs to relieve the homeless. They complain about the authoritarianism of the current Pontiff but participate in *Pax Christi,* read the *Commonweal,* and support the claims of Catholic feminism. One may wonder how these opposing types of Catholics can come out of the same Catholic school system or whether the bases for their ideology should be sought elsewhere.

JOSEPH H. FICHTER, S.J.
LOYOLA UNIVERSITY OF THE SOUTH

# *Preface*

I have yet to meet anyone of my generation—I was born in 1929—who has not given thought to the decades of change we have seen, felt, and taken part in. They resonate differently for each of us but whose list could omit the civil rights struggle, the war in Vietnam, relaxation of sexual mores, widespread use of drugs, shifts in the ways women and men relate to each other, and skepticism of authority? These have touched our personal and family lives, often in ways that render the changes anything but cultural abstractions. Now, I am wary of conjuring up a past of received stabilities and reliable standards, as though our parents and grandparents' generations experienced some kind of static universe. After all, the one grandfather I knew growing up unflatteringly contrasted the 1940s and 1950s with the good old days of an Iowa farm life: everyone knew everyone else and a man was as good as his word—and he found few good words for much of what he saw in mid-twentieth-century California. But the changes my generation knows still seem to me more corrosive of past traditions than anything our parents or grandparents experienced or could imagine.

I belive this sense of weakened traditions is most keenly felt in pondering the lives of our children. What can and what ought we to pass on to them? Few of our forebears found themselves wondering what to do, if anything, about a son or daughter living with a girlfriend or boyfriend, or whether Doug or Jennifer is into drugs, or what to say to the college sophomore who asks why work so hard when a nuclear war will erase the future anyway. I am not suggesting that no parents succeed in transmitting clear standards and firm securities to their children; obviously many do. But I do know that the loss or severe crippling of a taken-for-granted tradition that promised reliable principles for our children makes that task harder. This is no small matter. As a parent and as a college instructor, I encounter young people struggling to find sensible guidelines and questioning whether adults and adult institutions of politics, education, religion, and work are capable of providing any. As a sociologist, I think about the broader cultural and institutional changes that have contributed to the erosion of tradition; I consider the ways in which young people react to the situation I am describing and what they put in place of what seems to them irrelevant or outmoded.

I am not alone in thinking about these things, of course. Parents and counselors of adolescents today are aware of young people's reluctance to look for moral and spiritual guidance in a church they think is rigid in its doctrines, untrusting of people, and outmoded in its moral teaching. Furthermore, many parents of today's adolescents are themselves from a baby-boom generation that called into question many traditional values. What should they pass on to their children? Psychologist Ann Caron captures their dilemma:

> Can the current parents of young adolescents help them to figure out why some behavior is morally wrong? . . . I suggested that young parents want to give their kids attention and guidance but they are at a loss about how to do it. I know this from listening to mothers in my workshops. These parents of our current teenagers experienced both the days of revolution and the days of self-indulgence and now don't know what to pass on to their children. . . . The stress on individualism that this generation emphasized after their flirtation with communal living has diminished the ability of these parents to provide strong leadership within their families. ("Mom, Dad, the Kids are Listening." *The National Catholic Reporter*. September 1, 1989, pp. 1 and 18)

To the extent this portrait is accurate, the role of the value-oriented religious school certainly assumes importance. Can a Catholic school successfully impart values and norms in the face of this moral and spiritual uncertainty? My answer in this book is yes it can, but it takes a thoughtful and creative set of teachers, actively engaged with their students, to make it happen. In addition, the high school seniors and their teachers featured here do not interact in some timeless vacuum. Both come from a tradition whose impact cannot be ignored or wished away. Remembering what this tradition was like, how and why it shifted so rapidly, and where it has arrived today in an age impatient of history is essential, I believe, to appreciating both the possibilities and limitations of what the schools can do. This is the promise of the pages that follow.

\*　　\*　　\*　　\*

I wish to thank the following reviewers for their most helpful comments on an earlier draft: David Bromley, James Davidson, Phillip Hammond, Michael Hornsby-Smith, Gary LaFree, Peter McLaren, and Clark Roof. I appreciate, too, the enlightening statistical advice of the "blackboard and chalk whizzes" at Brigham Young University during a memorable visit in 1987: my host, Darwin Thomas, with Larry Young, Tim Heaton, Marie Cornwall, Bruce Chadwick, and Jim Duke. Finally, no author could ask for a more professional editorial staff. To Rosalie Robertson, Marilyn Semerad, Bernadette LaManna at SUNY, and David Prout, thanks for all the help and encouragement.

# Introduction

I write this book out of concern for a changing tradition, one whose authority has diminished in recent years for many of those belonging to it. Whether applauded or deplored, this erosion of tradition is a process sociology's founders knew well. Let me elaborate briefly. Karl Marx, Max Weber, and Émile Durkheim lived and wrote in times of dissolving traditions and the emergence of new pathways in politics, social relationships, science, art, and religion. The Enlightenment a century before had decried the tyranny of autocratic rule and the superstitions of revealed religion, confidently proclaiming that human societies could be made better if rearranged and ordered according to laws that human reason could discover.

Sociology's classic authors found themselves in a later intellectual climate that reacted to the apparent failure of the French Revolution to fulfill its promise of a rational, well-ordered, and enduring society. The Romantic movement that so affected Saint-Simon and Comte, and later Durkheim, brought back into focus concepts discarded by Enlightenment rationalism: authority, status, and ritual — in a word, tradition itself. For Karl Marx in neighboring Germany, of course, these notions were the stuff of ruling class ideology perpetuating a false consciousness of societal unity that aided the elites in retaining control of the means of production. But French social thinkers, closer to the turmoil generated by the French Revolution and the nineteenth-century aftermath of successive liberal and reactionary regimes, sought out sources of an organic social order that would ensure stability. Yet these men assumed that any new social order could not be traditional in substance or content, for they were in accord with the basic Enlightenment critique of traditional religion: the medieval Catholic belief and worship system that supported monarchy and privileged classes of priests and nobles stood in the way of progress. Furthermore, the industrial revolution made possible by science had ushered in, for Saint-Simon and Comte, the final scientific stage of human evolution that rendered previous theological and metaphysical stages obsolete. Durkheim adopted this perspective, but acknowledged that the loss of traditional religion had left a vacuum of moral authority with its consequences of anomie and loss of firm boundaries for human aspirations and behavior. His solution was to relocate the source of moral authority within industrial society's emerging division of labor. Professional and occupational groupings should be encouraged, for within

1

these associations people could find the social and moral support to counteract anomie on a personal level and social anarchy on the collective level. Traditions would develop from these new associations to replace those formerly upheld by church and guild.

The views of Max Weber on tradition are more complex and have become classic themes of social theory. Tradition constitutes one of three "pure types of legitimate domination" based on "immemorial traditions and the legitimacy of those exercising authority under them."[1] Weber discusses several subtypes of traditional authority, but all are rooted in the time-honored status of the ruling figure to whom obedience is owed personally. Traditional authority is foreign to any formally established regulations. It is challenged historically by charismatic personages. The latter's authority, as the charismatic figure passes from the scene and his or her successors try to institutionalize the legacy left them, is itself subject to routinization and becomes, in time, a tradition. The third type, so characteristic of modern societies, is rational-legal authority, which becomes possible "with the triumph of juristic rationalism."[2] Submission to legal authority is based on "an impersonal bond to the generally defined and functional 'duty of office'."[3] Its authority, then, is one of rules "purposely thought out, enacted, and announced with formal correctness."[4] As modern states came into being, rational-legal authority took bureaucratic form. Though bureaucracies existed in ancient civilizations, the modern era is distinguished by the universal spread of bureaucratization, which for Weber, became an expression of the modern drive toward rationalization, that is, the progressive subjection of belief systems and activities to systematic planning designed to achieve a definite and predictable outcome.

Tradition, in Weber's view, would not survive this latter tendency in modern society toward rational bureaucratic management. Traditions worldwide would diminish, even disappear, under the onslaught of modernization. More specifically still, the rise of science and administrative rationality left little room for religious beliefs derivative from tradition. In the words of Edward Shils, Weber

> thought that rationalization had made such progress in the West that the world was being emptied not only of magic but of the meaning which great religions offer; he thought that this rationalization entailed the expulsion from the world of the power of divinity and of whatever powers are located beyond what is apprehensible by the senses."[5]

The Roman Catholic tradition I write about in this book has survived these forces of modernization and bureaucratic rationalization, but this does not mean it is wholly comfortable in contemporary America. Its strong corporate and communal core is sharply at odds with the individualism of

Americans interviewed in a celebrated book, *Habits of the Heart: Individualism and Commitment in American Life* (1985). In that book Robert Bellah and colleagues discern in the upwardly mobile Americans they interviewed between 1979 and 1980 a "culture of separation" set against "communities of memory" both "biblical" and "republican" that "tell us about the nature of the world, about the nature of society, and about who we are as a people."[6] These memories or traditions are carried mainly by families and churches, by cultural associations, and more tenuously, by our nation's schools and universities. The culture of separation is represented by Sheila Larson, a young nurse interviewed who described her personal faith as "Sheilaism." Affirming her belief in God, she added, "I can't remember the last time I went to church. My faith has carried me a long way. Its Sheilaism. Just my own little voice."[7] Bellah and colleagues discovered that their mobile middle-class respondents typically resorted to the language of self-reliant individuals. The language of tradition and commitment, the words indicating shared rhythms of corporate and communal life were by no means dead, but Americans utilized them and their meanings only secondarily. The language of the achieving individual occurred to them first.

This shift from the corporate to the individual resonates well with the reflections of sociologist Phillip Hammond on identity. He discusses two notions of identity: the first refers to the relatively unchanging aspects of individual personality, "the slowly changing core . . . that shows up in all of a person's encounters, irrespective of differing role partners."[8] This kind of identity is often involuntary, i.e., given in such basic institutions as the family, the ethnic group, and traditional churches. Allegiances arising from this familiar kind of identity are strong and largely taken for granted. We are back to a traditional world that bestows a solid "ontological security" on its members (see discussion in Chapter 1). A second kind of identity speaks to "transient and changeable" selves as we shift social locations and partners. Occupational and educational roles provide examples of transient identities that people routinely experience. Hammond rightly points out that in modern societies, some institutional spheres—he cites religion and ethnic group membership as examples—may be shifting "from being important in the first sense, to being important only in the second sense."[9] Such a shift would entail a change in meaning of this sphere (religion or ethnic membership) for individuals undergoing the transition. Moreover, the loss of the first kind of identity makes possible or opens up the way for the second. I can voluntarily re-enter an ethnic identity only when the "overlapping primary ties" that make the first identity so central and powerful have been broken.[10] Thus, as chapter 1 will point out, Catholic identity of the "collective-expressive" (first) kind was salient precisely because Catholic institutions exerted a powerful pull on most American Catholics—parish, schools, and clubs (Catholic Boy and Girl Scouts, for example), all working together to make

Catholic identity a taken-for-granted phenomenon. But when these institutional ties are attenuated, when few memberships overlap any more, "individual-expressive" religious and ethnic identities come into play. People feel free to choose. In Hammond's trenchant summary, "The very forces that free them from mandatory involvement are forces that encourage their voluntary involvement."[11]

I write in this book of young Catholics Americans who, like those interviewed in *Habits of the Heart*, are carriers of both tradition and change. The 1987 visit of Pope John Paul II set off a flurry of media commentary that echoed recent national surveys showing a tendency, particularly among younger Catholics, to select from their tradition only what they wish to believe and to practice. They have taken on, in other words, an individual-expressive identity reminiscent of their Protestant neighbors: voluntary adherence to tradition is the norm. Indeed, this shift among Catholics is predictable from their newly arrived middle- and upper-middle-class status. Why should they not be affected by the culture of separation and the prevalent language of individualism? After all, no tradition persists unchanged indefinitely. Is American Catholicism an exception? Edward Shils is again helpful: "At every point in time in the course of its growth, a tradition of belief or rules of conduct is an amalgam of persistent elements, increments, and innovations which have become a part of it."[12]

Identifying these persistent elements along with increments and innovations in post Vatican II Roman Catholicism has preoccupied many authors, including Andrew Greeley,[13] Richard McBrien,[14] and most recently, John Seidler and Katherine Meyer.[15] almost without exception, however, they write on what social scientists call the macro level: global Catholicism, European Catholics, and the American Church, respectively. I have little quarrel with these approaches; indeed, they are indispensable for an adequate understanding of the changes within tradition that have beset the American Catholic Church over the past two decades.

What we lack, however, are studies on a micro level, that is, approaches focusing on the everyday lives, views, reflections, and behaviors of Catholics living through this period of shifting tradition. We lack firsthand accounts in their own words, with all the nuances of affirmations, denials, doubts, ponderings, and feelings. That is what this study is about.

The heart of this book is a multiyear case study of a single Catholic high school in a southwestern city. Through close friendship with the school's senior theology teacher, I was permitted to administer a survey to virtually every senior in the graduating classes of 1977 through 1989. Over 2000 young men and women answered both fixed-choice and open-ended questions. I also contacted a second group of 54 graduates of the classes of 1978 and 1979 who agreed to be resurveyed at a later date to assess changes over time in their beliefs and practices. I recontacted them in 1987, mailing to them their original questionnaires. I asked them to note changes in each item and to supply current biographical information. I also included an open-ended question I considered central to gauging their experiences of religious change and sense of religious identity eight or nine years after graduation (see Chapter five). Finally, I conducted personal interviews with members of the school's theology department to assess their views on changing traditions and their strategies of imparting religious teaching in the face of the religious individualism manifested by their students.

In sum, this book attempts to demonstrate, through the opinions and reflections of the Catholic high school seniors, what elements of tradition do persist in their lives, what has been set aside, and how this selective process is expressed in and affected by classroom dialogues with their teachers.

I believe the case-study approach yields several advantages. First, national survey research does not readily lend itself to open-ended questions. Thus, many issues are necessarily left unexplored. National data, invaluable as they are—and I rely heavily on them in interpreting my own survey findings—fail to tell us why respondents choose one answer over another, how they have arrived at the answer(s) they select, and what emotions or feelings lie behind the answers they set down. As I pointed out in my 1984 presidential address to members of the Association for the Sociology of Religion,

> The distinctive ethos of a group of people consists of much more than belief systems or worldviews. People make sense of their world both emotionally, feeling-wise, as well as cognitively, in terms of clusters of symbols we call meaning systems and these should be our units of analysis, complex as they may be. And to grasp how people fashion and shape their lives through, by, and around these symbols we must ask them to tell us, helping them open personal doors as best we can. By definition this involves ethnographic research.[16]

Now my research is not ethnographic, except for the interviews I conducted. But open-ended questions and invited comments on fixed-choice items in a survey can be a kind of halfway house between participant observation, field research, and/or interviews on the one hand and standard survey research on the other. In any case, I believe the data presented and analyzed will yield a greater understanding of the change processes experienced by younger Catholics than is available through national survey research alone.

Another advantage of the case-study approach, in this instance, focusing on students from one high school, involves a trade-off in reliability. On the one hand, I cannot generalize easily to all young American Catholics:

these young men and women do not represent all American Catholics ages 18 to 28. But a case study does pinpoint a population or subpopulation of particular theoretical and/or policy interest and explores this population in ways unavailable to national surveys. Let me explain. Sociologist Dean Hoge's "assimilation hypothesis" of behavioral and attitude change among younger Catholics assumes that "change will be faster among educated young adults than others in the community, since they assimilate faster," and that "change should be faster in locations in the society away from the immigrant ports of entry . . . The main locus of innovation and experimentation in Catholicism today is in the Midwest and West." Finally, this hypothesis suggests that assimilation itself will "speed up value and attitude shifts more in middle-class urban areas and least in ethnic enclaves or isolated rural areas."[17]

The school I selected contains a student body drawn heavily from middle- and upper-middle class Catholics in a Southwestern city. In chapter 3, I set down the socioeconomic backgrounds of these students, who represent precisely the stratum of Catholics Hoge describes in the above passage. They come from relatively affluent and highly educated parents; the school's location is in the Southwest but several hundred miles removed from a Mexican port of entry; the school itself is situated literally between the two major shopping centers, each a block from the school, of the state's largest city. These students are in every sense upwardly mobile—young urban Catholics from families who have attained comfortable status in American society. By comparing them with young Catholics nationally, one can perform a kind of test of the assimilation hypothesis.

Because of its location in the Southwest, this school contains a sizable (almost one-third) subgroup of Hispanic students. The research literature on Catholic Hispanics suggests that they retain, as a group, strong loyalties to Catholic identity. Do they? If so, how do they compare, in terms of various measures of Catholicity to their "Anglo" counterparts? Few are the studies of *young* Catholic Hispanics, and we have almost *no* studies of upwardly mobile young Hispanics. This focused study can shed light on this substratum of young Catholics.

Finally, in a broader context, this study is about people. I am not writing about "American Catholicism" or analyzing "changes in the Catholic Church." Others have written on these topics, and I acknowledge my indebtedness to them in the pages that follow. I am writing about young Catholics from relatively well-off families whose high educational and occupational aspirations stamp them as the stratum from which substantial financial and personal support for the institutional Catholic Church would be expected to come. But will it?

Asking this question returns us to the central issue of identity: what sense of being Catholic emerges from the self-portraits of young people in this book? As later chapters portray them, this sense is not rooted in the tradition historian Jay Dolan terms "devotional Catholicism" that character-ized the "immigrant generation" of Catholics, parents or grandparents of these young women and men.[18] These seniors' distinctive sense of who they are cannot be captured in the fixed-choice format of survey research or the quick responses to telephone interviews. Open-ended questions and face-to-face interviews that invite respondents to reflect on aspects of their lives, are much more likely to tap this important dimension of consciousness, as will be evident in the responses of the seniors and their teachers in the pages to follow.

But why is this sense of identity "a central notion?" Two interrelated reasons occur to me. First, some writers focusing on current American Catholicism, such as journalist John Deedy, deal mainly (though not entirely) with the Catholic Church as an institution.[49] Deedy discusses the new active role of Catholic bishops, problems faced by Catholic priests, controversies surrounding the role of women in the Church, the Church's relationship to minority groups of recent arrival, and issues of freedom and authority symbolized in the recent cases of Archbishop Hunthausen and theologian Charles Curran. But surely the vitality of the Church as an institution depends principally on how much individual Catholics care about it, whether they see any reasons to take their Church seriously enough to sustain an interest in the various problems cited by Deedy. An attenuated sense of identity as Catholics is sure to weaken support for the agendas, issues, and reforms Deedy portrays—issues that indeed preoccupy American Catholic leaders today.

Second, the issue of identity is important both in terms of social theory and in generating fruitful policy discussion of lay Catholics' involvement in their Church. Individual-expressive identity may well underline an *American* identity at the expense of a *Catholic* one, as Catholics achieve social and economic security in this country.

Historian Dolan understands the transition to socioeconomic security very well, though he does not phrase it in theoretical terms. In the concluding chapter to his *The American Catholic Experience*, Dolan notes that Catholics no longer struggle with the issue of what it means to be an American. That time has passed; Catholics now enjoy a firm taken-for-granted sense that they have arrived occupationally, educationally, on a par with other Americans. *That* identity receives reinforcement on all sides in both intimate and more formal settings. But not so with what it means to be *Catholic*. That is another matter.

Just when they had solved one half of the riddle—what it meant to be American—the other half became unraveled. For the first time in modern history, Catholics no longer agreed on an answer to the

question of what it meant to be Catholic. Vatican II was largely
responsible for forcing Catholics to rethink the meaning of Catholicism
in the modern world.[20]

Part of this "rethinking" involves the whole question of authority. As
identities shift to Hammond's individual-expressive mode, skepticism toward
church authority increases. Individual decision-making is less likely to be
based on authoritative pronouncements. I review in this book the historical
factors leading to the loosening of authority within American Catholicism
(chapter 2). But my main interest is how younger Catholics, given this
attenuation of authority and their sense of "little difference" between
themselves and other Americans their ages, *see themselves* as Catholic,
particularly when they are asked in an open-ended question to contrast their
own sense of "being Catholic" with that of their parents. Are their Catholic
identities as distinctive as their parents'?

I think it important to raise these questions for, should younger
generations of Catholics possess mainly individual-expressive bonds to their
Church, how will this affect their relationships to Catholic parishes, schools,
and other voluntary organizations, including their willingness to sustain them
financially? Furthermore, to take a specific issue I address in this book, if
Church leaders, aware of the voluntary character of current Catholic identity,
embark on a policy of asking Catholics to take a critical or "prophetic" look
at an American economy that has been good to them as the latest upwardly
mobile group in American society, what response can they expect? If
younger Catholics, in particular, assume a Catholic identity in Hammond's
second sense—a voluntarily, situationally salient "I" that feels free to
engage, or to disregard—can Church leadership expect widespread attention
(much less adherence) to messages that cut against the grain of the culturally
validated, the taken-for-granted comfort of middle- and upper-middle class
lifestyles and an economy beneficent to many families in the 1980s?

\*    \*    \*    \*

I have divided this book into two parts: Part I addresses these
questions: how to portray the "baseline" American Catholic tradition set
aside—at least in part—by the young Catholics described in Part II? What
legacy was left to them following the Second Vatican Council and the
changes it set off in this tradition? What kinds of theory best interpret these
changes? If a younger generation now carries convictions of individual
autonomy, of each person charting his or her own course with religious
tradition just one guidepost among many offered by the culture, this defines
a sensibility differing profoundly from the world of devotional Catholicism.
There, its enveloping securities and sense of a universe set in place become

threads in a tapestry woven by others, worn but still vibrant and distinctive in color and texture. If these threads (or some of them) have become unraveled, how did this happen?

Part II portrays the young women and men, along with their teachers, of Martin's High School. It invites them to speak for themselves. We will hear their personal versions of selective Catholicism and their responses to a Church leadership asking their involvement in solving global social and economic problems. It will be obvious that they see themselves, as Catholics, much differently than their parents and grandparents.

## Chapter Outline

*Chapter 1:* Catholic writers evoke the world once known by the forbearers of St. Martin's seniors. A once secure Catholic universe has given way to another less clear and certain to these young people. Seldom has this contrast been written about, yet it forms a gateway to comprehending the religious consciousness of the younger, post Vatican II generation. I complement this portrait with studies by social scientists in the years immediately following World War II, for these writers—Joseph Fichter, Will Herberg, Gerhard Lenski, and William Halsey—chronicled changes of a different sort affecting American Catholics. Assimilation into the ranks of middle-class Americans was in full swing. But Catholic religious consciousness had yet to experience the impact of the Second Vatican Council and is best captured by historian Jay Dolan's concept of devotional Catholicism with its "four pillars": authority, sense of sin, ritual, and openness to the miraculous. Chapter One concludes with a sketch of the theoretical concepts and perspectives I shall use throughout the book. I borrow from the dynamic nonfunctionalist framework of sociologist Anthony Giddens to make sense of the creative reactions and adaptations of the young people and their teachers as they confront a "Catholic world" at odds with their parents'.

*Chapter 2*: I review the impact of the Second Vatican Council upon belief and worship patterns of American Catholics, utilizing theoretical concepts of social change and deviance. Adopting this strategy affords an understanding of how devotional Catholicism gave way to the selective Catholicism, or theological and moral individualism, among younger cohorts of American Catholics. I review the extensive surveys of Father Andrew Greeley and colleagues that document the emergence of selective Catholicism. I utilize recent research by Gallup and Castelli and by D'Antonio and colleagues that profiles American Catholics in the late 1980s. I pay some attention to survey findings of Catholics' less intense regard, when compared to their Protestant neighbors, for religion's importance in life. I close by outlining the American bishops' recent development of social teaching that, in effect, "prophetically" challenges a laity "comfortable" in

American culture by raising questions about nuclear war policy and about economic justice in American life. This chapter sets the stage for the case study of high school seniors: how do they respond both to traditional doctrinal-moral teaching and to the newer social initiatives of the bishops?

*Chapter 3:* American Catholic high schools, though suffering severe attrition since the mid-1960s, continue to educate over half a million young Catholics today. Due to sharply rising costs, schools located in areas serving predominantly middle- and upper-middle class Catholics continue to thrive, while those in inner-city locations struggle to keep open. The present case study represents the more "thriving" high school, educating young Catholics from predominantly business or professional families. I analyze survey results of seniors over a thirteen-year period (1977 to 1989), representing over 2000 respondents. I discuss the seniors' selective Catholicism, or primacy placed on personal conscience. I assess their receptivity to teaching regarding personal morality as well as broader sociomoral issues, utilizing demographic and attitudinal controls not found in previous studies of Catholic high school students.

*Chapter 4:* Seniors' viewpoints are formed to a considerable extent in interaction with their theology teachers, who are responsible for seniors' socialization into the teachings of the Catholic Church. Interviews with the teachers reveal their understanding of the "primacy of personal conscience" characterizing their students. I show how teachers have responded to this primacy by creating paradigms of gradation of Catholic teaching from solemnly defined doctrines to those of lesser weight, with the attendant risk of contributing to the very selective Catholicism they find problematic among the students. Seniors' responses show they appreciate the nonauthoritarian teaching approaches of their instructors, which, in turn, dispose many seniors to take seriously viewpoints they might otherwise find unacceptable. I indicate how these results find interpretation within Giddens's analysis of change processes occurring inside social systems as actors contribute varying understandings and discover accommodations and compromises that are "livable with."

*Chapter 5:* I analyze findings from the resurvey of a sample of senior "volunteers" from the graduating classes of 1978 and 1979. These 54 graduates agreed to be recontacted at a later date so that I could assess changes in their attitudes and values over the years. I contacted them in the spring of 1987, eight or nine years after graduation. While consideration attrition is evident in their religious practice, they are, for the most part, orthodox on moral issues (excepting sexual morality) and "liberal" on social issues. I also develop a typology from their answers to an open-ended question asking them to compare themselves with their parents on the meaning of "being a Catholic." Generational differences in sense of identity emerge from their responses.

In the *Conclusion*, I comment on the value of Giddens and other authors in interpreting the historical and contemporary changes affecting Roman Catholics. I discuss the shifting identities of young Catholics today and what bearing these shifts may have upon Catholic responsiveness to both older and more recent themes of Catholic teaching and practice.

# PART I

# 1 From Ghetto to Suburbs: The Decline of Devotional Catholicism

> History is the structuration of events
> in time and space through the
> continual interplay of agency and
> structure, the interconnection of the
> mundane nature of day-to-day life
> with institutional forms stretching over
> immense spans of time and space.[1]

In *The Company of Women,* novelist Mary Gordon introduces Father Cyprian, whose strong personality and convictions made him a kind of spiritual center for the five women forming the book's central characters. His retreats, his Masses, his spiritual advice flowed from a man sure of himself and his universe, convinced that while "Protestants had nature . . . Catholics have the word of God."[2] He knew each of the women almost better than they knew themselves, recognizing distinctive strengths and weaknesses. His firm guidance was reassuring and sustaining.

> All those years he had not failed her. He had kept her on the path. He had reminded her of the love of God which was beyond her understanding. He told her God had chosen her for a special trial and that she might be, without knowing it, a channel of extraordinary graces.[3]

Father Cyprian visualized "the whole sewer of the modern world, the great dark stink of it . . . only this remnant was left to him: women whose lives had gone bad in one way or another, who came to him in times of crisis. He was there, wearing the great distinction of his priesthood like a cloak cut big to hide the body."[4]

The novel succeeds grandly in portraying the certain world inhabited by American Catholics of the pre–Vatican II era, a world not only of respected priestly authority but one in which to be Catholic meant being other, set apart, and expected to conduct one's life differently from one's Protestant and Jewish neighbors. Indeed, Mary Gordon stands in a long tradition of American Catholic writers who knew this world intimately and portrayed it unforgettably. James T. Farrell immortalized Studs Lonigan, who despite his youthful waywardness, never found himself outside the reach of his parish church and what it represented:

Studs muttered the words of the Act of Contrition over and over again. He wished last night undone, like he had almost never wished for anything. The bell, the sudden feeling of change in everyone at Mass, the knowledge that he was to witness the greatest of mysteries, the changing of bread and water into the body and blood of Jesus Christ, the memories of other masses, other Christmas days, catechism lessons, all converged in him. He was lonesome, and contrite, and adoring. He felt himself a part of the great and powerful Catholic Church, built upon the rock of Peter, a member, however unworthy, and he vowed to be more worthy.[5]

In *Memoirs of a Catholic Girlhood* Mary McCarthy evoked this atmosphere of certainty by recalling her teenage challenge to church teaching. Confronting a Jesuit retreat master whom the nun-teachers had summoned to talk to her, McCarthy felt the force of his closing admonitions:

The priest shook his head sorrowfully. "I cannot tell you my child . . . I cannot open eyes that blindly refuse to see. Can inert matter give birth to spirit? Did inert matter give you your conscience?" His hollow voice reverberated as if he were addressing a whole dockful of secular philosophers, arraigned in a corner of the room. "Oh, my child," he concluded, rising, "give up reading that atheistic filth. Pray to God for faith and make a good confession." He left the room swiftly, his cassock swelling behind him."[6]

Perceptive outsiders felt this same sense of envelopment in a distinctive world. Theologian Harvey Cox remembers boyhood brushes with the Catholic Church in his Pennsylvania home town:

In the Catholic Church thirteen-year-old boys must absorb a lot about the mystery of the Mass, the power of gesture and sacrament, the objective *otherness* of the holy, by serving as altar boys and acolytes. The Catholic religious sensibility includes, from very early on, the feeling of being *part* of a vast, ancient, and relatively fixed reality. Like the grace that was promised to me in those sermons, the church itself, for Catholics, was not something you had to do anything about. It just *was,* and all you had to do was accept it. I could sense that even in my Catholic cousins and playmates.[7] (emphasis in original).

No wonder that Catholic writers of the post–Vatican II era sounded nostalgic even as they voiced approval of Council changes in Church worship and authority. John Cogley in *Catholic America* referred to the "ghetto culture" of American Catholicism in the 1940s and 1950s, a culture "often at odds with powerful currents of American life."[8] Catholics were content to inhabit "the one true church" and to regard Protestant neighbors, some the closest of friends, as "invincibly ignorant" and "victims of an erroneous system of theological thought."[9] Priests were generally forbidden to participate in anything smacking of "ecumenical" discussions with clergy of other denominations. For Cogley, the pre–Vatican II Catholicism he knew was a closed world in many ways. But it was also a richly evocative universe perhaps nowhere better captured in retrospect than by Gary Wills in *Bare Ruined Choirs,* his 1972 reflection on how it used to be:

> The habits of childhood are tenacious, and Catholicism was first experienced by us as a vast set of intermeshed childhood habits— prayers offered, heads ducked in unison, crossing, chants, christenings, grace at meals, beads, altar, incense, candles; nuns in the classroom alternately too sweet and too severe, priests garbed black on the street and brilliant at the altar; churches lit and darkened, clothed and stripped, to the rhythm of liturgical recurrences; the crib in winter, purple Februaries, and lilies in spring; confession as intimidation and comfort (comfort, if nothing else, that the intimidation was survived), communion as revery and discomfort; faith as a creed, and the creed as catechism, Latin responses, salvation by rote, all things going to a rhythm, memorized, old things always returning, eternal in that sense, no matter how transitory."[10]

Not that all writers took things so seriously, of course. Novelist John R. Powers could look back upon the Catholic universe of pre–Vatican II days and find a lot to laugh about. In 1973 he treated his readers to a delightful remembrance of his eight years in a Chicago parochial elementary school complete with references to a Catholic life revolving around the parish church. *The Last Catholic in America* adds a funny touch to the motif seen above: a world of clearly defined and, for the most part, unquestioned obligations and expectations:

> Lent was a time of "give ups." At the beginning of the forty days, fathers would give up smoking and swearing, mothers would give up nagging, and children would give up sweets. A few more weeks and we'd all give up. . . . About the only people who kind of looked forward to Lent were the fat Catholics. Throughout the Lenten period, everyone between the ages of twenty-one and fifty-nine was allowed to

eat meat only once a day. Snacks between meals were also prohibited. In addition, two of the three daily meals could not equal in size the main daily meal. Of course, if you ate like a madman at your main meal, you could still manage, within the rules, to gorge yourself two more times a day and still remain in good standing with the Church. [11]

While the novelists and essayists sketched a Catholicism of clear and clean definition, the social scientists focused a different lens upon American Catholics. Second- and third-generation Catholics in the 1950s seemed well on their way out of the "ghetto" and on up the ladder of socioeconomic mobility. Post–World War II America bestowed its prosperity on the sons and daughters of immigrants; many a Catholic veteran was the first in his family to attend college under the GI Bill. "Assimilation" was a key theme, raising the question of whether Catholics were remaining distinctive from their non-Catholic neighbors. Not all social scientists answered this question in the same way.

### Catholic Assimilation: An Earlier View from Social Science

#### Joseph Fichter

The first systematic portraits of American Catholics emerged in the 1950s. Father Joseph Fichter, Jesuit priest-sociologist, published *Southern Parish* in 1951, based on field work he did from 1949 to 1950. Fichter wrote a subsequent reflection on this study in 1954, *Social Relations in the Urban Parish*. He then shifted to Chicago for another field study, publishing *Parochial School* in 1958. Fichter's books, taken together, give us a detailed picture and analysis of everyday Catholicism as mirrored in the lives of lay people, priests, and nuns of early post–World War II America. Catholics remained distinctive, Fichter would conclude, but the assimilative pull of postwar America seemed irresistible.

In his 1954 reflections on *Southern Parish,* Fichter stated a theme echoed by other observers of the decade: American Catholics were feeling the pull of the larger American society. They were surging into middle-class status, helped in no little way by the opportunities offered World War II veterans in education, housing, and employment. The great upward movement of the sons and daughters of the immigrant generation was under full steam. Fichter pointed out, for example, that in the Louisiana parish he studied, parishioners' Catholicism was not the principal factor either in attitudes or in social relationships. Thus, in recreational pursuits like bowling, bridge, poker, and athletic teams, personal associations easily crossed parochial and "Catholic" lines, having little or nothing to do with religious affiliation. Nor were Catholics immune to the ethos of the business world. "The Catholic's proximate conformity to the role demands and vocational values of the business institution may imply his growing distance from the ideals of the religious institution. His economic role may have little integration with his familial role and even less with his religious role."[12] Fichter pointed especially to "marginal Catholics," those barely performing their religious duties who, he felt, were "being pulled toward the center of one or more other institutions."[13] The modern urban parish, then, no longer resembled the ethnic-centered solidaristic community one thinks of in early twentieth-century Chicago of Philadelphia or Boston of New York. Other institutions play a larger role:

> This seems especially true in the so-called leisure time activities of urban Catholics. Radio and television, the picture magazines, commercial movies, sports and dances, are now enjoyed outside the context of the parish. They are also generally outside (or at least indifferent to) the system of typical religious values.[14]

In other words, the weight and pull of "secular" American institutions involved pressures to change, change which, as Fichter saw it, moved "away from religious patterns toward secular patterns of behavior."[15] Catholics were strongly affected by these trends; resistance was difficult. Voluntary organizations were becoming increasingly prominent in American life, and Catholics were feeling this attraction and finding themselves through them in increasingly close contact with Americans of other outlooks and beliefs.[16]

In *Parochial School,* Fichter pursued this theme of assimilation in tension with American values. Demographic data signaled major trends under way. By mid-decade, increasing proportions of Chicago Catholics were native-born. Less than 5 percent of the school children's parents were foreign-born; almost three-quarters of families had parents of different ethnic backgrounds as intermarriage took place. Finally, a large majority of the children themselves were already fourth-generation Americans. The ethnic cultures—German, Irish, Italian, Polish, and Bohemian—that had contributed to a distinctive Catholic subculture were eroding. St Luke's appeared to Fichter as "the Catholic parish of the future," which meant

> the acceptance of American cultural values and behavior patterns, the continued urbanization of life, the tendency to intermarry, the pursuit of American economic and political goals, are removing these people further and further from their immigrant ethnic background. The urban parish has reached a point of assimilation at which the dominant cultural influence is the American urban influence.[17]

Fichter was among the first, then, to notice the rapid postwar upward mobility of Catholics and to assess its significance for maintaining a distinctive Catholic subculture. Evidence of change seemed to lie all about him. Compared to males of the same age group in Chicago (ages 30 to 44), the fathers of St. Luke's students had more schooling, and more went to college. Few had only an elementary school education. Fichter even surveyed public school youngsters using the same items with which he queried the parochial school students, discovering that both sets of children "share . . . in the same cultural milieu the popular choices of movie stars and of television programs" and nominate "exactly the same great historical persons in the same order as did the public school children."[18] St. Luke's indeed inculcated distinctive Catholic attitudes and practices and was notably successful in doing so. But Fichter could still conclude that "St. Luke's is clearly part of the stream of culture which gets into the molding of the middle-class consciousness, the broad attitudinal basis of the American urban democracy."[19]

### Will Herberg

Perhaps the most widely read sociological portrait of American religious communities in the 1950s was Herberg's *Protestant-Catholic-Jew*. Herberg was forthright: American Catholicism had witnessed a transformation from "a group socially and culturally alien into a thoroughly American religious community."[20] He noted the "revision of Catholic thinking on the problem of church and state and to deny that Catholics would tyrannically curtail religious freedom of others were they to become a majority.[21] America was seen by its Catholic citizens, lay and clerical, as "intrinsically pluralist." An earlier separatism had been forsaken. Irish Catholics had led the church in achieving this change. Bishop Fulton Sheen symbolized, in his large television audience, the arrival of the American Catholic Church as an accepted, even respected, institution. Tensions between Catholics and Protestants continued to crop up from time to time, Herberg acknowledged, but American Catholicism was now part of Herberg's "American Way of Life".[22]

Herberg's basic thesis, of course, was that all three great religious traditions expressed in the book's title had become so domesticated within the larger American culture, so caught up in celebrating "prosperity, success, and advancement," along with peace of mind, that they had lost their prophetic voices. Assimilation with a vengeance seemed to be the chief outcome of post–World War II booming America. Americans—and Herberg did not except Catholics—were becoming church members and attending church in greater numbers than ever before but were simultaneously more secularist in the sense of "the practice of the absence of God in the affairs of life."[23] Both secularism and the religious revival of the 1950s were, for

Herberg, generated out of the same social conditions making the American way of life seem natural and overwhelming attractive. Both developments appeared to assure an American of "the essential rightness of everything American, his nation, his culture, and himself."[24]

### Gerhard Lenski

Lenski begins his analysis of the 1958 Detroit Area Study survey, which compared samples of Protestant and Catholic adults, by noting an assertion of Herberg: modern urban living creates in people a need for communal relationships. Urban dwellers find compensation for the impersonality of city life, a feature stressed by classical sociologists like Toennies and Durkheim, in relationships broader than the nuclear family but narrower in scope than the larger society around them. Ethnic and religious subcommunities are examples of groups providing this sense of community belonging.[25]

But Lenski's *The Religious Factor* continues with a broader thesis. Drawing on the legacy of Max Weber's *The Protestant Ethnic and the Spirit of Capitalism,* Lenski asks whether, given Herberg's thesis that Americans were turning in greater numbers to one of the three major faiths, these allegiances resulted in differing economic and political orientations? Lenski's answer is yes. Catholics and Protestants were different in important ways. Urban residence had *not* melted down different orientations within some common broth of impersonality and anonymity. Both working-class and middle-class Catholics, Lenski discovered, were more "glued" into their communities than their Protestant counterparts. This communal orientation meant that Catholics interviewed were more likely to believe that family connections were of greater importance than striving for success, were less likely to be self-employed, less apt to believe in intellectual independence, and tended to have larger families. The upshot of these findings: being Catholic tended to *hinder* upward mobility; more precisely, strong involvement in a religious subcommunity whether Catholic or Protestant dampened prospects for upward mobility, and Catholics were much more likely than Protestants to be so involved, even when one controlled for social class membership.

In his concluding chapter, Lenski reflected that since the Catholic urban birth rate appeared to be higher than that of Protestants, the future might well be characterized by such trends as declining importance attached to intellectual independence, a shifting of interest from work group to kinship groups, a slowing of the rate of material progress and perhaps even of scientific advance, restrictive attitudes concerning the right of free speech, restraints on Sunday business and divorce and perhaps even birth control, and declining sanctions on gambling and drinking.[26]

In other words, Lenski called into serious question the assimilationist themes implicit in the works of Fichter and Herberg. Detroit Catholics did *not* appear to Lenski to be rapidly blending into some great American way of life. Lenski referred to data showing increasing intermarriage across ethnic lines in the Catholic community (such as the Irish marrying Poles) and believed that the religious subcommunity was gradually replacing the ethnic one as a basic unit "in the system of status groups in American society."[27] And those religious subcommunities looked like they were here to stay. In fact, Lenski continued, American society might well, as the 1960s began, see "heightened tensions between socio-religious groups."[28] Could America possibly be heading toward a "compartmentalized society" like Holland and Lebanon, in which "virtually all the major institutional systems are obliged to take account of socio-religious distinctions" and "political parties, families, sports teams, and even business establishments are generally identified with one or another of the major groups"?[29] Lenski drew back from the praise usually heaped upon the ideal of a "pluralistic society."[30] Suppose pluralism led to increasing loyalty to one's own subcommunity at the expense of a sense of responsibility for "outsiders" and even for the nation as a whole?

But Lenski's findings and interpretations did not go unchallenged. Priest-sociologist Andrew Greeley, drawing upon a national sample of 1961 college graduates, found that Catholics were as likely as Protestants to plan on attending graduate school, to choose an academic career, to major in the natural sciences, and to plan a life of research. Nor was there any evidence of anti-intellectualism or anti-achievement economically among Catholics. Lenski, suggested Greeley, in having no data on ethnic subdivisions within the Detroit community he surveyed, may have been characterizing mainly later-arrival Catholic immigrant groups such as Poles and Italians. A national sample of graduate students cited by Greeley indicated that descendants of earlier-arrival Catholic groups, i.e., British, Irish, and Germans, were more college-oriented and had a higher estimate of their own abilities when they were younger than the graduate students from ethnic groups arriving later.[31]

In his concluding comments, Greeley ponders a theme he himself would elaborate greatly over the next two decades. A major change seemed to be taking place among American Catholics, "a change which has accompanied the emergence of American Catholics as the social, political, and economic equals of their fellow Americans."[32]

## A Historian's Interpretation

The social historian's task is to deepen our understanding of major turning points in the trajectories of social institutions. Recall that the social scientists just reviewed above focused their lenses on the changing socioeconomic status of post–World War II Catholics, asking if assimilating Catholics were beginning to resemble their fellow Americans. Notre Dame historian Jay Dolan's recent book, *The American Catholic Experience*, turns instead to what kept Catholics *distinctive*. He distills for us the major characteristics of the Catholicism described above as a prelude to the post–Vatican II changes he later analyzes. The late nineteenth century saw a worldwide spiritual revival within Roman Catholicism, Dolan tells us, best captured in the phrase "devotional Catholicism." Its four characteristics—authority, sin, ritual, and openness to the miraculous—together "had a major influence in shaping the Catholic worldwide."[33]

*Authority:* Laity and clergy spelled two categories of persons with an unmistakable subordinate relationship of people to priesthood. The local parish priest was this authority's closest and most visible symbol. Through him, Catholics learned the Commandments, the Laws of the Church, and regulations regarding membership. He reminded parishioners of times of fast and abstinence, holy days of obligation, and the importance of regular Mass attendance and sacramental reception, especially of Confession and Holy Communion. In turn, the very centrality of Mass and sacraments, dispensed only by priests, enhanced clerical authority. "Raised in such a culture of authority, Catholics were taught to be docile and submissive."[34]

*Sin:* Catholics scarcely had a monopoly on the concept of sin, shared, of course, by other churches, but resembled Puritans in being thoroughly inculcated with a sense of transgression. It was eased only by the ritual of going to Confession (as Studs Lonigan could testify). Prayer manuals plus devotions such as the Sacred Heart and the Immaculate Conception only reinforced how sinful people were and how sin must be expiated. Parish missions, vividly recalled by many older Catholics today, played a key role in reinforcing the sense of sinfulness, with emphasis on sins of impurity and of drunkenness. Strength to combat these temptations was present in the Mass and sacraments and devotion to the saints, particularly to the Blessed Virgin Mary, symbol of purity and freedom from all sin. Mercy and forgiveness followed and allayed guilt. Dolan is on the mark in observing that "the dominance of sin in the Catholic culture meant that guilt was a very important influence in shaping the minds of people."[35]

*Ritual:* In all their detailed prescriptions and recommendations, as an earlier quotation from Gary Wills suggests, rituals fostered two notable qualities. First, an *individualism* in which personal salvation was the highest goal for the Catholic man and woman, boy and girl, and the Gospel one heard preached from the pulpit carried themes of individual salvation from sin and bondage. Little of social responsibility and corporate evil was present in this culture of an individual before a stern God. Second, the devotions promoted by ritual prescriptions were also "riddled with emotionalism and sentimentalism, qualities identified as feminine," though these characteristics were perhaps more pronounced in late nineteenth- and early twentieth-century Catholicism, in which women were the predominant Mass attenders and "clients" of the Church's devotional life.[36]

*Openness to the miraculous:* No one growing up in pre–Vatican II Catholicism escaped exposure to stories of miracles at Lourdes and Fatima. Accounts of supernaturally accomplished cures and healings were a part of the culture. Travellers "knew" that St. Christopher had rescued them from a near accident or that St. Anthony was behind the unexpected finding of a lost ring or wallet or purse. Scapulars and relics in one's possession were especially powerful, particularly if invoked with confident prayer.[37]

In sum, devotional Catholicism bestowed on Catholics a set of beliefs and practices that formed a distinctive worldview and a set of moral boundaries serving to reinforce a sense of cohesion and differentness. Yet, as Fichter's work underlines, Catholics were beginning, by the middle of this century, to move into the American middle class, believing and asserting that they were solidly part of the American mainstream.

Complementing Dolan's portrait of devotional Catholicism is William H. Halsey's analysis of American Catholic intellectual history from 1920 to 1940. The philosophy of St. Thomas Aquinas became standard fare in Catholic colleges and universities, a situation lasting well into the mid-1960s, as those of us attending them at the time vividly recall. Halsey notes a stance prevalent among American intellectuals during the interwar years: disillusion with any prospects of rational world order. World War I and the gradual rearmament of western countries in the 1920s and 1930s prompted thinkers like Walter Lippman to bemoan the lack of conviction that mankind could find "security and serenity in the universe."[38] Thomism, on the contrary, bestowed on those Catholics exposed to it, a sense of certitude and rectitude, of "right thinking." Even if *others* despaired of the power of reason, Catholics possessed a system of thought that validated it.

> Thomism in the hands of American Catholics did not probe reality but charted it. It paved secure avenues for Catholics to confront the challenges of life . . . it delivered Catholics from the burden of carrying the weight of the universe on their shoulders. It was extremely adaptable to the American desire to get confidently on with life.[39]

Of central importance, Halsey insists, was that Thomism enabled the increasing number of Catholic college-educated laity to reaffirm faith in the "promises of America." Catholics were "sensitive to the charge of being un-American." Armed with a philosophical system emphasizing human ability to discover basic truths, "unearthed through human reason and demonstrated by logic and common sense," Catholics could begin an upward climb toward being comfortable with American culture, optimistic about the country and their place in it, even if many American intellectuals apparently could not.[40] This "innocent optimism," as Halsey terms it, would last, as we shall see, well into the mid-1950s. It formed an important element in the assimilation of American Catholics. Graduates of a Catholic college in the two decades following World War II could easily assume that faith and patriotism were mutually reinforcing.

\*   \*   \*   \*

I have drawn from novelists, social scientists, and historians in this chapter to evoke a very powerful and formative tradition familiar to many Catholics. I do so, however, not to summon up nostalgic recollections or bemoan the loss of earlier clarities and securities. Many Catholics, including those of my generation, resonate with John Cogley's view that "ghetto Catholicism" was all too smug, simple, and self-satisfied in conferring a sense that we were blessed with "the true faith," however understandable this smugness may have been. Besides, Catholics of all ages surveyed since 1970 say they like the changes they have seen—Mass in English, altar facing the congregation, more relaxed and easygoing relationships with bishops, priests, sisters, and brothers; faith as personal quest rather than as delivered certitudes, a church readier to identify with the poor and oppressed.

But this is not the whole story. I suspect the assimilative pull of American culture—a trend only intensifying over the last two decades—has continued the effect first postulated by Fichter and Herberg, that is, a diminished sense of being different or distinctive *because* one is Catholic. Is it the case that being a Catholic *makes less difference* both for oneself and in the eyes of others, than it did in times evoked by the writers I have cited? I do not imply that such a change (to the extent it is true) is either good or bad. I am not sure. But I do think this "Catholic sensibility" is very seldom measured or captured in national survey research purporting to tell us how Catholics have changed, and yet it is this diffusely felt shift that strikes Catholics whose memories span the pre– to post–Vatican II decades, at those moments when generational differences surface—a conversation with a daughter or son, a teacher-student exchange, past-present comparisons at a class reunion.

I think there are ways of exploring this shift in sensibility among Catholics, but this exploration must take into account three other major and related transformations receiving recent and extensive commentary, which I see as being joined in a fateful relationship that will characterize American Catholicism for decades to come: (1) theological individualism or "selective Catholicism" (discussed in the following chapter), (2) a diminished Catholic sensibility or sense of distinctiveness, (3) the recent (mid-1980s) initiatives of the American Catholic bishops to invite—and challenge—American Catholics to reflect upon and apply their faith to significant social and economic problems of American society and to be critical at times of American governmental policies. I refer, of course, to the pastoral letters on war and peace (1983) and on the economy (1986), both the focus of wide media publicity and commentary from Catholics and non-Catholics alike, much of it controversial. I could not agree more with Archbishop Rembert Weakland, chair of the American Bishops' Committee on Catholic Social Teaching and the U.S. Economy, when he writes,

> The Church in the United States is passing through a new and critical phase with regard to two aspects of its life: (1) how its clergy—and especially its bishops—will relate as teachers to its highly trained laity, and (2) how the Church as a whole will enter into the debate in American society on political, social and economic issues. These two questions are intimately related.[41]

I ask whether this "highly trained" and upwardly mobile laity, affected by theological individualism and by a diminished Catholic sensibility, will prove resistant to the American bishops' new initiatives—a resistance perhaps impervious to the impact of Catholic schooling. This question will receive attention in the case study featured in chapters 4 and 5.

As a sociologist, however, I think it important to move beyond descriptions of events and trends toward a broader framework that makes sense out of complex changes. Let me sketch briefly the theoretical perspectives I shall use for interpretation.

## A Theoretical Focus

This book deals, in part, with the question of how people negotiate their way through, and sometimes around, the constraints of social institutions. I am less interested, as I have stated, in using up pages to discuss broad institutional change within Roman Catholicism. Others have done that very capably. What *does* interest me is how people find a secure world in tradition, why it is important to them, and how they and their children react and try to make new sense of their lives as that tradition shifts. Instead of viewing these change dynamics under the familiar canopies of moderniza- tion, rationalism, individualism, and similar abstractions, I borrow in the following pages from the "structuration" perspective of British theorist Anthony Giddens. I think his approach is helpful in three principal respects.[42]

First, like any social scientist, Giddens is respectful of the "givenness" of social structure in our lives. But he is wary of the conventional functionalist approach that sees structure as really "prior" to human subjects or actors, as though our families, schools, churches, businesses, and voluntary organizations are "out there first" to be "entered into" by people. In viewing these structures as given *and* constraining and the human actors shaped by them (as indeed we are), functional approaches neglect the creative capacities of human actors in social systems, actors whose reflexive understanding on what Giddens calls "the level of practical consciousness" makes us anything but "puppets" of social structures and institutions. For we human beings are active, knowledgeable agents who, through our day-to-day activities *reproduce* the structural features of social systems. Such features—the four characteristics of devotional Catholicism, for example— exist only insofar as they are chronically reproduced in time and space by their participants. These structures, in turn, "act back" upon participants and influence them, but would not exist at all or *continue* in existence but for the knowledgeable participation of system actors who have a very practical understanding of "how things work" and are thus capable of "projecting" the system forward in time and space.

As we "actors" monitor the flow of daily social activity with the everyday understanding we have of how things work, our actions continually produce consequences we did not intend. Here is a major source of social change. As knowledgeable as we may be about the social structures we "inhabit," our comprehension of the actions we take is bounded or limited. History plus everyday experience testify to the ways in which our actions have unforeseen and unintended consequences. Functionalism regards such consequences as important, but not as principal engines of social change. Robert Merton's essay on manifest and latent (unintended) consequences identifies them as clarifying apparently "irrational" patterns (a rain dance may not produce rain but does reinforce group solidarity), and enabling social scientists to set aside "naive moral judgments" for sounder sociological analysis. Thus, political machines do afford needed services to immigrant groups who might otherwise not receive them, "corrupt" as these machines may appear from a moral or legal standpoint. Sociological understanding is thereby improved and researchers' attention directed to "fruitful fields of inquiry."[43] Structuration theory, on the other hand, gives front billing to unintended consequences as constantly recurring sources of change: a pope summons a worldwide ecumenical council and formally states its mandate. Yet its results several years later were clearly unforeseen and unintended. Ensuing consequences then return to form new conditions of further activity. The importance of a particular "strip" of action or decision-making depends on the strategic placement of an actor in a social system. A pope making a decision will have a greater impact, in all probability, than a lay person in an American parish.

Structuration theory also takes into account time-space contexts of social interaction, since these settings are influential in the sustaining of particular frameworks of meaning. For example, American Catholicism's principal time-space context is that of being located and operative in an upwardly mobile immigrant-descended population. This contexuality is an element essential to any analysis of change involving American Catholics and American Catholicism as an institution.

Second, tradition and changes that affect tradition are explicitly analyzed within structuration theory. Participants or actors "reproduce" a traditional social system *not* by actively attempting to control and alter the circumstances of its existence: devotional Catholicism confronted believers as something divinely sanctioned, a legacy handed down from age to age beyond the normal processes of change. It was to be accepted, not questioned. Active human intervention for change is a characteristic of post-traditional or modern societies in which social actors are *consciously aware* of how the system works and how they may effect changes in it, making use of knowledge bestowed by social science and historical understanding. The Second Vatican Council, as we shall see, departed from previous church councils in not embracing defense of tradition as its mandate but instead attempted to "update" church teachings and practices in a world changing rapidly and which itself contained developments and trends worthy of praise—a stance departing from a long-standing tendency to condemn the world. By contrast, social actors in *traditional* societies reproduce social structure by habitually entering into the routinized practices, feelings, and thoughts that tradition prescribes. Tradition thus becomes, in Giddens's phrase, both *medium* and *outcome* of their activities. The medium is the fourfold world of devotional Catholicism that constitutes the environment in which the actors go about their lives and act out their socially prescribed roles. This environment is a powerful conditioner of their behavior and viewpoints. The outcome is how they express this "devotional world" in their everyday lives, both in the entire culture (or in this case, subculture) and the structures that "carry" it (such as rituals, schools, and customs) are maintained and pushed forward, so to speak, in time and space. *Time,* in Giddens's framework is "reversible" in traditional contexts; that is, the same events (religious holidays, for example) recur at predictable intervals, helping to create a sense of a universe stable and dependable in its yearly renewal. Whether one decides to continue living in or by this tradition is quite another question, as Mary McCarthy's *Memoirs* suggests. But accepted or rejected, this universe looks and feels fixed and permanently in place to its members. It can be relied on as a secure place to which a Studs Lonigan can return for reassurance and inspiration.

Psychologically, as Giddens indicates, this kind of world, because it *is* routinized, provides a sense of what he calls "ontological security," which is precisely what Dolan and others define as a key feature of devotional Catholicism. The anxiety of believers in a culture often hostile to them (some would say American society remained so until the election to the presidency of John F. Kennedy in 1960) is allayed by the subculture of devotional (or traditional) Catholicism. The *context* of system reproduction, or as Giddens phrases it, "the contexualities of interaction," involves "time-space boundaries" symbolically marked. The very sacramentalism of devotional Catholicism created a rich symbolic environment whose contents served as behavioral guideposts of Catholics and endowed them with a sense of differentness vis-à-vis fellow Americans who were not Catholic.

Context also involves, as Giddens says in acknowledging his indebtedness to Erving Goffman, actors "in co-presence," using body, gestures, facial expressions, language, and other kinds of face-to-face communications. Social actors are knowledgeable about the systems in which they act out their social identities and use their knowledge to influence and control, if possible, the flow of interaction. In devotional Catholicism, one can point, for example, to the co-presence of laity and clergy, or laity and religious order members (e.g., teaching nuns). Catholic priests, sisters, and brothers rarely experienced any questioning of their authority in the climate of devotional Catholicism, for they alone were the legitimate performers or enactors of the defining practices characterizing Catholicism. This entire sphere of interaction served to confirm or "reproduce" the lines of authority and power.

Giddens's perspective can now be reapplied. Devotional Catholicism constituted a firm and long-standing tradition. It simultaneously reinforced and reproduced Catholics' sense of distinctiveness *and* strengthened and renewed their sense of "second-classness" within the larger Protestant culture. In any case, the panoply of symbols referred to set them apart, a conclusion historians are unanimous in affirming and which finds reinforcement in the contemporary sociology of emotions and ritual expression.

Third, change in tradition, set in motion by the Second Vatican Council (1962 to 1965), is a major theme of this book. The sheer number of books and articles on the Council would fill a good-sized office library. I see no need to tread again over familiar ground, but I do wish to look at the Council's impact on American Catholicism within the specific context of American Catholic upward mobility. Structuration theory pays a good deal of attention to change in tradition in tradition through two basic concepts: *social change* and *deviance*. Both are helpful in understanding how the Second Vatican Council set off far-reaching changes in the tradition we have seen as devotional Catholicism. These changes form the legacy of contemporary young Catholics.

In summoning the bishops worldwide to the Council in 1962, Pope John XXIII proclaimed that the Church was out of date. The Council was to be an important step toward making the Church relevant to the world rather than condemning that world, as had been the traditional stance of papacy and church for several centuries. In his explanation of this goal, the pope made the fundamental and, as it turned out, fateful distinction between the *truths* of the Catholic faith and their *modes of expression*. As Jesuit author William McSweeney remarks, no Council bishops and certainly not the pope himself were prepared to admit that "the Church might have erred on matters of doctrinal or moral substance."[44] Yet Pope John also charged the assembled bishops with the task of formulating church teaching in ways that would encourage new relationships with non-Catholic Christians and non-Christians. The solution, which forms a dramatic example of *unforeseen consequences* of social action, was a set of eloquent documents laced with ambiguity in formulation, reflecting and bringing into the open the disputes that hitherto had been kept under wraps in theological journals. The very disagreements of the participants were "incorporated into the Council documents themselves and made manifest in the official teaching which that *magisterium* is believed infallibly to express."[45] Those theologians previously held as suspect now found, or thought they found, their viewpoints legitimized in Council documents. Doctrinal and moral teaching were, in consequence, tinged with relativity, their content "never finally captured in any particular form of expression for all times and for all cultures."[46]

In a word, the social change processes just reviewed had a major unforeseen and unintended result: *deviance and its ultimate consequence, relativity, were set loose within a traditional institution.* Dissenting theologians at the Council were not required either to submit or face the choice of leaving the church if they dissented, as was the case in the First Vatican Council in 1870. A coercive strategy was absent a century later, if only because practically the entire Council proceedings took place under intense media coverage. What emerged was a kind of victory for the newer formulations of doctrine and practice, insofar as more traditional views of the nature of the church, relationships with non-Catholics, and so on were deemed "to be neither correct nor erroneous but simply traditional—one perspective among many equally valid."[47] Thus, it was not wrong to hold to the time-honored view of the Church as a hierarchical organization with clear lines of authority from top to bottom, but one had to allow for the acceptability of other views that Council documents elaborated, e.g., the church defined as the People of God. Preservation of tradition is obvious in "People of God," but it does "flatten out" the more rigid hierarchical concepts of traditional ecclesiology.[48]

Let us stand back for a moment and consider the implications of these changes. Tradition, as Giddens emphasizes, involves, as do all social systems, active monitoring by "constituent actors" of the "reproduction of mutually linked role relationships."[49] But in a traditional context, this monitoring is designed to keep things just as they have always been, and "does not take the form of an active attempt to control or to alter the circumstances of reproduction."[50] Until the Second Vatican Council, these formulations fit precisely the control strategies of the Roman curia, for whom, indeed, tradition represented "the moral command of 'what went before' over the continuity of day-to-day life."[51]

But Vatican II's context was different. "What went before" had to be reexamined, without loss to doctrinal and moral essentials, in order to make the church more "relevant" to the modern world. In fact, McSweeney terms the outcome "the triumph of relevance." First of all, the Council documents themselves were ambiguous in many formulations, reflecting the bishops' desire to make room for differing theological concepts. Varying interpretations were thus possible, and were made by theologians following the Council. In this respect, we return to Giddens's first point concerning change in tradition: literacy or the written document gives rise to the possibility of diverse interpretations, a point doubly true considering the ambiguity of Vatican II documents just referred to. Secondly, a kind of reexamination of tradition had gone on in Europe prior to the Council through such social movements as the priest-worker and the liturgical and ecumenical experiments whose thrust was to loosen the grip of tradition in the name of relevance and promote participation from the rank-and-file laity. Aiding this thrust toward a kind of democratization was loss of one of the most effective means of bureaucratic control, secrecy. Information control was rendered extremely difficult because of the massive media presence at the Council. The press, particularly the recently established lay-owned and operated Catholic periodicals such as the American *National Catholic Reporter,* erased for all practical purposes the frontstage-backstage distinction essential for top-down bureaucratic control. Audience and backstage were now linked together as never before; the center's activities and deliberations became visible to observers on the periphery. Furthermore, the traditional Vatican control agency, the Curia, had been nullified in its attempts to intervene by Pope John's sometimes tacit, sometimes explicit support of more "progressive" theologians, again as an example of a "key actor's" importance in situations in which opposing forces are closely matched in power.

Thus, McSweeney does not hesitate to trumpet the "triumph of relevance" in both dogmatic and ethical or moral theology. In the latter case, the findings of social science were often imported to make an argument. For example, *The New Catechism,* published in 1967 under the auspices of the Dutch bishops, in treating of homosexuality, masturbation, contraception, and living together without marriage often cited psychological and social consequences of these actions as among principal reasons for their immorality. A Commission of cardinals appointed in 1968 to review and modify the *Catechism* took issue with such analyses *but,* rather than condemn what it regarded as erroneous, praised the authors' intentions, indicating only that the authors should have *added* material on the "objective" immorality of these actions.

I find McSweeney's conclusion persuasive: "the legitimation of dissent" was established at the highest authoritative levels, and from now on, dissent would be decidedly more difficult to sanction and control. This "authority to dissent" was a major outcome of the Council and perhaps its most important unintended consequence.[52] For once a plurality of viewpoints or models, e.g., of the nature of the Church, was admitted as legitimate, who and on what authority would draw the boundaries of the permissible?

\*    \*    \*    \*

In any case, few Catholics would have guessed that in the early 1960s their traditional Church would shortly undertake an epochal self-transformation and that they themselves were entering a decade destined to set off great changes affecting their religious beliefs, practices, and sensibilities. If their own lives were on the move toward comfortable affluence in the great American middle class, as Fichter and Herberg suggested, their church also seemed unchanging and solidly rooted in its long traditions and destined to help keep them "different," as Lenski indicated. Like themselves, their church seemed to be flourishing, for devotional Catholicism constituted a tradition that, in Giddens' framework, reproduced the rules and resources bestowing an "ontological security." It delivered a solid social identity and confidence that "the natural and social worlds are as they appear to be."[53] For the growing numbers of college-educated Catholics, Thomism reinforced a sense of bedrock security, of standing on a dependable base in a relativistic world of shifting ideas and morals. And they were as American as any neighbor on the block. What was right and true seemed clear and in place; what was wrong and out of place was equally apparent. Reinforcements abounded to confirm Catholics' plausibility structures: converts in the 1950s were familiar faces; their accounts echoed the theme of "at last" finding a church that had these securities and traceable credentials leading back to Jesus Christ, the founder. A Catholic school system flourished throughout the United States turning out the "knowledge-able agents" or "competent actors" of structuration theory who could, in considerable measure, give an account of what they believed and practiced and why.

How this confident and secure world shifted into the "selective Catholicism" embraced by many of today's younger Catholics is the burden of the next chapter.

# 2

## "According to My Conscience": Young Catholics and the Rise of Selective Catholicism

### Threads Unravel: Vatican II and Humanae Vitae

Just how the Second Vatican Council affected American Catholicism continues to generate lively debate. What seems to me incontestable is the fallout from the 1968 "birth control" encyclical letter of Pope Paul VI. *Humanae Vitae* set off a reaction in the American Catholic Church that simultaneously affected two elements of devotional Catholicism: *authority* and *the sense of sin.*[1] The unanticipated events following this declaration show dramatically how great numbers of American Catholics, in pursuing the American dream of upward social mobility, had shed the "ghetto" distinctiveness noted in the preceding chapter. They were prepared to react like their Protestant and Jewish neighbors, with supreme regard for the individual conscience and a disregard of authority attempting to enforce norms in the name of a sacred tradition. No less than the meaning of "being Catholic" was suddenly and unexpectedly at stake.

As we shall see in succeeding chapters, it is precisely this sense of "being Catholic" that constitutes a problematic legacy for your Catholics today. How did the devotional Catholicism taken for granted by an older generation begin to unravel?

Between 1968 and 1969, Catholic laity were treated to the spectacle of those traditionally representing authority publicly dissenting from a solemnly pronounced papal teaching.[2] Instead of bowing submissively, some clergy and even some bishops seemed, at least tacitly, to be saying, "make your decision according to your own conscience." Furthermore, had not the Vatican Council asserted the right of the individual conscience to be free from outside coercion in its *Declaration of Religious Liberty?* At stake was no less than the authority of the Church itself. In Dolan's trenchant summary,

> The encyclical and the harsh reprisal against dissenting clergy undercut this *Declaration* and created a severe credibility gap for the Church. Catholics were not only disappointed, but disillusioned. For these

reasons, *Humanae Vitae* was a shattering blow to the euphoria that flourished after Vatican II.[3]

The sense of sin seemed to be diminishing as Catholics were exposed to dissent from within the ranks of the clergy themselves. The issue of divorce with remarriage soon joined that of birth control. While the proscription of divorce with remarriage was officially unchanged, bishops and priests were scarcely unaware of the growing numbers of Catholics divorcing and remarrying, or wishing to remarry. Soon ministry to the divorced, with an accompanying attitude of compassion, replaced for many clergy a former attitude of condemnation. Annulments grew. In 1967, the American Church granted 700 annulments; by 1978, the number grew to 25,000. The departure of many priests and nuns from active ministry raised questions about the requirements of celibacy and the value of a life vowed to poverty, chastity, and obedience.[4] Did Catholics sin in practicing birth control, remarrying after divorce, or leaving the priesthood and sisterhood? Could an authority command respect and obedience when, in 1966, it no longer required abstinence from meat on Fridays, whereas before this date, deliberately eating meat on Friday was a mortal sin meriting eternal punishment?

In retrospect, it is hardly surprising that survey research conducted in the 1970s and 1980s demonstrates significant changes in beliefs and practices among American Catholics. Particularly affected were members of the baby-boom generation coming to maturity from the mid-1960s on. Many of them are today the parents of the high school seniors portrayed in the chapters to follow. "Selective Catholicism," or theological individualism, in which the individual considers himself or herself the final arbiter and judge of what is to be believed and practiced, is a stance frequently found among these younger American adults and their children. I summarize below the findings of two decades of survey research that illustrate facets of these important shifts.

### *Young Catholics in the 1970s: The Rise of Theological Individualism*

The massive research of Father Andrew Greeley and colleagues stands as the premier source of information on post–Vatican II American Catholics. As Senior Study Director of the National Opinion Research Center (NORC) affiliated with the University of Chicago, priest-sociologist Andrew Greeley, both as author and co-author with colleagues, has written a series of books, articles and research reports which taken in toto constitute a detailed profile of American Catholic belief, worship, and practice over the last twenty years.

I now summarize briefly the findings I think best illustrate the concept of theological individualism, for it is this shift in religious consciousness that distinctively stamps the young Catholics profiled in the pages that follow.

A good place to start is Greeley's concept of "the Communal Catholic." Survey findings from 1973 and 1974 showed Catholic laypersons distrustful of the Church's teaching authority and unwilling to take it seriously. Yet, insisted Greeley, this lay alienation did not extend to a rejection of their Catholic heritage or identity. Young Catholics skeptical of Church leadership were not switching from Catholicism to other denominations; "communal Catholics" did not forsake Sunday Mass. They would remain Catholic in self-chosen identity yet exhibit a "self-consciously selective style of affiliating with the Catholic tradition."[5] Their social location was a well-educated younger stratum "who find themselves on the fringes of the nation's intellectual and cultural elites, either trying to gain admission or conscious of the barriers that bar admission."[6]

By 1979, Greeley was focusing explicitly on younger Catholics. In *Crisis in the Church,* he returned to "the very serious problem of the Church's almost nonexistent credibility in the area of sexual ethics." Seventy-three percent of Catholics *under* thirty years of age approved of premarital sex among engaged couples; by contrast, only 30 percent of those *over* thirty lent their approval.[7] In fact, a Chicago archdiocesan survey indicated that among those under thirty who reported receiving Holy Communion weekly and praying daily, "approximately two-thirds . . . approved of premarital sex among the engaged and approved of divorce and birth control."[8]

In the 1981 publication of *Young Catholics,* based on a 1979 survey of American and Canadian Catholics under thirty, and authored by Joan Fee and colleagues, findings were in continuity with previous research: 25 percent of those eighteen to twenty-nine years old had left the Church; 35 percent of the entire group (fourteen to thirty years old) attended Mass weekly; three-quarters went to Confession once a year or less. Yet almost half of both current and former Catholics said they felt very or moderately close to God, and approximately a third of each group reported praying daily.[9]

The authors note that by the time young Catholics reach their late twenties, they tend to "drift back" to more regular religious practice. The drift, they suggest, is an aspect of "a more general alienation from all social institutions," while the return is linked with marriage, particularly if the spouse is also Catholic. This return is also associated with "warm religious imagery" and "a sexually fulfilling marriage with such spouses," as well as with Catholic schooling.[10]

In 1985 came *American Catholics Since the Council: An Unauthorized Report.* Four years later Greeley published *Religious Change in America.* Both books summarize previous survey research. By 1975, any decline in church attendance had leveled off. The dropoff between 1969 and 1975 did not signal a young generation of Catholics turned "irreligious" and remaining so throughout their lives. Catholics in their twenties are just like Protestant young men and women—slightly under a third attend church weekly. This percentage jumps into the high forties for both traditions if one adds "at least once a month" attenders. In fact, higher attendance accompanies each successive age grouping. By the time they are in their early forties, over half of Catholics attend every week, or almost so—a figure rising to 67 percent if one includes the "at least once a month" category. In other words, as young Catholics enter their thirties when marriage and the raising of children became responsibilities, their attendance "rebounds" a good deal.[11]

### Catholics in the 1980s

The early 1980s are covered by *The American Catholic People* (1987), a comprehensive view of Catholic beliefs, attitudes, and practices in the United States.[12] In 1987, *The National Catholic Reporter* sponsored a national survey conducted and analyzed by four sociologists, William D'Antonio, James Davidson, Dean Hoge, and Ruth Wallace. Their report, *The American Catholic Laity in a Changing Church,* appeared in the fall of 1989.[13]

I turn first to the three major conclusions of the Gallup-Castelli study.

First, in an overall sense, the authors agree with Greeley's assessment: church attendance has been stable from 1975 through 1985. The so-called decline phenomenon was short-lived. In fact, Catholics are back to religious activities such as confession, saying the rosary, involvement in parish life, and Bible reading. Increases among young Catholics in these devotions parallel those among older Catholics. Catholics *do* expect "liberalizing" changes in their church: ordination of women and married men, permission to practice birth control, remarriage following divorce, and abortion under some circumstances (rape, incest, or a deformed fetus). Trend data supported these expectations: Forty-seven percent of Catholics in 1985 supported ordination for women, as opposed to 29 percent in 1974.[14] American Catholics still show respect for the priesthood and for nuns. The church, however, received low marks from its members on how it treats separated, divorced, and remarried Catholics.[15]

Second, of interest to the present study, Hispanic Catholics, 70 percent of whom are Catholic nationwide, are singled out for analysis. Hispanics surveyed in 1978 by the Gallup Organization would like to see more evidence of Hispanic culture and tradition in church services. This is less the case as the respondents' income and educational levels increase. Three-quarters would like to see more Hispanic priests, but "only 56 percent say they would want a son of theirs to become a priest. This drops to 46 percent among those age eighteen to twenty-four".[16] Fifty-one percent would approve of a daughter becoming a nun. Hispanics are, the authors suggest, more vulnerable to recruitment by non-Catholic churches due to "weak institutional ties to Catholicism," e.g., 10 percent of those surveyed reported doing some kind of work currently for their church (though an additional 41 percent said they would be willing to do so if asked.[17]

Third, young Catholics are *not* leaving the church for good. Gallup and Castelli agree with Greeley that lower rates of attendance are most likely life-cycle effects. College-educated Catholics are no less likely to be involved in the Church; three-fifths of them rate the Church as "excellent" or "good" at meeting their needs.[18]

The D'Antonio, Davidson, Hoge, and Wallace study indicates no turnaround from previous trends in the late 1980s. Younger Catholics (eighteen to twenty-nine years old) as contrasted with those age thirty and older, are less likely to say the Church is an important part of their lives, to attend Mass weekly, and to read the Bible on a regular basis; they donate less money to the Church.[19] On moral issues of sex and marriage (sexual relations outside marriage, homosexual behavior, remarrying without annulment, and practicing birth control), young Catholics were joined by those ages thirty to fifty-five (in contrast with those over fifty-five) in believing that "final moral authority" should lie "with the individual or with a collaboration of church leaders and individuals."[20] This is perhaps the first indication from survey research suggesting that the parents of many of today's teenage Catholics are no less "liberal" in some issues relating to Church authority than are their offspring. However, for all ages, frequent Mass attendance notably increases willingness to accept Church authority.

While the authors found that Catholic laity wish to participate in joint decision-making with church leaders ("working toward a model of Church as voluntary association"), they also discovered that

> never did more than one-third of the laity acknowledge that the ultimate source of moral authority (who should decide what is morally right or wrong) should rest with the hierarchy alone. Contemporary Catholics see themselves as the proper sources of moral authority, with or without the teaching of church leaders as an aid to guide them. Rejection of Vatican decrees is greatest among the young and better educated.[21]

### Catholics as "Less Intensely Religious"

While the preceding portraits carry no overwhelming message of mass defection from the Catholic Church, some findings from the Gallup-Castelli study seem relatively negative and deserve further reflection. The two authors point to "a greater erosion of outward concern about religion among Catholics than among Protestants."[22] This erosion they label "the intensity factor." It shows up in responses where Catholics find religion *less* important than Protestants; whereas Catholics were *more* pious than Protestants in the 1950s, they are less so today.

On a ten-point scale, for example, Catholics are less likely than Protestants to give high priority to helping those in need. Slightly less than half (49 percent) of Catholics give this moral ideal a nine or ten rating, while 64 percent of mainline Protestants and 74 percent of evangelicals do so. Catholics and Protestants do not differ significantly on political self-description (left, right, or center). But using the same scale, Catholics are more liberal than Protestants "concerning values toward sex, morality, family life, and religion." Just 19 percent of Protestants placed themselves in liberal categories in these areas, while 29 percent of Catholics did so.[23]

Surveys also show Catholics to be tolerant as a group in attitudes toward nonbelievers, homosexuals, and unwed couples living together. In addition,

> The Catholic worldview also asserts itself in attitudes toward other religions, as seen in the greater sensitivity toward Jews and the astonishing difference revealed in the fact that, unlike Protestants, a majority of Catholics would not be deterred from voting for a qualified presidential candidate who happened to be an atheist.[24]

Catholics list salvation fourth in importance when ranking personal needs in life, while Protestants place it first (Catholics list physical well-being, love and affection, and a sense of meaning in life ahead of salvation).

Catholics are *less* likely than Protestants to say that:

1. they have a personal relationship with God (though an overwhelming majority say they do, of course).

2. deepening a relationship with God is "very important" to them.

3. they have been influenced by a presence or power different from their everyday lives.

4. a person can't be a good Christian without going to church.[25]

Seventy-two percent of Catholics agree that "God doesn't really care how he is worshipped as long as he is worshipped." Catholics are more inclined to view the Devil as an impersonal force causing people to do wrong, whereas Protestants incline to see the Devil as a personal being; just 51 percent believe that God will punish evil for all eternity.[26] Catholics are more "accepting" than Protestants, viewing fewer actions as sinful and believing that salvation is possible without belief in Christ. Grappling with problems in this world seems more important to Catholics who "are more likely to emphasize love of neighbor and to rank broader social concerns about personal evangelization" — in a word, a more private and less enthusiastic approach to spreading their faith to others.[27]

Yet another survey conducted in 1985 discovered that 25 percent of those claiming to be Catholics considered religion "largely old fashioned and out of date;" a further 27 percent had "no opinion" on the same question. Less than half (48 percent) of Catholics could bring themselves to state that religion was "relevant and did supply answers in their lives," compared with 66 percent of Protestants who found religion relevant and a mere 15 percent who termed religion "out of date".[28]

Fifty-two percent of Protestant teenagers consider religious faith to be a very important quality, whereas only 37 percent of Catholic teenagers feel the same way.[29]

These findings, like all survey results, lie open to a variety of interpretations. I think Gallup and Castelli are too benign in recurring to the metaphor of "intensity." They suggest that U.S. Catholics are simply more pragmatically accepting of the world around them; they are less "personal" in their approach to religion when compared to their Protestant neighbors. I would agree instead with author John Deedy that the United States contains large numbers of "cultural Catholics" or "individuals for whom Catholicism is not so much a compelling spiritual experience as it is a social circumstance, a shared history, an accident of birth rather than an actual spiritual and intellectual choice."[30] Perhaps the holding of old orthodoxies means less than "keeping in touch with their roots," so that being a Catholic is part of a distinct *cultural* identity rather than a mark of distinctive belief, worship, and morality. Devotional Catholicism, of course, emphasized almost exclusively the "orthodox" dimension and, in so doing, provided elements of a distinctive identity, as we have seen. But these findings suggest that whatever remains of devotional Catholicism has become ensconced in a strictly personal, private sphere, contributing little to spiritual identity or distinctiveness. To the extent this interpretation is plausible, it may reflect an upwardly mobile Catholic population tending to invest much more in occupational and educational identities than in "personally religious" ones. The latter assume less salience as "ghetto Catholicism" has receded and its symbols, once so forcefully inculcated by religious authority figures, are now less evocative of and indeed necessary for one's sense of security, place, status, and personal identity.

The meaning of being a Catholic, in short, has not just changed in content; it appears to have diminished in importance to Catholics. This is the sense in which I suggest that Catholic distinctiveness or "differentness" has receded over the past two decades. This development is yet another indication of a profound change in the *tradition* called Roman Catholic as believers understand and profess it. Catholics seem to have blended all too smoothly into what Herberg called "the Great American Way of Life." He is echoed by recent research on a broad spectrum of American Catholics. David Leege, a director of the Notre Dame Study of Catholic Parish Life, points to Catholic educational attainment in recent decades:

> The legitimacy accorded church authority is no longer traditional, but increasingly rational; Catholics have known both education and life away from ancestral parishes; they are accustomed in their jobs and daily life to means-end calculations and have to be won to the reasonableness of a policy. They live in a society and have been socialized through an educational system that seldom accords absolute authority to any human being. They are accustomed to owing loyalty to an institution while still accepting or rejecting specific policies of its leaders. They find no great inconsistency in accepting the central mysteries of the church and, in recent decades, rejecting some of its teachings.[31]

### Summary

Recent survey evidence leaves no doubt that selective Catholicism, or theological individualism, continues visibly and firmly in the 1980s. Catholics "make up their own minds" and set Church authority aside on certain issues. Problems of divorce, credibility on the issue of birth control, and on "everything related to sex" remain. "When it comes to sex, church leaders are preaching to an audience that is simply not paying any attention."[32]

I have reviewed this large body of research in some detail if only because it demonstrates empirically better than any abstract argument the substantial shifts in the tradition labeled "devotional Catholicism." I say "shift," because the changes clearly have been neither drastic nor totally transforming. Here survey research joins the contemporary experience of many Catholics to underline how much of devotional Catholicism remains intact: the clergy continues to be respected; sin and repentance are acknowledged, reduced though the list of sins may be; ritual involvement confers on many a sense of community and of comfort; and some believers find the miraculous retains its force in their lives as prayers for "hopeless cases" are unexpectedly answered.

But tradition *has* eroded in some clear respects, particularly (though by no means exclusively) among younger Catholics for whom the principle of selectivity seems well entrenched in areas of birth control, sexual attitudes, abortion under certain circumstances, and divorce with remarriage. Catholics have simply defined these areas as outside the legitimate range of external authority. They are subject mainly to individual experience and judgment. Add to this the apparent loss of intensity pointed out by Gallup and Castelli, and the question poses itself: is being a Catholic any longer a badge of distinctive identity?[33]

## Bishops and "Prophetic Challenges"

It is no small irony that the American bishops, in the face of more American Catholics saying, "I will decide for myself what I believe," have recently summoned their collective authority to bid Catholics apply their faith to contemporary social problems. Theology programs in Catholic high schools are now instructing students in these teachings, which call American Catholics to apply God-oriented beliefs and practices to love for one's neighbor and to the conditions of that neighbor's life.

In fact, the bishops have set forth over the past two decades a body of teaching that challenges American Catholics to bring their beliefs and values to bear on important social issues such as nuclear deterrence and the American economy. How did this new emphasis come about?

Inserting themselves into the arena of controversial issues was neither a sudden nor unprecedented strategy. Not lost on the American bishops was the Second Vatican Council's admonition to learn, analyze, and make judgments based on "signs" from the world around it, a world no longer simply to be condemned as the arena of sin and distraction. Among the unmistakable "signs" for post–World War II American bishops was not only the civil rights movement approaching its most conflictful stages in the mid-1960s, but disturbing accusations internationally. Why had the Church seemingly been silent in the face of Nazi genocide during World War II? What about the traditional church policy of making convenient concordats even with brutal dictatorships to ensure church "freedom" to operate in those nations? Whatever bishops might say—or not say—could scarcely ignore human rights issues.

Reorganizing their national offices into an episcopal conference in 1970, the National Conference of Catholic Bishops accelerated the pace they had set from 1963 through 1969 when they denounced discrimination and supported the war on poverty, launching in 1969 a Campaign for Human Development pledging to raise fifty millions dollars over ten years earmarked for organizations working on behalf of the poor.

Beginning in 1971 with a letter stating that the Vietnam War was no longer justifiable, the bishops widened the range of domestic issues they addressed: welfare reform, environmental, immigration, degradation problems, eliminating hunger; energy, housing, the handicapped, and minority groups.[34]

### Letters on War and Peace and on the Economy

The stage was thus set for the bishops to search their consciences when the nuclear freeze movement gained momentum in the early 1980s—no time to sit silently on the sidelines. Much has been made of the subsequent 1983 Letter on War and Peace and how it challenged some basic tenets of national policy in regard to nuclear deterrence. But no less important was the *manner* in which the bishops went about formulating the letter's content, a manner or process repeated in the more recent letter on the American economy, and in drafts of the letter on the status of women in the Church. I call attention to the process because it reveals the bishops' perception of the changed status, i.e., upward mobility, of the laity and their recognition, at least implicitly, of the "selective Catholicism" practiced by many American Catholics.

Both letters (peace and the economy) were prepared through wide consultation with those deemed knowledgeable or expert—an exercise in what Giddens terms "reflexive self-regulation." Business executives, government representatives, military spokespersons, philosophers, labor leaders, and intellectuals from around the nation were invited to present their views and to be questioned by the bishops. Successive drafts of the letters then incorporated some of the suggestions emerging from these hearings.

The letters address two audiences, both church members and all Americans, a strategy never before employed. The bishops' self-conception, then, has shifted from representatives of a parochial minority in the 1920s, 1930s, and 1940s to one of speaking from a more secure status as leaders of mainstream Americans who now resemble other Americans in terms of shared apprehensiveness about the arms race and about a shifting economy in the 1980s.[35] The bishops clearly want to be among the voices heard in formulating national policy. As Thomas Gannon puts it, referring to the letter on the economy, this strategy of a dual audience helps

> ensure that the document will be judged as an extension and application of Catholic teaching and as a contribution to a public moral debate on the whole array of American economic and social institutions. The process of open consultation and revision also contributes to establishing credibility with an American audience and to safeguarding the bishops claim to be heard on a complex issue on which their expertise is obviously limited.[36]

The bishops make a clear distinction between universal principles or formal Church teaching and applications of these principles on the other: "We know that some of our specific recommendations are controversial. As bishops, we do not claim to make these prudential judgments with the same kind of authority that marks our declarations of principle."[37] Principles are binding on the consciences of believers; the applications are not. The dual audience is invited to take both seriously, but their own judgment is explicitly made room for. The bishops can therefore convey moral urgency without being authoritarian in tone. For example, they suggest that "the time has come for 'a new American experiment' to implement economic rights, to broaden the sharing of economic power, and to make economic decisions more accountable to the common good." The bishops follow this assertion by admitting that "There may be specific points on which men and women of goodwill may disagree. We look for a fruitful exchange among differing viewpoints. We pray only that all will take to heart the urgency of our concerns."[38]

The challenge theme in the *Pastoral Letter on the Economy* becomes salient in the late 1980s as millions of European-ancestry Catholics enjoy the benefits of upward social and economic mobility.[39] The bishops have prophetically challenged Catholic laypersons to a further dimension of "differentness," and one they clearly believe has costs attached. Their own words could not frame this challenge more starkly, urging American Catholics to

> control greed and selfishness, a personal commitment to reverence one's own human dignity and the dignity of others by avoiding self-indulgence and those attachments that make us insensitive to the conditions of others and that erode social solidarity. Christ warned us against attachment to material things, against total self-reliance, against the idolatry of accumulating material goods and seeking safety in them. . . . Together we must reflect on our personal and family decisions and curb unnecessary wants in order to meet the needs of others. . . . Are we able to distinguish between our true needs and those thrust on us by advertising and a society that values consumption more than saving? All of us could well ask ourselves whether as Christian prophetic witnesses we are not called *to adopt a simple life-style in the face of excessive accumulation of material goods that characterizes an affluent society.*[40]

From a theoretical viewpoint, we can see how markedly a shift of authoritative resources has altered the dialectic of power between church leadership and people. An educated laity does not expect bishops to "dictate" to them and is not prepared to comply in thought or action if they do. The bishops are aware that "persuasion" is their only effective mode of exercising authority. Only in this way do they have a chance to earn a respectful hearing from lay Catholics.

In the words of James Kelly, the bishops are aware in their drafting of these two letters,

> that in modern societies religious membership is largely voluntary and while they clearly seek to challenge the consciences of Catholics, they take particular care not to lose the good will of those Catholics whose occupational lives would be most adversely affected by following the moral principles they urge.[41]

## *Commentary*

In sum, the bishops' stances in writing these two letters in the 1980s reveals a continuation of the significant shift in tradition set off by the Second Vatican Council. The "environmental penetration" during the first half of the twentieth century moved one particular charismatic pope, John XXIII, to adopt a posture of dialogue with the modern world, exemplifying a historical consciousness that broke the grip of tradition in significant respects, as McSweeney insightfully analyzes. The Catholic Church entered as a "global actor" on the stage of worldwide struggle for social justice, disarmament and peace, and respect for human rights. This shift occurred while another major change was occurring in a basic "structural principle" of authority within the Church, i.e., the formation of national episcopal bodies enjoined to apply their own situations to the renewed call to place social justice as a major element in evangelization of the Gospel. The "time-space" setting to which Giddens calls attention was that of an American laity no longer characterizable as an "immigrant minority," but instead one well on its way toward full socioeconomic integration into the American middle-class mainstream (through many groups were still struggling). The stage was set for tension between the prophetic challenges from the bishops and the social location of a large stratum of "comfortable Catholics." How would they respond?

The answer will lie in the next few decades, but survey research provides some early straws in the wind. Even the redoubtable Andrew Greeley, ever quick to criticize Catholic leadership for emphasizing social teaching at the expense of pastoral reforms ("the bishops and the clergy are now greatly exercised about the rights of the poor, but singularly disinterested in the right of the laity to have the gospel effectively preached to them"),[42] professed surprise at the following findings: equal proportions (36 percent) of Catholic and Protestant Americans agreed *prior* to release of the Catholic bishops' 1983 pastoral letter on nuclear disarmament that "too much money was being spent on defense." *After* the letter came out, Protestant opinion did not change. Catholic opinion, however, went up to 54 percent on this survey item. Possessing little credibility on sexual morality questions, the bishops, said Greeley, seem to have, where nuclear policy is concerned, "probably more credibility than they themselves thought they possessed and certainly more than most outside observers would have anticipated."[43] Yet Greeley is cautious: in 1983, the nuclear freeze movement was at its zenith; Democrats, self-described liberals, and those who did not vote for Ronald Reagan were the Catholics most influenced by the pastoral letter. So perhaps the timing of the bishops' letter was fortuitous. It may be that the laity will bestow credibility upon bishops' social policy pronouncements in situations where they "decide that the bishops know what they are talking about".[44]

A more sobering view comes from a concluding chapter of *American Catholic Laity*. By 1987, four years after issuance of the Letter on War and Peace, only 29 percent of Catholic adults had heard of or read it. The comparable figure for the Letter on the Economy is 25 percent. The figures climb somewhat for highly educated, well-off, and active Catholics. Taken in all, these data suggest the bishops' efforts are far from penetrating into the consciousness of rank-and-file Catholics. A more encouraging datum is that, of those who *had* heard of the letters, two-thirds or more approved of their message.[45]

Two comments are in order, forming a bridge to Part II. First, more research is needed on Catholic attitudes toward social issues with controls for income and education of respondents. The study of D'Antonio and colleagues is a start, but it deserves a more detailed follow-up.[46] Second, we know very little about Catholic teenagers and how these future adults "profile" in terms of the issues raised so far: do they continue in the late 1980s to be "selective" in their allegiance to beliefs and moral norms? Does the "individualism" pervasive in contemporary American society inhibit their concern for other people and groups? Greeley suggested in 1985 that "early teenagers today" may be growing up "in an era much less troubled religiously and politically than the late Sixties and the early Seventies," and notes that they are frequently alleged to be "conservative."[47] Gallup and Castelli include a chapter on Catholic teenagers, finding them more liberal than Protestant young people on such issues as welcoming more sexual freedom, more liberal on use of alcohol and on tolerance of marijuana (though the last difference is a slight one). Despite the fact that Catholic teens are more likely than Catholic adults to attend church and read the Bible, they assign lower importance to religion in their lives. Conservatism may indeed be a trend: while a plurality of Catholic adults say they are Democrats politically, and Protestant adults place themselves in the Republican camp, among teens Catholics show "a decided Republican preference." The shift is recent (1984) and held throughout 1985. "There is statistically no difference between Catholic and Protestant teens in political affiliation," a shift the authors term "historic."[48] In any case, Gallup and Castelli note that "research into the religious life of American teenagers is still in its infancy," and that much remains to be explored.

The case studies I present in Part II represent a modest attempt to remedy this state of affairs. As I will explain, they focus on the high socioeconomic status (hereafter SES) of young Catholics educated in a Catholic high school. Some of the data stretch from 1977 through 1989. Information on attitudes toward the bishops' recent social teaching covers the period from 1983 through 1989, representing over one thousand seniors as they are about to graduate (the survey was typically administered in late April each year). Has exposure to Catholic doctrine and moral values disposed them to accept the latter and render them in some respects distinctive from other young Americans, as they see themselves *and* as they respond to survey items? To what extent does their family SES affect their reactions to what they are taught?

In a word, the focus in Part II is on teenage Catholics and their teachers as "strategic actors," knowledgeable about both the *larger* institution (Catholic Church) of which they are members and the *smaller* institution (school), which in important ways I shall explore, *represents* to them the larger institution during these four critical years of their education. Within this setting, students are presented with Roman Catholicism by teachers who are well aware of the theological individualism characterizing the boys and girls in their classes and, thus, of student resistance to any manifestation of "old-fashioned" exercise of authority which says, in effect, accept this because this is what the Church teaches. At issue, then, is the teachers' search for some kind of authoritative leverage or purchase that promises success in persuading their students that the teaching presented "makes sense," that it is reasonable (or at least, not unreasonable) to give the teaching serious consideration. These issues of authority are by no means simple ones, as we shall see. At the same time, teachers are concerned to avoid the impression to both school administrators and to parents that they are imparting a kind of doctrinal and moral relativism contradictory to their mission of student religious formation. Keeping these two in balance is no easy task. What we shall see is a kind of extended dialectic or conversation between teachers and students that has a definite bearing on the way these Catholic high school seniors form their consciences and internalize the traditions with changes that are a part of post–Vatican II American Catholicism.

Chapter 4 also focuses on the sense of identity communicated by these young women and men. How do they see themselves as Catholics in comparison with their parents' generation?

In sum, as the 1980s came to a close, survey research demonstrated the enthronement of individual conscience, particularly in the lives of younger

Catholics, as the ultimate arbiter of what is believable or not believable, right or wrong, for each individual. "Selective Catholicism" seemed firmly in place. Catholic leadership appeared little inclined to challenge this phenomenon directly. Instead the American bishops in the 1980s took a leaf from another Vatican II theme, insertion of the Church into the world's agenda of socioeconomic issues. Exhibiting their own brand of "historical consciousness," they urged American Catholics to bring their religious heritage to bear on questions of nuclear war and disarmament and on issues of social justice and the more equitable distribution of wealth within the American economy as well as to consider whether the pursuit of affluence and acquiring consumer goods is compatible with Christian values. How receptive younger Catholics, in particular, may be to these appeals is an issue of central importance if the bishops are not to be "playing to an empty house." Catholic leadership confronts a laity whose "time-space" context in late twentieth-century United States is one of rapid assimilation to middle- and upper-middle-class (professional) status. A key issue in subsequent chapters is young American Catholics' receptivity to this new "prophetic thrust" articulated by their leadership.

# PART II

# 3

## Social Class and Social Viewpoints: The St. Martin's Senior Survey

> It is clear that Catholic teenagers are
> growing up in a world that is neither
> the world of their parents nor the
> world of other teenagers.[1]

### Introduction

A socially conscious Catholic leadership seems no longer satisfied with "producing" Catholics who attend Mass regularly and contribute to the collection plate. Attitudes of caring for those who have less, for issues of social and economic justice are central concerns to Catholic educators today. In a word, American Catholic leaders and educators are trying to broaden the meaning of being Catholic in today's America. This case study of St. Martin's High School seniors asks how well its teachers succeed in imparting a social consciousness to their students, *especially* in view of the rising socioeconomic prosperity of today's American Catholics. St. Martin's seniors represent families for whom the American dream has become reality. How open are they to the invitation extended by Church leaders to develop a moral sensitivity to problems of social and economic justice? I assign this question a certain primacy in the pages that follow.

Personal religiosity and moral viewpoints also come in for exploration. These issues obviously concern teachers, not to mention parents, of these young Catholics. At stake here is the preservation and handing on of tradition as many Catholic adults have known it. Premarital sex, sexual freedom, and abortion are not just abstract moral issues; they are obviously capable of affecting people's lives very deeply. Many, if not most, Catholic parents and educators believe traditional answers have much to offer since they safeguard the primacy of human life and the right of each person to be treated with dignity and respect. Are these understandings shared by young Catholics graduating from a Catholic high school? Religious practices and attitudes toward religion take on obvious importance in a school explicitly dedicated to Christian formation of its students. How "religious" do these seniors appear?

Before turning to St. Martin's High School, however, let us briefly contrast flourishing Catholic schools of the 1950s with today's beleaguered counterparts.

## A Historical Context

Catholic schools in midtwentieth century, as Father Fichter's research has highlighted, were instrumental in promoting values and ideals of American citizenship and self-improvement even as they socialized young Catholics into the religious traditions of their parents and grandparents. Church historians have pointed to World War I as a watershed event in which Catholic participation in the war deepened Catholics' sense of identity as both Catholics and Americans. Their schools began to mirror this dual identity. Instead of defending ethnic loyalties and protecting children of immigrants against a hostile environment, the schools, as newly confident Catholic educators saw them, were now simultaneously producing "Catholic Americans" and "American Catholics." Faye Veverke well expresses a vision

> institutionalized in the "Catholic ghetto" where the family, parish church and school, the press, and neighborhood, fraternal and professional organizations all served to sustain Catholicism in the U.S. as a distinct cultural reality. The educational counterpart of this social vision was, appropriately enough, a "permeation" of religious education that maintained the inseparability of the tasks of education in the faith and socialization into the culture.[2]

Parochial schools, like their public counterparts, promoted American-ization of foreign-language Catholics in the decades following World War I. English alone became the language of instruction. Underlined were ideals of both "solid citizenship" and devotional Catholicism. Little changed following the Second World War, as Fichter's research tells us, and on the eve of the Second Vatican Council in 1962, Catholic schools were flourishing. Over four million students filled parochial elementary classrooms; another 800,000 attended Catholic high schools. Separate schools for boys and girls was the predominant pattern.[3]

"Struggling" and "disappearing" are words best describing Catholic schools in the post–Vatican II period. While a declining birth rate drained the potential elementary school population, a more powerful dynamic was at work: sharply rising costs. Priests, nuns, and teaching brothers were either leaving their religious orders or their dioceses for secular occupations or persuading their superiors to place them in inner city ministries they deemed more relevant to the needs of the poor and minorities. Higher budgets for lay teachers' salaries have contributed to the closing of many schools in recent years. The heyday of the 1950s is over. From 1964 to 1984, "40 percent of the nation's Catholic high schools and 27 percent of its elementary schools closed their doors."[4] In fact, eighty-seven Catholic high schools closed between 1984 and 1989.[5] Few new schools have been built. No matter that Catholic laity continue to favor Catholic schools, or that Catholic schooling makes a significant positive difference in later adult religious behavior and outlooks.[6] They seem increasingly unaffordable.

When Catholic high schools *are* open and operating, what do they look like? The postwar years witnessed a series of studies focusing on Catholic high schools. Father Fichter was again in the forefront.

*Fichter's Study of Jesuit High Schools.* In 1966 and again in 1968, Joseph Fichter surveyed students in Jesuit high schools throughout the United States. Fichter asked whether religious and character formation improved in these all-males schools between freshman and senior years and compared freshmen in 1968 with freshmen surveyed in 1965 as well as seniors with seniors in the same time frame. Fichter termed the results "dismal": the religion curriculum "became less palatable the longer the student stayed in schools, and there was no demonstrable improvement during the three-year period between surveys."[7] Students considered religion a "dull subject" less interesting than almost everything else in the curriculum. Whether religion was taught well or badly made little difference in measures of Christian formation, ethical behavior, and moral attitudes. Students themselves made a distinction between Christian formation and character formation; Fichter concluded that the Jesuit high school system was more successful in building character than in forming Christian outlooks.

Most important is that the majority of students, who came "from well-advantaged families decidedly above the American average in social class," were little affected in their outlooks by Catholic social teaching. They remained skeptical of programs aimed at alleviation of poverty and unfavorably disposed to the idea of social welfare payments. In fact, these attitudes became more unfavorable as students progressed from freshman through senior year. Family and cultural environment persisted as influences from freshman through senior year; attending a Jesuit high school "promotes and reinforces the social attitudes of this class of people."[8] Fichter speculated that as the proportion of lay faculty increased and Jesuit faculty decreased, this situation would "worsen," since students who felt attracted to lay teachers expressed more "secular" outlooks less appreciative of spiritual and religious ideals proposed by the school and its theology faculty.[9]

### Recent Studies of Catholic High Schools

Catholic schools located in the inner cities of major metropolitan areas enroll mainly low-income minority students, including substantial numbers of non-Catholics. Father Andrew Greeley points out how well these schools serve their students. They educate them at a less per-pupil cost than public schools, even when lower teachers' salaries in Catholic schools are taken into account. Catholic high schools motivate their students to do more hours of homework per week than public school students and to perform better on standardized tests—measures of success that hold as well for minority students whose parents have low incomes and/or have not attended college.[10]

The early 1980s also saw the first of two institutional studies of Catholic high schools sponsored by the National Catholic Educational Association (NCEA). Sixty-two percent of high school principals, representing 910 of the 1464 Catholic high schools in the nation responded to an extensive survey. As would be expected, the principals' collective portrait of Catholic high schools is basically a favorable one. But three common problems gave them pause: (1) poor funding resulting in underpaid teachers and a tuition rate increasing yearly, a situation aggravated by declining subsidies from religious orders staffing many of the schools; (2) high teacher turnover, largely due to the first factor; (3) recruiting and retaining minority students. Forty percent of the principals rated their schools as "fair" or "poor" in this respect. Forty percent of schools serving high proportions of minority students had income insufficient to match expenses, and their enrollments were declining more than other schools.[11]

Most telling, however, is the portrait of schools whose enrollments were *increasing* from 1978 to 1983: students with higher academic achievement, higher family incomes ($35,000 per year average compared to $28,000 in declining enrollment schools), and more courses required for graduation. These "flourishing" schools tended to be in New England and in the western states, regions that have experienced stronger economies in recent years. It is hard to resist the impression that where Catholic high schools have growing enrollments, they do so by catering precisely to the stratum of Catholics that forms the principal focus of this chapter, the rising middle/upper-middle classes whose children are college-bound. Obviously these families are willing and able to afford the rising tuition costs of Catholic high schools.

*Effective Catholic Schools.* The second NCEA-sponsored study focused on seven high schools in Boston, Baltimore (two schools), Cleveland, Louisville, San Antonio, and Los Angeles—institutions considered representative of the nation's Catholic high schools. Findings echo many of those in the previous study. Five out of the seven schools are characterized as "primarily college preparatory." Tensions were reported in "schools with the strongest academic reputations" between parents choosing the school mainly for academic reasons ("attendance would enhance one's chances of admission to a premier university") and the religious goals of the school, "particularly with regard to social justice and responsibility. . . .

Balancing the emphasis on academics with a commitment to Catholic values and action can be a real dilemma for schools." This findings fits with the principals' study just cited: the principals identified their *own* chief goal for their schools as the building of community, while assessing the *parents'* chief goal in sending their children to be academic achievement.[12]

*Effective Catholic Schools* also emphasizes the dim future prospects of inner-city schools with a pessimistic observation "that many inner-city schools serving large numbers of minority children are likely to close." The contrast is made with "established religious order and suburban diocesan schools" that in the face of declining subsidies from religious orders, parishes, and dioceses can mount development and fund-raising programs — avenues closed to inner-city schools "serving predominantly minority populations not so fortunate."[13]

What about research on students themselves? Unfortunately, survey research is all too rare. A study conducted in 1982 included 2769 seniors (96 percent of the state's total) in thirty-three Wisconsin Catholic high schools. Seniors filled out the REKAP questionnaire (religious education, knowledge, attitudes, and practices) developed by the NCEA. The study's findings sound familiar in the light of research reviewed in chapter 2.

Slightly less than half the seniors agreed that "the Church is an important source of sound guidance on matters of sex and marriage," with 23 percent disagreeing and 30 percent unsure. Less than one-third said the Church's position on birth control "makes sense to me" with 38 percent disagreeing and 31 percent in the "unsure" category. Almost half agreed that "for some couples, living together before deciding on marriage is the intelligent thing to do," while 30 percent disagreed and 24 percent were unsure. "Sexual intercourse outside of marriage is always seriously wrong" drew agreement from one-quarter of the seniors, disagreement from 46 percent and an unsure response from 29 percent.[14] The issue of abortion found seniors more orthodox. Two-thirds disagreed that "the birth of an unwanted child is a worse evil than abortion." Another 20 percent were unsure; 15 percent agreed.

Social morality was probed as well. Fifty-three percent of the seniors disagreed that "the best way to improve world conditions is for people to concentrate on taking care of their own personal and family business," with 18 percent agreeing and 28 percent in the unsure column. "There are private social activities from which I could in good conscience exclude certain people because of their race" was rejected by 71 percent of the seniors, while 9 percent agreed and 19 percent were unsure. When asked if "white people have a right to live in all-white neighborhoods if they choose and blacks should respect that right," 31 percent agreed, 49 percent disagreed and 21 percent were unsure.[15]

A strong majority (70 percent) attends Sunday Mass "regularly"; few go to Confession (57 percent "rarely" or "never"), and three-quarters of the seniors "seldom" or "never" read the Bible nor "talk with a priest in my parish."[16]

The report controlled only for type of high school attended (single sex or coeducational) and for sex of respondent. Senior girls were consistently less likely than boys to disagree with Catholic moral positions on sex and abortion, but *more* likely to disagree on birth control. No difference by sex was evident with regard to the Church as "an important source of sound guidance" in sex and marriage. In terms of social morality, girls were more "liberal" on questions involving race but no different from boys concerning "the best way to improve world conditions," for example. Girls also scored higher on personal religiosity items than boys, except that they are *less* likely than boys to go to Confession, to have talked with a priest in their parish or to have read the Bible regularly or occasionally.[17]

A 1983 study of 784 seniors randomly chosen from ten Catholic high schools in the Archdiocese of Washington, D.C., is the subject of *Faith Without Form: Beliefs of Catholic Youth,* by E. Nancy McAuley and Moira Mathieson. The study includes questions on "family background, religious beliefs, value systems, hopes for the future, and the transformation taking place in their lives."[18] In addition, eighty students were interviewed for approximately one hour on the topics just mentioned. Results closely match those of the Wisconsin study on items dealing with premarital sex and birth control. Questions not included in the Wisconsin survey dealt with homosexuality as an acceptable life-style (31 percent agreed, 49 percent disagreed, and 20 percent had no opinion). Seniors were asked "whether the church should take public stands on important political issues such as the nuclear arms race, busing for school integration, equal rights and the like." Fifty-nine percent agreed, 24 percent disagreed, and 17 percent had no opinion.[19]

Personal interviews predictably reinforced the survey responses. In fact, they underlined the "selective Catholicism" and moral individualism discussed in chapter 2. "The students' tendency to see God as a friendly 'something' out there, asking only that they should be well-intentioned, led them to assume that they could define sin according to their own desires and convenience."[20] A senior remarked, "Basically, if you have thought about what you are doing and whether for you it is right or wrong, it really wouldn't cross my mind that it would be a sin. It would be just a normal everyday thing."[21] In a chapter entitled "The Church and Religion," the authors report "a widespread sense that the Church was too authoritarian,"[22] that the Church was allowed "very limited authority" in the lives of those interviewed, and that "many students believed that they could more or less design their own 'Catholicism.' "[23] Again, from a senior interview,

I believe that the way a person would prefer to practice religion should be left up to them. Yes, there should be different denominations, to be used as guidelines only. A person should not be considered a sinner or unholy if he does not practice the beliefs that his religion has. The choice should be left up to the person. The church's views should be just that, a view, not a law or rule to follow.[24]

The authors utilized no controls in reporting their findings.

### Summary

Catholic high schools in the 1980s continue to attract the support of higher status families. They can afford the tuition. They value the schools for their high academic and college-preparatory competence. Principals and (at least some) teachers view the primary purposes of the schools as building community and forming consciences according the Catholic ideals of social justice and personal morality. They see tension between these goals and the goal of academic excellence and college preparation desired by parents.

Catholic seniors of the early 1980s held liberal attitudes on matters of racial justice. A slight majority exhibited concern for improving world conditions over simply attending to one's personal concerns. Three out of five Catholic seniors supported their Church taking public stands on sociomoral issues such as the nuclear arms race and racial justice. The Fichter research, however, raises questions about the effectiveness of any Catholic school in challenging its students to transcend the influences of middle- and upper-middle-class status with its generally conservative ideologies concerning the socially disadvantaged.

Close to half of the seniors regarded the Catholic Church as a sound guide in matters of sex and marriage, but half or more disagreed with specific teachings. Seniors scored quite high on measures of personal religiosity with the exceptions of going to Confession and reading the Bible. In addition, few say they talked with a priest. Seniors embraced a moral individualism. Conscience formation was a highly personal matter allowing very little authority to the Church's teachings.

On the face of it, the research just summarized seems thoroughgoing enough. But it is not. As mentioned, the studies utilize few background controls other than sex of respondent. Particularly absent (except for Fichter's research) are measures of sociomoral sensitivity, a gap badly needing to be filled in the light of the Catholic bishops' emphasis in the 1980s upon application of Catholic teaching to contemporary matters of social justice and charity.

The following case study of St. Martin's High School attempts to fill this gap by focusing on a high school catering to relatively affluent Catholic families whose worldviews, as Fichter's research suggests, may well collide with the recent social justice emphasis of the American bishops. Before proceeding to the case study, let us ask on what basis such a collision between well-off young Catholics from relatively affluent families and the bishops' social teaching might occur.

*SES and Ideology.* In a recent study entitled *Beliefs about Inequality: Americans' Views of What is and What Ought to be,* James Kluegel and Eliot Smith cite the so-called new class thesis, i.e., the period beginning in the mid-1960s has given rise to "a group of especially liberal, college-educated people who now have assumed upper-middle-class occupations."[25] Their liberal views, however, are expressed mainly in beliefs and attitudes about race, gender, and related social policy issues concerning welfare, affirmative action programs and support for the Equal Rights Amendment. Their "liberalism," however, stops where that of most other Americans does, that is, in "dominant ideology beliefs about how the stratification order does and should work."[26] Most Americans believe the existing order is just—that those who are wealthy and those who are poor by and large deserve to be where they are. "Economic elites" differ from most other Americans in their unwillingness to attribute responsibility for poverty to failures of other institutions, for example, private industry, in not producing enough jobs. Explanations for poverty and wealth tend to be individualist only, e.g., hard work, initiative, and taking advantage of opportunities explains economic success, while their opposites (e.g., laziness) explain why some are poor.[27]

Research by Jackman and Jackman supports these conclusions. Regardless of SES, "people in all social classes heavily endorse the norm of unequal rewards based on personal achievement."[28]

*Focus on Social Morality.* The previous chapter indicated how the American bishops, particularly in their 1986 Pastoral Letter on the American Economy, asked American Catholics to examine the economic system under which so many of them have recently benefited, and to raise questions about its basic justice and fairness. Given that research on transmission of sociopolitical attitudes suggests that parents pass their worldviews to their children, one may expect St. Martin's seniors, coming from relatively well-off families, to show liberal attitudes in matters of race, gender equality, and world hunger. They will be *less* likely to endorse social justice norms of alleviating poverty or correcting social inequities.

St. Martin's High School (a pseudonym) represents the more "flourishing" type of Catholic high school referred to in the Introduction, i.e., one serving middle- to upper-middle-income Catholic families. Seldom, if ever, has this type of school been the subject of study. In the most general terms, I will ask how well the school succeeds in imparting a *distinctive* Catholic value system or ethos, given the tensions between the parental "goal" of academic excellence and the school's goal of value formation, especially in the light of a largely upper-middle-class student body likely to reflect individualist legitimations of wealth and poverty. Once more, how receptive are these relatively well-off young Catholics to themes of social justice and its application as formulated in the Bishops' documents discussed previously? The question is not one of merely academic interest, for these young people educated in Catholic schools are the source of future lay leadership, not to mention financial support. While the Gallup and Castelli surveys suggest the presence of "dovish" and socially liberal stances among a substantial segment of American Catholics, the more fundamental questions concern views on social justice and how these views are related to measures of religious commitment, to socioeconomic status, and to attitudes toward the Church's role as teacher in socioeconomic policy issues. Research on Catholic high school students tells us much about their outlooks on personal morality and their areas of resistance to orthodox Catholic teaching. Little of this surprises, given Father Greeley's "communal Catholic" model suggesting that upwardly mobile and younger Catholics do maintain Catholic identity, support parochial schools, and attend Mass with some regularity. But they remain "selective" in such matters as sexual expression and abortion under certain circumstances. St. Martin's seniors are likely to exercise this same doctrinal selectivity.

*A Question of Assimilation.* Let us recall at this point Dean Hoge's "assimilation hypothesis" reviewed in the Introduction. It simplifies the above argument, in a fashion, by pointing to a convergence of Catholic attitudes and practices with those of other Americans, especially among the younger and better educated. Catholic "distinctiveness" consequently erodes in several areas. Indeed, Hoge and Moberg, reviewing two decades of Marquette University students' views and practices from 1961 through 1982, conclude that by the early 1980s,

> Assimilation was far advanced. Catholics were increasingly a part of education's mainstream, and the uniqueness of Catholic attitudes among youth was almost a thing of the past. . . . The students shifted toward positions held by non-Catholics. We expect that this pattern will continue among young educated Catholics—that their attitudes will be pushed in the direction of the surrounding American middle-class culture.[29]

This chapter, then, undertakes a detailed examination of high school seniors graduating from a Catholic college preparatory high school from the mid-1970s through 1989, a school drawing its student body mainly from middle-class and increasingly in the 1980s, as we shall see, from upper-middle-class or professional family backgrounds. As the NCEA studies suggest, graduates of such schools are expected as adults to assume leadership roles in the Catholic Church. Possessed of educational and financial advantages superior to those of most Catholics, they are to bring their Church's viewpoints and values into both family life and marketplace. This charge presupposes a basic respect for the Catholic Church's authority and teachings, a respect inculcated through their theology courses and the entire tone of the school. Research on religious value formation tells us, of course, that the school cannot be expected to offset the influence of home, family, and even neighborhood. Nevertheless, the impact of the school is worth investigating, even if hard to measure, for its purpose is to influence young Catholics favorably toward the Church and motivate them to take its teachings seriously. In fact, one could argue that only in this way could the school hope to graduate young people who have a viewpoint *distinctive* from that of other young Americans.

### St. Martin's High School: A Description

St. Martin's is the only Catholic high school in a southwestern metropolitan area of half a million people. The school's location is highly urbanized, situated directly between two adjacent major suburban shopping centers. It draws students mostly from surrounding residential neighborhoods. Coeducational from its beginning in the early 1960s, the school today averages between 800 and 900 students. Ninety percent of its financial support comes from tuition. The remaining 10 percent derives from the diocese and from donations. Local parishes contribute little, if anything. Tuition by the 1987–88 school year had reached $2075 for Catholics and $2825 for non-Catholics, who at any time comprise between 5 and 8 percent of the total student body. Those receiving partial financial aid (full tuition scholarships are given rarely) vary between 5 and 12 percent in any given year.

"College preparatory school" is an accurate designation of St. Martin's, reflecting policies enacted in the late 1970s by the school board (composed mostly of parents of current students), as well as by a principal who fully encouraged this direction. Ninety-nine percent of graduating seniors go on to college (compared with 83 percent nationally). Eighth grade applicants take an entrance test each spring. From 1982 to 1984, the school admitted a little over half of such applicants. Due mainly to declining numbers of parochial school eighth graders in the mid-1980s, the ratio of test-takers to those accepted has dropped somewhat. In 1985, for example, 75 percent of those taking the entrance exam were invited to register the following fall. The high tuition and low number of scholarships, however, ensure a student body of high socioeconomic status.

Academic excellence is a goal cherished by school administrators and parents alike. A four-person counseling staff spends much time advising seniors about college choice and entrance requirements, frequently involving prestigious and selective institutions. The school has been notably successful in obtaining numerous scholarships and awards for its outstanding seniors and, during the mid-1980s, could count several International Science Fair and Westinghouse Science Competition winners among its student body (its chemistry teacher was voted the state's outstanding science teacher in 1982).

Hispanic students regularly comprise around one-third of the entire student body; students reporting mixed Hispanic ancestry make up an additional 10 percent. Female students comprise slightly over half of each senior class.

*The Senior Survey.* I was asked in 1976 by a friend who has been both dean of students and junior-senior theology teacher at St. Martin's to conduct a yearly survey of seniors each spring semester. He had in mind an assessment of the effectiveness of the school and, more specifically, its theology department on the religious formation of the students. We worked together to develop the questionnaire, which was first administered in the spring of 1977.

This teacher was concerned because students each year seemed to be coming from families of higher socioeconomic background and exhibited some resistance to accepting the doctrinal and moral authority of the Catholic Church. He was not unaware of the trends already cited but wondered if the theology program might attenuate the "deviant" views his students shared with their counterparts throughout the United States.

Limitations on the survey instrument quickly became apparent. After consulting with other members of the schools' administrative staff, the principal asked that no "personal questions" be asked that would arouse parental antagonism should seniors comment at home on the questions. As a result, parental religiosity items were excluded, as were questions on family income. In addition, behavioral moral indicators were ruled out, e.g., of student drinking, drug usage, or sexual practices. The revised questionnaire covered the following areas:

1. Sociomoral views, that is, whether seniors acknowledged responsibility for sharing with those who have less and for opposing practices in society that unjustly harm people. In addition, from 1983 through 1989, reflecting the Catholic bishops renewal of social teaching, the seniors were queried about views on the nuclear arms race, racial discrimination, and world hunger, and from 1987 to 1989, about economic justice. On these issues, the seniors were asked not only if they believe it to be their *own* responsibility to be involved with these issues, but whether they thought it was the *Church's* business to be involved as well. In other words, does the Church's legitimate authority, in their eyes, extend to these areas?

2. Personal religiosity, including Church attendance, importance of religion, degree of conviction, membership in a religious group.

3. Personal moral views on premarital sex, abortion, and sexual freedom.

4. The impact of the theology program. Seniors were asked if they thought their theology courses made the teachings of the Catholic Church more (or less) credible and to rate the program (excellent, good, fair, or poor).

5. From 1983 through 1989, conscience formation, i.e., the extent to which the individual ought to acknowledge the authority of the Catholic Church in forming one's conscience.

6. Future participation in parish or church. Do seniors foresee themselves, as adults, taking an active part?

7. Background variables. None of the high school studies cited above utilized an extensive array of background controls. This study controls not only for gender, but for occupations of mother and father (on a two-digit occupational prestige code), for ethnic background of the respondent, for the importance of this background to the respondent, for language other than English spoken in the home, for type of elementary school attended— Catholic, non-Catholic, or mixed—and whether, if not a Catholic school, the respondent took religious education classed (Confraternity of Christian Doctrine or CCD). In addition, items were inserted concerning parents' political stance (very conservative to very liberal), whether the father spent eight or more years in the military, and overall grade point average at graduation. From 1983 through 1989, father's and mother's education was also asked.[30]

8. From 1983 through 1989, the open-ended question, "Looking back over four years, what do you think is the major difference between you as a St. Martin's graduate and graduates of other high schools (public and private) in the city?" Responses to this question will be explored in the following chapter.

9. From 1987 through 1989, a second open-ended question, "Obviously, 'being a Catholic' has different meanings for different people, and sons and daughters may differ in this respect from their parents. In your case, how would you say 'being a Catholic' differs

in meaning for you—if at all—comparing yourself to your parents?" Responses to this question are also set down in the succeeding chapter.

In summary, the present study offers several advantages absent from previous research:

1. Measures of agreement with social teaching. While personal religiosity has received considerable attention in the studies cited above, rarely have measures of social sensitivity found their way into surveys of Catholic young people.

2. Attitudes toward involvement of the Church itself in teaching on issues. Previous studies have not inquired about attitudes toward the Church's authority to teach on nuclear war, racism, economic justice, and other social issues.

3. Controls for a considerable array of background factors, including ethnic identification. Rarely have socioreligious values of young Hispanics been studied. A national sample survey of Hispanic Catholics was conducted in 1984 and 1985.[31] U.S.-born Hispanics showed a marked decline compared to foreign-born Hispanics in religious belief and practices. The present Hispanic seniors are almost entirely descendants of Hispanic families who settled in the Southwest over a century before. A reasonable hypothesis, then, is that they will differ little from their "Anglo" counterparts. The survey also indicated that a vast majority (88 percent) of Hispanic Catholics were not involved directly in their parishes (though a majority said they had never been invited to do so). Hispanic seniors are unlikely to exhibit more interest in parish involvement as adults than are Anglo seniors. Hispanic female seniors will follow the national pattern of more regular church attendance than males, though as daughters and sons of upwardly mobile families, they will (again, following national patterns) show diminished church attendance. Two-thirds of Hispanic Catholics firmly believe abortion to be always wrong. These seniors are likely to match them. The national survey, constructed with a pastoral emphasis, had almost no questions on the social issues represented in the St. Martin's survey. The senior survey, then, easily lends itself to Anglo-Hispanic comparisons.

4. In terms of personal morality, while these issues have received

attention in previous survey research, they have not been explored with the array of background controls this study employs.

*Survey Administration.* Virtually all members of each senior class filled out the survey, which was announced prior to its date of administration as a regular part of the spring semester theology course. Owing partially to the high popularity and respect, in my opinion, accorded the senior theology teacher who invited my participation and also to the fact that the seniors seemed to enjoy filling out the questionnaire (a favorable impression was apparently passed along from year to year), no senior ever objected to filling it out. The result is perhaps one of the largest surveys undertaken of seniors at a Catholic high school, with an overall total of 2295 respondents from 1977 through 1989. I administered the survey personally each year, enabling me to speak to each classroom of seniors (approximately four each year) and explain the purpose of the survey. I encouraged them to fill it out completely and responded to questions. I believe this personal contact made for honest and accurate responses, as opposed to the "skips" and ill-considered or even flip responses more likely when someone other than the researcher administers the survey. I can report that the seniors frequently complimented the survey to me personally after its administration and, judging from both the length and content of many responses to open-ended questions, took the survey seriously.

The following analysis selects only those students reporting their religious affiliation as Catholic. The overall total from 1977 through 1989 in 2146 Catholic students; the 1983 to 1989 subtotal is 1173. (Note: Readers disinclined to wade through detailed data presentations may wish to skip to page 84, "A Note on the Classes of 1987 to 1989" followed by the concluding section on page 88.)

## St. Martin's High School: Findings of the Case Study

### Overall Summary (Frequencies)

Appendix 1 shows the variables, together with response frequencies, selected for analysis in this chapter. Taken globally over the twelve-year period (or six-year time period with some variables), the seniors appear in a positive light measured by Catholic norms of religious observance and attitudes, including social morality. Unsurprisingly, they match other young Catholics in terms of "liberal" views on sexual morality and sexual freedom. But a solid majority (62 percent) reject abortion "if the baby is likely to have serious birth defects." Seniors from 1983 through 1989 are generally willing to affirm the Church's right to be involved with social issues, and two-thirds see a personal responsibility to address social issues. Over three-quarters are willing to listen to the Church's teaching but believe conscience formation to be mainly the result of "making up my own mind." Among seniors graduating between 1987 and 1989, a majority extends Church teaching authority to "dimensions of economic decision-making," though a third disagree with this position; two-thirds affirm their personal responsibility to be involved with solutions to socioeconomic problems in our society. But these generally "rosy-hued" percentages can be misleading. I turn to an analysis of trend data that suggest the impact of rising socioeconomic status on seniors' beliefs and values.

### Background Characteristics

Figure 3.1 underlines the upward trend in SES of the seniors' families of origin. Father's occupation, asked each year of the survey, shows not only a decade-long rise in proportions of high-status fathers, but most importantly, a notable change beginning with the class of 1983. In that year, lower and upper professional fathers combined experience a rise that continues through 1989. In fact, professional fathers jump from 46 percent of the total in 1982 to 57 percent in 1983; though dropping to 48 percent in 1984, they then rebound to 62 percent in 1985 and remain at this high level throughout 1988 with a drop back to 53 percent in 1989. Father's *educational* attainment was asked only from 1983 through 1989. Parallel to the occupational analysis above, the educational curve *combines* college graduate and graduate degree

**Figure 3.1**
**Father's Occupational and Educational Attainments:**
**Percentages of Professional and College Graduates, by Year**

holders. There occurs a steady rise in these combined groups from 60 percent in 1983 to 69 percent in 1988, though 1989 shows a drop to 61 percent.[32]

Differences appear when Anglo and Hispanic seniors are compared by father's occupation over the decade (not shown in table). Hispanics have a decade-long underrepresentation of "upper" professionals. "Lower" professionals, however, show a pronounced upturn for Hispanic fathers starting in 1985, with corresponding downturns in blue- and white-collar occupations. Educationally, while proportions of those with "only" a college degree are almost identical in the two sets of fathers, Anglos are markedly more likely to have graduate degrees, with a rising gap between Anglos and Hispanics from 16 percent in 1985 to 29 percent in 1989. In any case, a marked rise in family SES of St. Martin's students, including Hispanics, characterizes the mid-1980s seniors.[33]

What explanation may be offered for these patterns? The most persuasive seems to be a policy decision by school authorities in the late 1970s to tighten admission standards, a policy taking effect approximately with the entering freshman class of 1979. As the only Catholic high school in a large metropolitan area, the school experienced strong enrollment pressures in the late 1970s. Higher cutoff points on the eighth-grade entrance examination were suggested by a new principal whose personal goal was to make the school competitive with a respected and highly selective secondary academy in the city. The school board approved the new policy that took effect mainly with the entering class of 1979. Entering freshmen from 1979 through 1984 came from families of higher occupational and educational backgrounds and were thus better equipped to pass the entrance exam successfully. Tuition also rose steadily during this period. In any case, I will analyze how this development in itself becomes a kind of "macro-variable;" that is, the shift in SES of entering classes visible for the first time in the senior class of 1983 is itself an important predictor of some responses.

Figure 3.2 indicates the proportions of seniors who attended Catholic elementary schools exclusively (as opposed to seniors who had at least some non-Catholic schooling but took religion classes (CCD); and seniors with no elementary school religious classes). What stands out is the diminishing percentages in the late 1980s who had graduated from Catholic elementary schools.

### Trends in Major Dependent Variables

Male-female differences are noted in the analysis that follows. Previous research suggests that females are "more religious." Thus, trends in religiosity measures may well reflect gender variations.

*Sociomoral Orientation.* "Sharing with others" and "opposing injustice" (tables 3.1 and 3.2) show an identical profile: from a peak of

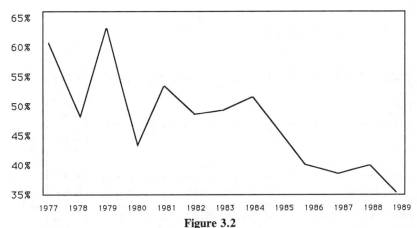

**Figure 3.2**
**Percentages of Seniors Having Attended Eight Years of Catholic Elementary School, by Year**

"liberal" attitudes around 1981, the "strongly agree" seniors steadily decline. But differences in the two items do appear: "share with others" shifts the mid-1980s "changers" mainly from "strongly agree" to "agree"—a kind of lukewarming effect. The "oppose injustice" item, on the other hand, slides toward "disagree" and "don't know" answers. In fact, in

**Table 3.1**

**Responsibility to Share with Others, by Year and Sex**

| | Strongly Agree | | | Agree | | | Disagree | | |
|---|---|---|---|---|---|---|---|---|---|
| | Gender | | | Gender | | | Gender | | |
| Year | Male | Female | Total | Male | Female | Total | Male | Female | Total |
| 1977 | 30.0% | 50.8% | 38.8% | 53.7% | 42.4% | 48.9% | 16.2% | 6.8% | 12.2% |
| 1978 | 36.8% | 52.9% | 45.8% | 54.4% | 40.0% | 46.4% | 8.8% | 7.1% | 7.8% |
| 1979 | 33.8% | 46.9% | 41.6% | 57.4% | 46.9% | 51.2% | 8.8% | 6.1% | 7.2% |
| 1980 | 49.3% | 38.9% | 43.4% | 47.8% | 56.7% | 52.8% | 2.9% | 4.4% | 3.8% |
| 1981 | 39.8% | 56.3% | 48.2% | 45.8% | 36.8% | 41.2% | 14.5% | 6.9% | 10.6% |
| 1982 | 46.6% | 40.0% | 42.9% | 41.1% | 53.3% | 47.9% | 12.3% | 6.7% | 9.2% |
| 1983 | 22.6% | 36.5% | 30.1% | 61.3% | 55.4% | 58.1% | 16.1% | 8.1% | 11.8% |
| 1984 | 24.0% | 33.8% | 28.7% | 53.3% | 48.5% | 51.0% | 22.7% | 17.6% | 20.3% |
| 1985 | 23.9% | 41.7% | 33.5% | 64.8% | 53.6% | 58.7% | 11.3% | 4.8% | 7.7% |
| 1986 | 26.9% | 31.3% | 29.3% | 59.7% | 58.7% | 559.2% | 13.4% | 10.0% | 11.6% |
| 1987 | 19.1% | 29.2% | 25.0% | 61.8% | 59.4% | 60.4% | 19.1% | 11.5% | 14.6% |
| 1988 | 14.6% | 31.9% | 22.4% | 65.2% | 58.3% | 62.1% | 20.2% | 9.7% | 15.5% |
| 1989 | 17.9% | 33.8% | 26.4% | 50.7% | 58.4% | 54.9% | 31.3% | 7.8% | 18.8% |

**Table 3.2**

**Responsibility to Oppose Injustice, by Year and Sex**

| | Strongly Agree | | | Agree | | | Disagree | | |
|---|---|---|---|---|---|---|---|---|---|
| | Gender | | | Gender | | | Gender | | |
| Year | Male | Female | Total | Male | Female | Total | Male | Female | Total |
| 1977 | 35.5% | 35.6% | 35.6% | 44.7% | 50.8% | 47.4% | 19.7% | 13.6% | 17.0% |
| 1978 | 48.5% | 46.9% | 47.6% | 27.3% | 38.3% | 33.3% | 24.2% | 14.8% | 19.0% |
| 1979 | 38.2% | 44.7% | 42.0% | 52.9% | 45.7% | 48.8% | 8.8% | 9.6% | 9.3% |
| 1980 | 49.3% | 42.7% | 45.6% | 35.2% | 42.7% | 39.4% | 15.5% | 14.6% | 15.0% |
| 1981 | 42.0% | 51.2% | 46.7% | 38.3% | 34.5% | 36.4% | 19.8% | 14.3% | 17.0% |
| 1982 | 39.4% | 49.4% | 45.0% | 45.1% | 36.0% | 40.0% | 15.5% | 14.6% | 15.0% |
| 1983 | 19.0% | 29.9% | 25.0% | 47.6% | 48.1% | 47.9% | 33.3% | 22.1% | 27.1% |
| 1984 | 15.3% | 27.4% | 20.9% | 51.4% | 54.8% | 53.0% | 33.3% | 17.7% | 26.1% |
| 1985 | 10.4% | 28.0% | 20.1% | 47.8% | 45.1% | 46.3% | 41.8% | 26.8% | 33.6% |
| 1986 | 19.7% | 29.3% | 25.0% | 40.9% | 46.3% | 43.9% | 39.4% | 24.4% | 31.1% |
| 1987 | 6.6% | 23.1% | 15.6% | 50.0% | 52.7% | 51.5% | 43.4% | 24.2% | 32.9% |
| 1988 | 14.0% | 22.5% | 17.8% | 43.0% | 50.7% | 46.5% | 43.0% | 26.8% | 35.7% |
| 1989 | 12.3% | 23.5% | 17.7% | 39.7% | 55.9% | 47.5% | 47.9% | 20.6% | 34.8% |

the late 1980s, the "disagrees" rise steadily toward a decade high of 36 percent in 1987.

Gender differences in yearly responses are quite striking. Female seniors, as proven in previous research on students in Catholic high schools, are notably more likely than male seniors to see sharing and opposing injustice as obligations. The discrepancy is especially glaring among those who disagree on the "oppose injustice" statement. Before 1983, male and females were fairly similar in their responses. After 1983, the gap widens. Males strikingly surpass female seniors in disagreeing about this item; by the close of the decade, a full 27 percentage points separated males from females. A corresponding gap opens if one glances at "sharing with others," widening to 10 points in 1988, but doubling to over 20 by 1989.

*Personal Religiosity.* Church attendance, importance of religion, and degree of religious conviction, all show downward trends (figure 3.3). As expected with Catholic adolescents living at home "under the thumbs" of their parents, attendance is still quite high. Nevertheless, a striking pattern is visible: through 1981, approximately three-quarters of the seniors reported weekly Mass attendance. A sharp decline begins in 1982, and from 1983 through 1989, a steady yearly drop in weekly attendance sets in. Only half the classes of 1988 and 1989 goes to Church each week. By the same token, the proportion of those saying they attend a few times a year or never has risen gradually since 1982, culminating in one-quarter of the classes of 1988 and 1989.

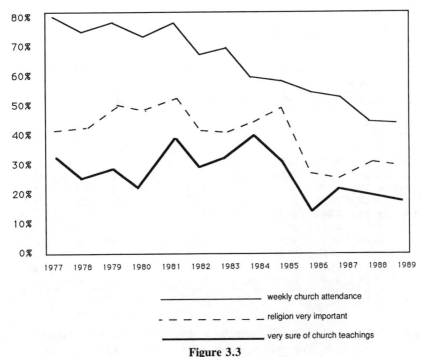

**Figure 3.3**
**Church Attendance, Importance of Religion, and Sureness of Church Teaching, by Year**

Seniors saying religion is "very important" in their lives fell to decade-low percentages in 1986 and 1987. "Unimportant" as a response doubled in 1983 and has remained at that level ever since. Religious conviction shows a similar pattern: those saying they are "not too convinced" or "not convinced at all" (responses combined) almost doubled in 1983, doubled again in 1986 (to 37 percent), and fell to one-fifth of the 1988 and 1989 seniors. Women differ from men only in assigning more importance to religion, not in attendance or conviction.

The trend data are crucial, then, in establishing the first indication of an arresting correlation: as seniors' overall family status has risen, personal religiosity and social sensitivity have diminished. Whether the two are causally connected, of course, is another matter. Let us continue examining the trends.

*Personal Ethics.* Fifty-eight percent of adult Catholics nationally in 1985 saw nothing wrong with premarital sex; 33 percent said it was immoral.[34] Seniors fluctuate considerably in their views over the years (table 3.3). About one-quarter thought it immoral in the first two years of the survey (1977 to 1978). But from 1979 through 1982, a more orthodox trend

**Table 3.3**

**"Premarital Sex is Immoral," by Year and Sex**

|      | Agree | | | Disagree | | | Don't Know | | |
|      | Gender | | | Gender | | | Gender | | |
| Year | Male | Female | Total | Male | Female | Total | Male | Female | Total |
|------|-------|--------|-------|-------|--------|-------|-------|--------|-------|
| 1977 | 26.2% | 33.3% | 29.3% | 68.8% | 51.7% | 61.4% | 5.0% | 15.0% | 9.3% |
| 1978 | 17.6% | 30.2% | 24.7% | 69.1% | 58.1% | 63.0% | 13.2% | 11.6% | 12.3% |
| 1979 | 31.5% | 42.4% | 37.8% | 56.2% | 47.5% | 51.2% | 12.3% | 10.1% | 11.0% |
| 1980 | 39.4% | 43.5% | 41.7% | 50.7% | 48.9% | 49.7% | 9.9% | 7.6% | 8.6% |
| 1981 | 43.5% | 52.3% | 48.0% | 44.7% | 34.1% | 39.3% | 11.8% | 13.6% | 12.7% |
| 1982 | 46.1% | 57.8% | 52.4% | 44.7% | 34.4% | 39.2% | 9.2% | 7.8% | 8.4% |
| 1983 | 28.1% | 26.2% | 27.1% | 51.6% | 46.2% | 48.6% | 20.3% | 27.5% | 24.3% |
| 1984 | 30.8% | 39.4% | 34.9% | 53.8% | 39.4% | 47.0% | 15.4% | 21.1% | 18.1% |
| 1985 | 39.0% | 40.0% | 39.5% | 46.8% | 36.7% | 41.3% | 14.3% | 23.3% | 19.2% |
| 1986 | 18.4% | 18.5% | 18.5% | 67.1% | 63.0% | 64.9% | 14.5% | 18.5% | 16.7% |
| 1987 | 28.7% | 27.2% | 27.9% | 58.7% | 64.1% | 61.7% | 12.5% | 8.7% | 10.4% |
| 1988 | 17.4% | 24.4% | 20.6% | 66.3% | 62.8% | 64.7% | 16.3% | 12.8% | 14.7% |
| 1989 | 19.1% | 21.4% | 20.3% | 68.5% | 62.2% | 65.2% | 12.4% | 16.3% | 14.4% |

set in, with over half in 1982 agreeing that premarital sex was immoral. In 1983, a very sharp drop, followed by a modest two year upswing, occurred. But the classes of 1986 through 1989 re-endorsed the liberal trend of the mid-1970s. Most remarkably, the class of 1986 increased 20 percentage points over the class of 1985 to 65 percent *disagreeing* overall—a level that has held fast through 1989.

Is this recent shift due mostly to young men changing their views? Given the traditional double standard, male seniors should be consistently more "liberal" than female seniors. Is this the case? In general, yes: the data from 1977 through 1982 speak clearly. But 1983 marks the opening year of a change. Males and females begin to even out and remain so through 1989. Majorities of both genders reject orthodox norms. But a glance at the *disagree* column shows an especially sharp upturn for both male and female seniors from 1986 through 1989. Obviously, 1986 marked a pivotal shift in seniors views: males' disagreement leaped ahead by 20 percentage points, while females outdid them with a 26 percent spurt which led to virtual parity with males for the rest of the decade. The late 1980s, then, reflected through the opinions of St. Martin's seniors, suggest the "sexual revolution" had wiped out any traces of "double-standard" thinking. Almost two-thirds of seniors, both women and men, disagreed that "premarital sex is immoral from 1986 through 1989.

But what about Hispanic seniors? Are they more orthodox than Anglo seniors? They are not. By the mid-1980s, both male and female Hispanic seniors were virtually indistinguishable from their Anglo counterparts. Once again, if a "sexual revolution" characterizes these late 1980s seniors, it has swept along a majority of Hispanics too.

"Welcoming more sexual freedom" appealed to teenage Catholics nationally in 1985 by a resounding two-thirds (69 percent).[35] Obviously, St. Martin's seniors were much more cautious (table 3.4). Only a third in the mid-1980s welcomed this freedom, a percentage rising to somewhat over 40 percent in 1987 and 1988. Notable is the one-fifth to one-quarter of seniors over the decade who were unsure or did not know. In fact, the classes of 1988 and 1989 represent the highest proportions of "don't knows" in the thirteen-year period. In any case, compared with Catholic teenagers nationally, these seniors are notably unsure, while holding to liberal views on premarital sex, whether more sexual freedom is a good idea. Senior women have been much more reluctant through the years to approve of "more freedom." In fact, from 1986 through 1989, while the men took a sharp upturn in agreeing, percentages of "approving" women rose slightly but remained from 20 to 25 points less in agreement than the men. Senior women, then, may be as "liberal" as their male classmates on premarital sex, but they seem much less convinced that more sexual freedom is a good idea. For them, perhaps, "the revolution" has gone far enough; maybe they wonder what more freedom would mean, anyway.

Abortion (if child is likely to have serious birth defects) shows the same patterns evident with premarital sex: 1977 and 1978 were "boldly

### Table 3.4
### "More Sexual Freedom a Good Thing," by Year and Sex

| Year | Agree | | | Disagree | | | Don't Know | | |
|------|-------|--------|-------|----------|--------|-------|------------|--------|-------|
| | Gender | | | Gender | | | Gender | | |
| | Male | Female | Total | Male | Female | Total | Male | Female | Total |
| 1977 | 46.9% | 26.7% | 38.3% | 32.1% | 45.0% | 37.6% | 21.0% | 28.3% | 24.1% |
| 1978 | 55.9% | 33.0% | 42.9% | 25.0% | 35.2% | 30.8% | 19.1% | 31.8% | 26.3% |
| 1979 | 52.8% | 26.3% | 37.4% | 23.6% | 54.5% | 41.5% | 23.6% | 19.2% | 21.1% |
| 1980 | 44.4% | 22.8% | 32.3% | 33.3% | 47.8% | 41.5% | 22.2% | 29.3% | 26.2% |
| 1981 | 39.3% | 20.0% | 29.6% | 41.7% | 57.6% | 49.7% | 19.0% | 22.4% | 20.7% |
| 1982 | 31.6% | 21.1% | 25.9% | 38.2% | 61.1% | 50.6% | 30.3% | 17.8% | 23.5% |
| 1983 | 35.9% | 27.5% | 31.3% | 40.6% | 48.7% | 45.1% | 23.4% | 23.7% | 23.6% |
| 1984 | 44.9% | 18.3% | 32.2% | 37.2% | 60.6% | 48.3% | 17.9% | 21.1% | 19.5% |
| 1985 | 36.4% | 29.7% | 32.7% | 40.3% | 53.8% | 47.6% | 23.4% | 16.5% | 19.6% |
| 1986 | 50.7% | 25.0% | 36.5% | 34.7% | 47.8% | 41.9% | 14.7% | 27.2% | 21.6% |
| 1987 | 57.5% | 32.0% | 43.2% | 28.7% | 45.6% | 38.3% | 13.7% | 22.3% | 18.6% |
| 1988 | 51.1% | 31.6% | 42.1% | 22.8% | 38.0% | 29.8% | 26.1% | 30.4% | 28.1% |
| 1989 | 52.2% | 28.3% | 39.7% | 28.9% | 37.4% | 33.3% | 18.9% | 34.3% | 27.0% |

liberal." The following year began a five-year conservative trend. But from 1974 to 1986, liberal attitudes again surfaced, though the graduating classes of 1987 and 1988 swung rather sharply toward a more orthodox stance (table 3.5). Significant differences appear by gender in just two years (1987 and 1989); none by ethnic background.

*Parish Orientation.* As table 3.6 makes clear, an upward shift in proportions of seniors seeing themselves in the future as either "attending but taking little or no active part," or "having little or nothing to do with parish or church" began in 1984. In 1983, the *combined* percentage of these two responses (labeled "little" and "nothing" in table 3.6) was 44 percent, but the following years saw the combined percentages jump to over 50 percent, rising to a thirteen-year high of 59 percent in 1987 and 1988. Male-female and Anglo-Hispanic differences (not shown here) are negligible, though male seniors are more likely than females to say they anticipate having "nothing to do" with the parish in later life.

## Summary

No bright, rosy-hued picture emerges from these data, nor do the 1980s studies reviewed earlier lead us to expect one. On the other hand, St. Martin's seniors hardly appear as sullen rebels against authority. The trend data tentatively suggest that the admission policy adopted in the late 1970s that brought large numbers of high SES students into St. Martin's, resulted in a mid-1980s student body (or at least, senior classes) less religious by survey measures, more resistant to orthodox teaching, less inclined to identify with ideals of social charity ("sharing") and social justice, and more reluctant to see themselves in future years as active participants in their parishes. Males contribute a good deal to the decline on social measures; few differences by ethnicity are apparent. No wholesale defections, of course, are evident. But a different kind of senior was sitting in St. Martin's classrooms. The next analytical task is to crosstabulate religious with background variables to see what relationship exists, if any, between these higher SES seniors of the 1980s and diminished religious outlooks and practice. Do occupational and educational attainments of parents significantly predict seniors' responses?

## Social and Personal Orientations: Bivariate Analysis

Nine dependent variables are singled out in the following section for bivariate analysis. Six of these were asked in all twelve survey years, 1977 through 1989, and were reviewed in the previous section: responsibility for sharing with others; responsibility for dealing with injustice; premarital sex; sexual freedom; abortion if fetus is defective; and future participation in the parish.

Beginning in 1983, I added several questions repeated through 1989. I

## Table 3.5

### "Abortion Acceptable if Child Defective," by Year and Sex

| Year | Agree* | | | Disagree | | | Strongly Disagree | | | Don't Know | | |
|------|--------|--------|-------|----------|--------|-------|-------------------|--------|-------|------------|--------|-------|
| | Gender | | | Gender | | | Gender | | | Gender | | |
| | Male | Female | Total | Male | Female | Total | Male | Female | Total | Male | Female | Total |
| 1977 | 40.5% | 28.8% | 35.5% | 34.2% | 30.5% | 32.6% | 16.5% | 28.8% | 21.7% | 8.9% | 11.9% | 10.1% |
| 1978 | 27.9% | 39.8% | 34.6% | 29.4% | 21.6% | 25.0% | 27.9% | 23.9% | 25.6% | 14.7% | 14.8% | 14.7% |
| 1979 | 17.1% | 33.3% | 26.4% | 27.1% | 21.5% | 23.9% | 47.1% | 36.6% | 41.1% | 8.6% | 8.6% | 8.6% |
| 1980 | 25.0% | 21.3% | 23.0% | 20.8% | 32.6% | 27.3% | 50.0% | 36.0% | 42.2% | 4.2% | 10.1% | 7.5% |
| 1981 | 7.1% | 12.3% | 9.7% | 46.4% | 18.5% | 32.7% | 41.7% | 67.9% | 54.5% | 4.8% | 1.2% | 3.0% |
| 1982 | 26.3% | 22.7% | 24.4% | 25.0% | 22.7% | 23.8% | 46.1% | 50.0% | 48.2% | 2.6% | 4.5% | 3.7% |
| 1983 | 23.4% | 22.5% | 22.9% | 34.4% | 25.0% | 29.2% | 34.4% | 37.5% | 36.1% | 7.8% | 15.0% | 11.8% |
| 1984 | 32.1% | 31.0% | 31.5% | 24.4% | 15.5% | 20.1% | 29.5% | 36.6% | 32.9% | 14.1% | 16.9% | 15.4% |
| 1985 | 33.8% | 26.4% | 29.8% | 29.9% | 28.6% | 29.2% | 22.1% | 29.7% | 26.2% | 14.3% | 15.4% | 14.9% |
| 1986 | 44.7% | 45.7% | 45.2% | 27.6% | 25.0% | 26.2% | 19.7% | 18.5% | 19.0% | 7.9% | 10.9% | 9.5% |
| 1987 | 33.7% | 23.3% | 27.9% | 46.2% | 31.1% | 37.7% | 15.0% | 35.9% | 26.8% | 5.0% | 9.7% | 7.7% |
| 1988 | 29.3% | 27.8% | 28.7% | 33.7% | 26.6% | 30.4% | 23.9% | 22.8% | 23.4% | 13.0% | 22.8% | 17.5% |
| 1989 | 42.2% | 31.3% | 36.5% | 32.2% | 24.2% | 28.0% | 21.1% | 30.3% | 25.9% | 4.4% | 14.1% | 9.5% |

* "Agree" combined the small percentages of "strongly agree" respondents with those stating "agree".

Table 3.6

**Willingness to be Involved with Parish, By Year and Sex**

| Year | Active Gender | | | Little Gender | | | Don't Know Gender | | | Nothing Gender | | |
|---|---|---|---|---|---|---|---|---|---|---|---|---|
| | Male | Female | Total | Male | Female | Total | Male | Female | Total | Male | Female | Total |
| 1977 | 25.9% | 26.7% | 26.2% | 35.8% | 43.3% | 39.0% | 29.6% | 26.7% | 28.4% | 8.6% | 3.3% | 6.4% |
| 1978 | 19.1% | 24.4% | 22.1% | 47.1% | 47.7% | 47.4% | 25.0% | 24.4% | 24.7% | 8.8% | 3.5% | 5.8% |
| 1979 | 26.0% | 21.0% | 23.1% | 34.2% | 51.0% | 43.9% | 37.0% | 25.0% | 30.1% | 2.7% | 3.0% | 2.9% |
| 1980 | 31.9% | 25.0% | 28.0% | 31.9% | 35.9% | 34.1% | 34.7% | 34.8% | 34.8% | 1.4% | 4.3% | 3.0% |
| 1981 | 30.6% | 34.1% | 32.4% | 31.8% | 31.8% | 31.8% | 37.6% | 33.0% | 35.3% | 0.0% | 1.1% | .6% |
| 1982 | 27.6% | 32.2% | 30.1% | 39.5% | 36.7% | 38.0% | 30.3% | 25.6% | 27.7% | 2.6% | 5.6% | 4.2% |
| 1983 | 25.0% | 20.5% | 22.5% | 29.7% | 37.7% | 35.2% | 31.3% | 34.6% | 33.1% | 14.1% | 5.1% | 9.2% |
| 1984 | 23.1% | 21.1% | 22.1% | 39.7% | 43.7% | 41.6% | 16.7% | 26.8% | 21.5% | 20.5% | 8.5% | 14.8% |
| 1985 | 11.8% | 30.8% | 22.2% | 48.7% | 39.6% | 43.7% | 19.7% | 22.0% | 21.0% | 19.7% | 7.7% | 13.2% |
| 1986 | 10.7% | 18.5% | 15.0% | 37.3% | 38.0% | 37.7% | 26.7% | 32.6% | 29.9% | 25.3% | 10.9% | 17.4% |
| 1987 | 17.5% | 22.3% | 20.2% | 45.0% | 50.5% | 48.1% | 20.0% | 21.4% | 20.8% | 17.5% | 5.8% | 10.9% |
| 1988 | 17.6% | 16.5% | 17.1% | 42.9% | 44.3% | 43.5% | 20.9% | 26.6% | 23.5% | 18.7% | 12.7% | 15.9% |
| 1989 | 16.9% | 16.2% | 16.5% | 33.7% | 43.4% | 38.8% | 34.8% | 28.3% | 31.4% | 14.6% | 12.1% | 13.3% |

select for analysis the following items created from these questions: (1) an index (CHRCHTCH) composed of three questions asking whether the respondent thinks it is the business of the *Church* to be involved with racial discrimination, world hunger, and nuclear disarmament; (2) a similar index (MEINVOLV) dealing with the same three issues, but asking whether the respondent feels it is the *individual's* responsibility to be involved with these issues. Finally, a question on conscience formation (CONSCNCE) asks seniors to choose one of three statements regarding the formation of one's conscience: (1) to base one's conscience on the Church's teaching regarding beliefs and morality; (2) to listen to the Church's teaching but then make up one's own mind as one's conscience suggests; (3) to reject the right of any authority to influence the formation of conscience, which should be left strictly to each individual.

### Findings

The following analysis highlights the social conscience variables of responsibility for sharing and for opposing injustice, the two indexes of personal involvement and of the Church's business to teach and the formation of personal conscience. I devote a briefer discussion to items of personal morality and of later parish involvement. The analysis employs both religiosity and background variables and adds two items relating to the school's theology program: (1) whether the theology courses make the Church's teaching more credible or less credible and (2) how would the respondent rate the theology program from excellent to poor on a five-point scale.

Let us turn first to two already familiar questions: responsibility for sharing and for opposing injustice. Appendix 2 displays responses to these two items taking into account the admission of higher SES students who first appeared in the senior class of 1983. That is, the analysis divides the entire eleven-year group into two sections, those graduating from 1977 through 1982 and those receiving their diplomas from 1983 through 1989. Answers are displayed according to an array of independent variables, both background and religiosity measures. Three responses are given under each year group: (1) those strongly agreeing with the item, (2) those simply agreeing, and (3) those disagreeing—a single category combining disagree with the very small number who chose "strongly disagree."

We have already seen the trend data indicating dramatic differences between the two senior year groupings. To repeat, the 1983 to 1989 seniors are much less likely to show "strongly agree" as a response on both items. But the *direction* of the shift differs for the "sharing" item as compared to the "oppose injustice" measure. In the "sharing" responses, the shift is mainly toward the milder "agree" statement and less toward the "disagree" column. But this is *not* the case with the "oppose injustice" statement. The jump from those who "disagree" between 1977 and 1982 to those who disagree between 1983 and 1989 is much higher for this item than for the "sharing" statement.

Let us examine both these variables in more detail, utilizing background and religiosity controls (Appendix 2). Focusing on "sharing with others," statistical significance accompanies only three items: gender, importance of ethnic background, and grade point average (GPA). In both year groupings, males show more resistance to "sharing." Also in both groupings, those affirming their ethnic background as "very important" are notably more willing to "share" than those deeming it less important; in fact, the relationship is straightforward linear between 1983 and 1989, with the "not very important" category most likely to strongly disagree. Those boasting the highest GPAs among the 1977 to 1982 seniors are much more likely to strongly agree than the "lower achievers." Among the 1983 to 1988 seniors, the highest *two* GPA categories together are sharply distinct from the bottom two.

Perhaps most striking is that neither father's nor mother's occupation distinguishes seniors' responses in *either* year grouping. Seniors from professional parents are no less willing to strongly agree—or disagree—than students from blue-collar or business-owner-manager families. Whatever is responsible for the "downward flow" of attitudes toward this item as we move into the mid-1980s, then, is apparently not directly the result of a larger influx of students from a higher family status into the school.

Background controls are even less significant in predicting responses to unjust practices in society. Two controls stand out: young women are twice as likely as young men to strongly agree on this item, though only among the 1983 to 1989 seniors. Again, those with top GPAs are the strongest supporters of this item across both year groupings. Parental occupations continue to be insignificant predictors. In fact, a slight (though insignificant) *positive* relationship appears, that is, the percentage of those strongly agreeing with this statement tends to *rise* with parental SES. Seniors from professional families are slightly more favorably disposed to agree than those from lower families status, a surprising finding.

*Religious Controls.* Religiosity questions turn out to be quite good predictors, better, in fact, than parental SES. Previous religious education in elementary school is the weakest. The others show a good deal of strength: belonging to a religious group, importance of religion, and strength of religious conviction are statistically significant across both variables and both year groupings. Yet while the religiosity items predict responses fairly strongly, *more* such items attain significance (statistically) among the *1983 to 1989* seniors than among the earlier group of graduates. Among cohorts (1983 to 1989) less disposed in the first place to agree with these items, the more "religious" seniors stand out in giving stronger assent to these statements.

But more than *personal* religiosity is operative among these seniors. Both theology program items are insignificant among the 1977 to 1982 seniors on both "sharing" and "opposing injustice." But they *are* operative with the 1983 to 1989 graduates to help distinguish the more from the less socially responsive seniors. In a word, personal religiosity and theology program variables had relatively little impact among the 1977 to 1982 seniors, who were more disposed as a group to agree with these items anyway. But among the 1983 to 1989 seniors, who appear more resistant to these social teachings or principles, being "more religious" and approving the theology program do have an impact, setting them apart from that growing proportion of seniors in the mid- and late 1980s who are not so "religious" or appreciative of the theology program. These measures of social sensitivity then, for the 1983 to 1989 seniors, are tied positively to religious attitudes and to favorable views about the theology program.

*Personal Involvement, Church as Teacher, and Conscience.* Keep in mind that these questions were asked only of 1983 to 1989 seniors. Tables for these variables are found in Appendix 3. As was the case with "sharing with others" and "opposing injustice," being religious does positively reinforce the item, "It is my personal responsibility to be involved with the question of racial discrimination (or world hunger or the nuclear arms race)." But the relationship is modest and the theology program items are insignificant (family values and peer attitudes not measured in this survey may well be the greatest influence on these issues). Which seniors, then, score highest on this Index? Those who are female, enjoy high GPAs, whose home language is Spanish and whose fathers have been in the military eight years or more are most favorably disposed toward personal involvement.

Religiosity variables are much stronger predictors of attitudes toward the *Church as teacher* ("It is the Church's responsibility to be involved with questions of racial discrimination [or world hunger or the nuclear arms race])." Only two background variables enjoy a modest relationship, with Hispanic (and mixed-Hispanic) students and students speaking Spanish at home more likely to acknowledge the Church's authority to teach on social issues. This is one of the few variables in which ethnic background is a significant predictor. Identity as Hispanic coupled with Spanish spoken in the home apparently dispose these seniors positively toward the Church as teacher; they bring less skepticism than Anglo students to the Church as teaching institution. Just as in the case of the "sharing" and "oppose injustice" variables, it seems to "require" personal religiosity reinforced by high regard for the theology program to bring out positive sentiment toward the Church as teacher. To some extent, then, the school assumes importance as a setting in which sensitivity to the Church as teacher is nurtured.

Conscience formation is related significantly only to religiosity variables. No background variables attain statistical significance.

*Premarital Sex, Sexual Freedom, Abortion, and Parish.* Again, no dramatic revelations await us in the tables displaying these variables (Appendix 3). Personal religiosity and theology program variables are strong predictors of all four items. Simply put, the more religious the student and the more he or she esteems the theology program, the more orthodox the senior will be on premarital sex, the less he or she will endorse more sexual freedom or abortion because of defects, and the more likely he or she will be to take an active part in a Catholic parish in the future. None of this is very surprising. I would like at this point to focus directly on background items, analyzing their relative value as predictors on the variables we have just seen.

### Background Variables: A Commentary

Among background items, gender and grade point average are most consistently represented as significant. Only these two are found across the four dependent variables of premarital sex, sexual freedom, abortion, and future participation in the parish. Female seniors and high grade achievers respond in a more "Catholic sense" to these items, perhaps because being female and being a superior student act as surrogate measures of identification with the school and school culture. Female seniors and good students may be more likely to identify with teachers and course themes than males and students with lower GPAs. Ethnic background—in this study, whether one is Hispanic or Anglo—is of little significance except for attitude toward the Church as teacher. Hispanic seniors are *less* likely to reject Church authority in social teaching. *More* importance than ethnic background on several items (responsibility to share with others, premarital sex, and parish involvement) is the *importance* of ethnicity to the respondent; furthermore, language spoken at home reveals that a Spanish-speaking background is positively related both to responsibility for sharing and personal involvement in world hunger and other issues as well as an acknowledgment of the Church's right to teach on these topics.

Measures of parental SES turn out to be inconsistent predictors. Father's occupation is relevant only for future parish participation, i.e., the more "professional" the father's occupation, the less likely the senior will indicate future active participation in his or her parish. *Mother's* occupation, though, has impact on premarital sex, sexual freedom, and abortion attitudes. The main "cutting point" is between mothers who are housewives (displaying greater orthodoxy) and those in the labor force, whether full- or part-time. Father's and mother's education (asked only from 1983 on) simply wash out as predictors, insignificant statistically to any of the dependent variables we are examining. This apparent insignificance may appear strange, of course, because the split between the two groupings (1977 to 1982 and 1983 to 1989) suggests a strong impact of the higher SES freshman entering the school in the late 1970s. Obviously, other factors besides parental SES were at work in accounting for the difference between the two groupings.

Agreement that the theology program makes the Church's teaching more credible is strongly and positively related to *all* dependent variables except for the personal involvement index. How each senior *rates* the program impacts on fewer items: premarital sex and sexual freedom, abortion, parish involvement, and church authority in social teaching. To explore these variable relationships in a different way, I turn to regression analysis.

### Variable Relationships: Regression Analysis

White the preceding bivariate analysis has pointed to background and religiosity measures significantly related to the major dependent variables, it does not address the question of which of these independent variables emerge as the strongest influence when one controls for all of them simultaneously? Will, for example, parental SES (occupation and education) turn out to be a strong predictor *when compared with other independent variables?* I turn to ordinary least-square multiple regression analysis to answer this question for each dependent variable examined above.

I also decided, however, in view of the apparent weakness of SES variables as predictors, to see whether the impact of the several independent variables (such as gender, ethnic background, and importance of religion) *changed after 1983,* considering the dramatic time-period shifts already seen. After 1983, for example, does the impact of social status (father's occupation and education) increase and that of religiosity decrease as more students with a high SES are admitted to the school? I thus recoded year of graduation as a binary variable (1 = 1977 to 1982; 2 = 1983 to 1989) and multiplied each independent variable by year of graduation to form a product term subsequently entered into each regression equation along with all independent variables. After inspecting the results for each dependent variable, I then dropped all variables but those emerging as statistically significant, entering only the latter into a "final equation" for each of the major dependent variables. The results are displayed in table 3.7 and 3.8.

In the analysis that follows, the explained variance is quite small for any single dependent variable, i.e., the predictor or independent variables account for no more than 16 percent of the explained variance for any one variable. But accounting for variance is not a key issue in this analysis. What is important is the *relative weight* of each predictor variable in comparison with others entered into the regression equation. Significant, too, is whether any of the independent variables shift in impact on the measures (dependent variables) when we move from the 1977 to 1982 to the 1983 to 1989 group. The product terms entered into each equation are designed to help answer this question.

*Willingness to Share with Others.* Table 3.7 indicates that willingness to share with others is most strongly related to importance of religion. But gender and grade point average are also significant (girls and high academic achievers are more willing to share). Father's occupation is not significant. While both year of graduation and religious conviction taken separately are weakly related to willingness to share, together as a product term they have an impact second only to importance of religion. In other words, conviction about the Church's teaching did not predict attitudes toward sharing from 1977 to 1982. Seniors during these earlier years apparently affirmed or distanced themselves from willingness to share, regardless of conviction. To return to the analysis made above, as the student body changed during the 1983 to 1989 group, seniors on the whole were less disposed to agree that they had a responsibility to share with those who had less. Seniors most strongly convinced of Catholic teachings, however, were significantly more likely to agree.

*Responsibility for Injustice.* Responsibility for doing something about injustice elicited grade point average and religious conviction as relatively important predictors. But the strongest variable by far is year of graduation (beta weight of 0.30). The shift in student body manifested in the responses of the 1983 to 1989 seniors had a powerful negative impact on proportion of seniors endorsing the quest for justice. The product term of year graduated and gender attains significance, that is, the difference in response patterns between males and females is much sharper among 1983 to 1989 seniors. Girls are much more apt than boys in the later group to acknowledge their responsibility to correct social injustices in society. Father's occupation attains a slight significance, but again not in the way suggested at first by the trend data. As the bivariate analysis revealed, seniors with high SES fathers are slightly *more* willing to "correct injustices" than lower status counterparts.

*Church as Teacher.* Is it the Church's responsibility to be involved with world hunger, nuclear war, and racial discrimination? (This question was asked only from 1983 to 1989.) Degree of religious conviction continues to be salient; father's occupation, insignificant in crosstabular analysis, develops a modest impact along with the two theology program variables. Again, seniors with higher status fathers are *more* likely to endorse Church authority to teach on social issues than are lower status fathers. As we have seen, approval of the theology program enhances seniors' willingness to acknowledge the Church's role as teacher on social issues.

*Willingness to Be Involved.* In terms of willingness to be personally

### Table 3.7

**Seniors' Attitudes Toward Sharing, Opposing Injustice, Church Social Involvement, and Personal Involvement: Regression Coefficients, Standard Errors, and Beta Weights for Predictor Variables**

| Independent Variables | Sharing | | | Unjust Practices | | | Church's Business | | | Personal Involvement | | |
|---|---|---|---|---|---|---|---|---|---|---|---|---|
| | b | SE | B | b | SE | B | b | SE | B | b | SE | B |
| Sex of respondent | -0.16 | 0.041 | -0.09 | -0.04 | 0.069 | -0.02 | — | — | — | -0.10 | 0.053 | -0.07 |
| Grade point average | 0.08 | .023 | .08 | .14 | .029 | .12 | .08 | .031 | .09 | .08 | .030 | .09 |
| Importance of ethnic background to respondent | .06 | .026 | .05 | — | — | — | — | — | — | — | — | — |
| Year grouping of survey (1977 to 1982 or 1983 to 1987) | .07 | .080 | .04 | .65 | .075 | .30 | — | — | — | — | — | — |
| Father's occupation | — | — | — | -.05 | .020 | -.05 | -.06 | .023 | -.09 | -.06 | .023 | -.10 |
| Conviction on teachings of Catholic Church | .03 | .024 | .04 | .12 | .019 | .14 | .09 | .029 | .14 | — | — | — |
| Importance of religion | .21 | .038 | .15 | — | — | — | — | — | — | .17 | .037 | .17 |
| Belonging to a religious group | -.15 | .053 | -.07 | — | — | — | — | — | — | — | — | — |
| Credibility of Church Teaching by theology courses | — | — | — | — | — | — | .10 | .047 | .10 | — | — | — |
| Rating of theology program | — | — | — | — | — | — | .10 | .042 | .10 | — | — | — |
| *Product Terms* | | | | | | | | | | | | |
| Conviction on teachings, year grouping | .07 | .030 | .13 | — | — | — | — | — | — | — | — | — |
| Sex of respondent, year grouping | — | — | — | -.31 | .100 | -.13 | — | — | — | — | — | — |

b = regression coefficient

SE = standard error

B = beta weight

involved in these issues, importance of religion is the single most important predictor. Seniors whose fathers are of lower SES are slightly less likely to say yes. Again, females and those with higher grade point averages stand out as supporters of personal involvement.

*Premarital Sex.* Three religiosity variables together with grade point average are major "actors" in predicting attitudes on premarital sex (table 3.8). Two ethnic-related variables—importance of ethnic background and language spoked at home—play a lesser role (again, no product terms are significant).

*More Sexual Freedom.* Advocacy of more sexual freedom, as one would suppose, is negatively related to the religiosity variables (table 3.8). But the latter, in a departure from the premarital sex variable, are secondary to sex of respondent and to the variable year. Seniors from 1983 to 1989 are significantly more likely to advocate more sexual freedom; males consistently through the eleven years "out-advocate" the female seniors. In a repeat of the pattern evident in "responsibility for sharing" above, importance of religion becomes a slightly more important predictor in the 1983 to 1989 group; once more, these seniors from a higher SES background "need" stronger religiosity in order to affirm that more sexual freedom is *not* such a good thing.

*Abortion if Fetus Is Defective.* Abortion if a fetus proves defective (table 3.8) is subject to the same variable relationship just noted: seniors from 1983 through 1989 are substantially more likely to support abortion in such circumstances. But throughout the thirteen years, church attendance and importance of religion relate negatively to support for abortion. Curiously, prior religious education, a mild predictor, receives support as a product term, meaning that from 1983 to 1989, its impact is stronger than in the previous six years (1977 to 1982).

*Parish Involvement.* Willingness to be involved in the future with one's parish reflects the impact of grade point average, mother's occupation, and religious education prior to high school. But the latter is the sole religiosity variable with any significant impact, making this response unique among those seen so far. Importance of ethnic background is moderately important over the years but, when combined with year graduated, tells us that believing one's ethnic background to be important has a much bigger impact in generating sentiment for future parish involvement among the 1983 to 1989 seniors than among their predecessors. In a word, an element of traditionality inserts itself to distinguish seniors who affirm parish involvement as a future goal from those who reject it (table 3.8).

*Conscience Formation.* This item (not shown on table) was asked from 1983 to 1989 only. It is distinguished by having *no* background items significantly related to it. It is affected only by religiosity questions, very

## Table 3.8

**Seniors' Attitudes Toward Premarital Sex, Sexual Freedom, Abortion if Fetus is Defective, and Parish Involvement: Regression Coefficients, Standard Errors, and Beta Weights for Predictor Variables**

| Independent Variables | Premarital Sex b | SE | B | Sexual Freedom b | SE | B | Abortion b | SE | B | Parish b | SE | B |
|---|---|---|---|---|---|---|---|---|---|---|---|---|
| Grade point average | 0.13 | 0.030 | 0.16 | −0.13 | 0.026 | −0.11 | — | — | — | 0.05 | 0.03 | 0.05 |
| Importance of ethnic background to respondent | .11 | .035 | .08 | — | — | — | .11 | .040 | .06 | .21 | .056 | .26 |
| Language spoken at home | .19 | .058 | .08 | — | — | — | — | — | — | — | — | — |
| Sex of respondent | — | — | — | .35 | .047 | .17 | — | — | — | — | — | — |
| Year grouping of survey (1977 to 1982 or 1983 to 1987) | — | — | — | .37 | .131 | .17 | −.44 | .161 | −.16 | −.12 | .13 | −.07 |
| Church attendance | .28 | .040 | .17 | −.10 | .035 | −.07 | −.34 | .049 | −.18 | — | — | — |
| Importance of religion | .28 | .050 | .16 | −.17 | .057 | −.11 | −.31 | .061 | −.14 | — | — | — |
| Conviction on teachings of Catholic Church | .13 | .023 | .15 | −.07 | .020 | −.10 | −.08 | .028 | −.08 | — | — | — |
| Belonging to a religious education | — | — | — | — | — | — | −.17 | .058 | −.09 | .09 | .03 | .07 |
| Mother's occupation | — | — | — | — | — | — | — | — | — | .04 | .02 | .05 |
| *Product Terms* | | | | | | | | | | | | |
| Importance of religion, year grouping | — | — | — | −.14 | .072 | −.14 | — | — | — | — | — | — |
| Prior religious education, year grouping | — | — | — | — | — | — | .17 | .086 | .12 | — | — | — |

b = regression coefficient
SE = standard error
B = beta weight

especially by importance of religion and religious conviction whose beta weights far surpass those of the other religiosity variables.

Before I draw some conclusions from this analysis, I turn to findings from the 1987 to 1989 senior surveys asking their reactions to the 1986 bishops' pastoral letter on the American economy. The question on personal responsibility for dealing with unemployment, poverty, and other issues may well tap what Kluegel and Smith (cited earlier) refer to as the dominant ideological beliefs about the stratification system itself. Here "new class" Americans are less likely to answer "liberally," since they believe the existing system naturally favors those who work hard and thus deserve the system's rewards.

### A Note on the Classes of 1987 to 1989

Two questions were added to the survey filled out by the graduating classes of 1987 to 1989, reflecting publication in late 1986 of the American bishops' pastoral letter, "Economic Justice for All." The first question contains wording taken directly from the pastoral letter. In paragraph No. 360, the bishops state the dual goal of the letter:

> to help Catholics form their consciences on the moral dimensions of economic decision-making and to articulate a moral perspective in the general societal and political debate that surrounds these questions.[36]

In tandem with the format used to ask seniors' views on the Church's teaching role on sociomoral issues and the individual senior's sense of personal responsibility on each issue, the questions were worded as follows:

1. "It is the Church's business to help Catholics form their consciences on the moral dimensions of economic decision-making, for example, in areas such as unemployment, poverty, immigration policy, national spending priorities, etc." (strongly agree, etc.).

2. "It is my own personal responsibility to be involved with solutions to problems such as those stated in the question above" (strongly agree, etc.).

It is instructive to compare answers on these two questions with those concerning racial discrimination, world hunger, and nuclear arms race (table 3.9). One relationship appears clearly: the more controversial an issue, the stronger the resistance to affirming the appropriateness of Church teaching on the issue. Thus, combining strongly agree and agree responses, world hunger receives 91 percent support from the seniors; combatting racial discrimina-

Table 3.9

**Authority of the Catholic Church and Sense of Personal Involvement in Issues of Nuclear War, World Hunger, and Racial Discrimination Compared with Issues of Economic Decision-Making St. Martin's High School, Classes of 1987 to 1989\***

**(N = 517)**

*1. Authority to be involved with*

| "It is the Church's business to be involved with teaching on . . ." | | | | "It is the Church's business to help Catholics form their consciences on the moral dimensions of economic decision-making, etc." |
|---|---|---|---|---|
| | Racial Discrimination | World Hunger | Nuclear Arms Race | |
| Stongly agree | 25% | 29% | 18% | 9% |
| Agree | 56% | 62% | 43% | 49% |
| Disagree[†] | 11% | 4% | 29% | 32% |
| Don't know | 8% | 4% | 10% | 10% |

*2. Sense of Personal Responsibilty*

| "It is my own personal responsibility to be involved with the problem of . . ." | | | | "It is my own personal responsibility to be involved with solutions to problems of unemployment, etc." |
|---|---|---|---|---|
| | Racial Discrimination | World Hunger | Nuclear Arms Race | |
| Stongly agree | 27% | 22% | 20% | 24% |
| Agree | 51% | 54% | 48% | 51% |
| Disagree | 13% | 13% | 18% | 14% |
| Don't know | 9% | 10% | 14% | 11% |

\* T-tests revealed no significant differences in means on these two items among the classes of 1987 through 1989. The data are therefore combined for the three years.

† Due to the small number of respondents choosing "stongly disagree" on these items, this response was combined with the "disagree" response to form one category for both questions.

tion, 82 percent, and reducing nuclear arms, 62 percent—all impressive majorities but still markedly distinct from one another. Very few say the Church has "no business" in these areas. But when the formation of consciences on economic decision-making enters the scene, just slightly over half (57 percent) agree that the Church has a legitimate role to play. This drop may, of course, reflect the phrase "form consciences" (used by the bishops in the letter itself), perhaps objectionable to some seniors as suggesting an authoritarian "mind control" rather than a presentation of teaching.

Keeping the focus on the first question (Church's role in forming consciences), background variable controls show *none* of the latter are statistically significant when brought to bear on this question. *Religious* controls, however, do manifest significant response shifts (table not shown here) making a difference in how favorably these 1987 to 1989 seniors view the Church's teaching role, particularly in economic matters. Church attendance, for example, is statistically insignificant with regard to the Church's role in racial discrimination, world hunger, and nuclear disarmament but *is* significant ($p<0.03$) on the economic decision-making issue. Controls for importance of religion and degree of religious conviction are more strongly related to all "Church role" items but much *more* forcefully to economic decision-making ($p = 0.000$). The "average senior," in other words, is generally approving of the Church's role in racial discrimination, etc., but when it comes to economic decision-making, he or she is much more cautious. It takes, so to speak, the more "religious" seniors to endorse a very favorable view of the Church's role in forming consciences where economic decision-making is concerned. The variable of attitude toward the theology program is also salient. Classroom teaching appears as a key factor in creating a positive sentiment toward the Church's outreach in socioeconomic moral teaching, as it did with other sociomoral issues seen previously.

With regard to the second question on personal responsibility only *one* background variable affected this response: those stating their ethnic background was important to them were twice as likely to "strongly agree" that they had such a personal responsibility than those saying background was "not important" (30 versus 15 percent). Just one variable related to religion made a difference: those who found Church teachings more credible due to their theology courses (or said they did not know) were much *less* likely to say they had no personal responsibility than those saying the theology courses made the Church's teachings *less* credible (12 versus 38 percent).

But what about the one-third of seniors who disagreed that the Church has any business in areas of economic policy? Seniors were invited to comment on their responses to this item. Most of those commenting were among seniors who checked "disagree." Their comments reveal the sentiment of theological individualism or the assumed right of "personal conscience" as brought to bear especially on sociomoral issues. The Church may inform, but the individual in his or her conscience is the ultimate arbiter. This objection often accompanies another (echoing complaints of many commentators on the bishops' letter) that the Church is outside its proper jurisdiction in pronouncing on these matters.

I think the Church should not interfere in some matters. They should make their opinion known but let Catholics decide for themselves.

The Church should provide the information, but it is my decision.

What if the Church's decision is wrong, as it frequently is? Just to make one example, rock music has done more for poverty than the Church ever has.

I believe the Church should inform Catholics on these issues, but not really help form their consciences. One must decide on his own.

It is the Church's responsibility to educate its followers, but it is our choice whether or not one is to become involved.

Church and government don't mix. I'm business oriented—a real capitalist.

I really don't think the Church can make decisions on such things as national spending priorities or nuclear disarmament because they are not experts in those fields. It is my personal choice to be involved in solutions and to accept responsibility.

I believe the Church should allow the information to be spread, but never attempt to sway personal opinion.

There is a separation of Church and State in this country, and recently the Church has been moving more and more towards the politics surrounding this country, which it shouldn't. It should be more concerned with mental and spiritual guidance, and not the guidance of this country.

One should listen to the Church, but make up one's own mind. Not listening can result in stubborn ignorance. Listening too much results in corruption and puppetry.

The Church is to each individual what he makes of it. It deals more with the person rather than government.

The reason for such a strong disagree answer I gave is the phrase "form their conscience." The Church has only the right to discuss matters. Thus the people can form their own consciences.

Apparent from the responses, then, is that the 36 percent objecting to the Church's conscience-forming role in matters of economic decision-making put a high premium on the supremacy of the individual conscience. The Church may advise, offer guidance, state opinions; but "forming a conscience" apparently sounded to these seniors like taking away their prized freedom to make their own moral (or sociomoral) decisions independently of any external authority—the hallmark of "selective Catholicism."

Yet more than half the seniors *did* acknowledge the Church's "business" in this area. The data again suggest that school-related factors, in this case, the theology program, do help to sensitize young Catholics favorably toward the Church's role as moral guide in the socioeconomic area and contribute toward their sense of personal responsibility for self-involvement in problems of poverty, unemployment, and other social issues.

## Conclusion

It would be easy to miss the forest for the trees at this point. The larger picture comes into focus if we consider three topical headings: social consciousness, personal morality, and religiosity.

### Social Consciousness

These seniors do not "come off" as self-centered and uncaring of others. An impressive majority over the twelve years show themselves to be socially "liberal" in overall views, even personally generous in their willingness to share with others in need and to oppose injustice; to become personally involved in issues of race, hunger, and the nuclear arms race; and to support their Church's right to teach on these issues. Fewer, as one would expect, support the *Church's* involvement in economic matters, but even here, a majority of the classes between 1987 and 1989 affirmed the Church's role. Almost three-fourths of these three senior classes agree they have a *personal* responsibility to be involved in such issues as unemployment and poverty. In these respects, St. Martin's seniors resemble seniors from other Catholic high schools in studies cited earlier.

But let us return to the puzzling finding that parental occupation (especially the father's) and, for the 1983 to 1989 seniors, parental education are either unrelated to the dependent variables or even positively related; that is, seniors from professional families are *more* likely to appear socially sensitive. How is this so? Father Fichter found the male seniors in Jesuit high schools little affected by Catholic social teaching; they seemed to reflect what he believed were attitudes of the broad middle class, little disposed to challenge American social attitudes and institutions. Fichter used more specific measures of racial attitudes, and these may account for the greater resistance of his 1964 and 1968 seniors; in addition, these years saw civil rights issues evoking strongly controversial reactions from those surveyed.

Whatever be the case, the present study is intended to probe more basic dispositions along two axes: willingness to share and willingness to oppose injustice, along with indicators of personal inclination to become involved in racial, world hunger, and nuclear arms issues. Finally, St. Martin's seniors were asked about support for their Church's involvement in these issues, and like the seniors in the McAuley and Mathieson study quoted earlier, positively endorsed the Church's role in matters of race, hunger, and nuclear arms.

To return to the issue posed above (why seniors from higher status families were slightly more "liberal" on these issues), recall the "new class" thesis by Kluegel and Smith cited earlier in this chapter. Educated younger Americans are quite liberal on matters of race, gender, and related social policy issues. The measures used in the St. Martin's study concerning sharing with others and opposing injustice, and among the 1983 to 1989 seniors, in terms of both personal and Church involvement in matters of race, world hunger, and nuclear war, speak more to issues on which "new class" Americans are *expectedly more liberal*. The "oppose injustice" issue seems less related to these items, but respondents may have experienced a kind of halo effect as they filled out the survey, so that working for social justice "took on the coloration" of responses relating to race, sharing with others, and so. These survey items, then, could well have tapped the more liberal attitudes of "new class" American families. Seniors not from these "new class" families but from lower SES families *do* show themselves more conservative on these issues.

Still problematic, though, is why the 1983 to 1989 seniors were so much less socially conscious than their counterparts in 1977 to 1982. The change is not due directly to the changing SES backgrounds of the seniors who first appeared in the class of 1983. In fact, few background variables in the study, outside of gender and GPA, have much impact. The answers may lie in factors not measured in this study. The change in admission policy referred to earlier stressed academics above factors many Catholic high schools give weight to in admitting freshmen: how active the family is in the parish or whether the boy or girl attended Catholic elementary school. I was present at several school board meetings in 1979 where admission policy was debated. Some pastors allegedly complained that children from "their best families" now couldn't gain admission to the school, in contrast with a more open policy in the past. The school was becoming "too academic." A respected pastor who was a board member at the time apparently polled fellow priests on the issue but admitted under questioning from board members that the complaining priests "were by no means a majority." Most pastors in the city were satisfied with the school. Whatever be the case, the senior survey indicates that the classes between 1986 and 1989 hit all-time lows in proportions of seniors who had attended Catholic elementary school and all-time highs in percentages of those who had *no* religious education prior to high school. Yet this factor, as a variable entered into the regression equation, was predictive only of attitudes toward abortion. Still, it is difficult to put aside the possibility that setting higher academic standards drew into St. Martin's a higher proportion, compared with previous years, of students whose families were less involved institutionally in the Church (not sending children to parochial schools) and less open to the religious socialization afforded through theology classes. A gap, so to speak, had opened up between students "religiously disposed" to be accepting of the teaching and students (numerically a minority) who were more resistive. "Less religious" senior classes, in any case, were on board by 1983. The survey data, however, permit no unambiguous reasons as to why the school, beginning in 1979, drew these students. As we will see in the following chapter, the theology teachers say they noticed this change in student body, but neither they nor school administrators offer convincing explanations for the shift.

What the survey evidence *does* suggest is that two forces work to enhance receptivity to the social teaching reflected in the survey. One is a kind of "traditionality" in which to be female (most surveys show higher religiosity of females over males), ethnically conscious (*not* Hispanic per se), and having a high GPA (taking studies seriously) apparently dispose students to be more receptive to the "messages" of their teachers. Such students may be, as suggested earlier, more identified with the culture of the school and its "official norms." That female students are more open to norms of both personal and sociomoral religious teaching is predictable from the studies of Catholic high school students cited earlier.

The other force is simply personal religiosity, in which church attendance, acknowledging religion to be important in one's life and, perhaps most significantly, being sure of one's beliefs and saying the theology program enhances these convictions act together to open students to consider positively the Church's role in the larger world. The strength of these combined influences suggests that both family background *and* high school influences work together to enhance receptivity to religious and moral teaching. Prior religious education in parochial schools or in CCD classes relates positively only to the abortion question and to future parish involvement.

But while the survey may not directly pinpoint causal factors, it does resolve a key issue: are these young Catholics receptive to their Church's involvement in social issues? The answer is a clear yes. Seniors are, on the whole, very well disposed to acknowledge their Church's teaching role in areas of racial discrimination, world hunger, and the nuclear arms race. They are somewhat less positive, by comparison, about the Church's role in dealing with socioeconomic questions; nevertheless, a majority does support this role. They are even more positive about personal involvement in these issues, acknowledging a responsibility to share with those who have less, and to oppose societal practices unjustly harmful to others. It is safe to say, then, that Catholic leadership finds in these young women and men an audience receptive to their recent social initiatives, willing to listen and disposed to involve themselves in solutions to the problems presented.

*Personal Morality*

Seniors, it is clear, share the moral individualism pointed out in the McAuley and Mathieson study cited earlier. Decisions about personal sexual morality are strictly individual with few, if any, cues taken from religious norms. Yet they are not "liberal" across the board. Abortion (for reasons of birth defects) is the best example. Even views on premarital sex have fluctuated. An orthodox trend in the late 1970s gave way to a more liberal trend in the mid-1980s—a trend sweeping up women, both Anglo and Hispanic, almost equally with men. A similar pattern emerges concerning more sexual freedom as a "good thing," though a solid quarter say they are unsure or don't know. Women seem particularly doubtful on this issue. More worrisome to Church leaders, perhaps, is the reluctance of increasing majorities of seniors over the decade to be more actively involved in their parishes. This may reflect personally unsatisfactory experiences or may suggest an "early start" on the often validated survey finding that young persons from 18 to 29 years old characteristically are underrepresented in *all* mainline churches but drift back during their thirties when raising families arouses concern about religious values and practices.

Hispanic seniors in this survey "stand out," so to speak, by appearing to follow their Anglo peers, thus blending into the "great mass" of seniors. This is not the case, however, for those speaking Spanish at home, who tend to be more orthodox and conservative. Once this home language factor is removed, though, Hispanic students as such exhibit very few attitudes—save for their apparently greater respect for the Church as teacher (again, no small matter)—differentiating them from Anglo students. Once speaking Spanish at home disappears, they fit a profile of highly assimilated young men and women as their families rise in SES.

\* \* \* \*

The question of tradition is central to this book. The viewpoints of the St. Martin's seniors on personal, especially sexual matters, show they vary little from other young Catholic Americans, though they seem to be moving away from orthodox teaching here in increasing numbers during the late 1980s. They apparently do not share the moral understandings of their parents. Traditional teaching goes unheeded; contemporary sexual mores carry the assumption that this area of life is "strictly personal" and outside the legitimate range of any external authority. It is tempting to wonder whether, in this case, tradition has simply yielded to the culture. This is an oversimplification, of course, because, as we have seen, Church leadership insisted in 1968 on maintaining a moral norm—prohibition of artificial birth control—in the face of (even at the time) majority rejection in practice of the norm itself. This is not to say the Catholic Church "erred," a judgment outside the scope of any sociological (or nontheological) analysis. But it points sharply to the practical impossibility of eliciting compliance once a moral precept has been widely judged to be irrelevant or, in this case, even possibly injurious to personal and family welfare. And of course, research by Greeley and others had demonstrated, subsequently to the issuance of *Humanae Vitae,* that the entire area of sexuality became one in which ecclesiastical authority was judged to be "off limits," even sheerly incompetent to legislate. Reinforcing this conviction, as many commentators have noted, was the central emphasis associated with the youth culture of the late 1960s and early 1970s upon personal experience. This emphasis in turn formed a powerful dynamic in which virtually all doctrinal and moral norms had to pass through the gates of experience and "relevance" before gaining acceptability and assent. This overall dynamic is almost certainly at work among the St. Martin's seniors and is apparently immune to challenge in the area of sexual attitudes.

Are these same shared cultural assumptions at work in the seniors' views on *social issues?* The large majority of seniors affirming the Church's right to teach on racial discrimination, world hunger, and the nuclear arms race may simply "tap into" the majority American cultural consensus concerning these issues. Agreement comes easily when "liberal" views on these themes receive considerable endorsement from the culture. Even the seniors' willingness to be involved personally in solving these problems, while not to be downplayed, doubtless finds some reinforcement from current notions of "worthwhile causes," such as the Live Aid concert and movement a few years ago on behalf of starving peoples. On the nuclear arms issue, as well, majorities of Americans by the mid-1980s had come to favor a mutually verifiable agreement to reduce or even eliminate stockpiles of atomic weapons.

But when American Catholic bishops take on questions of "economic justice," one suspects that it may be "a new ball game." At this writing (late 1990) it seems too early to tell; after all, the survey by D'Antonio and colleagues cited previously tells us that a mere 25 percent of Catholic adults polled nationally had even heard of the pastoral letter. And while 70 percent of those who had gave it their support, one wonders how much they knew about it.[37]

The point is this: if Catholics, especially younger ones being taught contemporary Catholic doctrine, are to take seriously and "internalize" the teaching, their teachers have to confront, and themselves take seriously, the theological individualism of their students. As the area of sexual mores makes clear, if what is taught runs counter to strongly reinforced cultural norms, teachers will have a hard time indeed getting students to accept the Church as teacher. St. Martin's instructors have not done badly; 54 percent of the seniors affirm the Church's role in forming consciences on economic decision-making. But the teachers themselves acknowledged the problem exemplified in 46 percent either disagreeing or remaining unsure as to whether the Church has a legitimate guidance role in the economic realm. The teachers' task is not an easy one, as we have seen, since *Economic Justice for All* sets forth moral and policy challenges to assumptions and normative patterns widely accepted in our country. What is said obviously runs against the grain of what Americans support and even take for granted, *especially* middle- and upper-middle-class families of whom St. Martin's seniors are broadly representative. These are not readily acceptable points of view, and the teachers have their work cut out for them. As one of them remarked to me, arguments in class on these issues "ran hot and heavy." But the teachers, all of whom were veterans of at least ten years teaching at the school, are deeply aware of both maturational and ideological factors at work in their students. They know they and their students live in what sociologist Ann Swidler terms an "unsettled period" in which cultural assumptions compete with one another.[38] But they also echo Swidler in being aware, at least implicitly, that they and the students interact together in an institution—a Catholic high school—which provides "structural and historical opportunities that may determine which cultural systems succeed."[39] They realize, as one of them put it simply, that "we have a golden opportunity during these formative years to get some basic values across to them—but you really have to work at it these days. They certainly don't want to hear everything you have to say." In other words, they are cognizant of and willing to confront the theological individualism of their students, but also know they cannot resort to traditional invocation of authority to gain assent to what they are teaching.

### Personal Religiosity

The steady decline in weekly Mass attendance over the twelve years of the survey finds no ready explanation. As suggested earlier, if Catholic families less institutionally involved in the Church were sending their children to St. Martin's in the mid-1980s, one would expect religiosity indicators to drop somewhat. This is also the case with importance of religion and conviction about the Church's teachings. While one might argue that combined "weekly" and "two or three times a month" attendance still adds up to an impressive majority, room for concern remains among educators and parents about the downward trend itself, for the latter seems to confirm the Gallup and Castelli finding that Catholics seem less "religiously concerned" on a number of measures than Protestant Americans. In any case, the class of 1989's 50 percent weekly attendance is a sharp drop from the 1983 Wisconsin Catholic high school seniors' 70 percent rate, and more immediately, from earlier years of St. Martin's seniors. It remains to be seen whether other studies will show similar drops in the late 1980s.

On the other hand, as the following chapter will disclose, seniors *do* accord their teachers respect and are willing to listen to their presentations and the arguments they put forward. Their agreement with Catholic teaching, however, is partially a response to the ways in which teachers exercise their authority, given the theological individualism held by their students. How the teachers "manage" this resistive dynamic in the students is an important theme in the next chapter. We will enter into the culture of the school itself, through the responses of seniors to open-ended questions contained in the survey, and through the reflections of their theology teachers whom I interviewed. The chapter opens with students' attitudes toward the school as they compare themselves with graduates of other high schools in the city, affording us insights into the school's culture. I then examine the seniors' attitudes toward conscience formation, illustrating the "essence" of theological individualism, followed by the teachers' strategies for "reaching" their students. The chapter closes with seniors' varying descriptions (through a typology I developed from their responses) of what being a Catholic means to them as compared with their parents. This chapter will exemplify more than any other the importance of focusing on the initiatives of social actors working within a given social structure, but finding ample scope for creative "conflict" and adjustment through negotiated arrangements they work out, sometimes explicitly, most often tacitly. The second section of the chapter raises again the issue discussed in the Introduction: the distinctive Catholic identity (or lack of it) which these seniors manifest.

# 4 "Selling More Than Telling": Portraits of Seniors and Their Teachers

> I miss something reading the results of
> the surveys, some kind of
> understanding that lies in the shadows,
> in nuances surveys cannot quantify
> and shadings cannot hint at (Louise
> Bernikow)[1]

This chapter invites students and teachers to speak for themselves. I go beyond the survey findings just reviewed into how seniors see themselves in relation to their school, their classes, and their teachers. So far the phrase "theological individualism" has assumed a kind of abstract quality, visible only through the "agrees" and "disagrees" of responses to questionnaire items. Here the phrase comes to life as seniors say what being Catholic means to them, and teachers muse about the challenge of presenting doctrine to the young women and men sitting in front of them. The structuration perspective of Anthony Giddens, in turn, comes into play; for each set of social actors continuously responds to what they are confronting in a setting where traditional guidelines are called into question, and new strategies of communication seem necessary if any "value formation" is to take place. The interaction of students and their teachers inevitably involves questions of *authority;* I spend some time reflecting on how seniors respond to the manifestations of authority, given their insistence on the primacy of "personal conscience."

## Students and Teachers

From 1983 through 1989, I appended the following open-ended question to the senior survey: "Looking back over four years, what do you think is the major difference between you as a St. Martin's graduate and graduates of other high schools (public and private) in the city?" Most students listed two or more characteristics. *Seven* themes emerged from their answers. I list them in order of frequency:

1. School's academic strengths (334)

2. Experience of community (239)

3. Personal growth (161)

4. Religion and theology program (143)

5. School discipline (81)

6. Moral values (religion not cited) (73)

7. School as sheltered environment (49)

I believe sample comments from the first five categories—academic strengths through school discipline—yield important insights into the distinctive school culture of St. Martin's.

*Academic Strengths.* Clearly, a plurality of seniors values the school for just the reason most parents in the high school principals' survey chose a school: a strong academic curriculum and a chance to gain admittance to a college or university of their choice. Many contrasted the school's small size with the surrounding public high schools, commenting on what they thought was the superiority of St. Martin's curriculum.

> I think the major difference is that we really learned in high school. My GPA might not be as high as some of the public school grads, but I didn't take plastics, gymnastics, dance, etc., my senior year. I believe [St. Martin's] is there to make sure the students learn what they're taught and that has helped me greatly in these past four years.

> I feel I have been given much more experience to deal with people and situations I will face in the 'real world.' Attending [St. Martin's] has given me much more confidence in myself and my abilities. After two years at a public high school, I think that wasn't even good enough to prepare me for high school, much less college. Of course I disagree with some policies such as the dress code, but many rules were needed to learn discipline.

*Experience of Community.* For many seniors, St. Martin's was a fulfillment of the goal most Catholic high school principals set: building of community. Some seniors were remarkably eloquent, noting that St. Martin's small size contributed greatly to the close bonding they experienced. Some explicitly included teachers and counselors.

People at this school care more about each other because we are a small school and everyone knows just about everyone. They also prepare us for college a great deal more. . . . All the seniors love one another and we are all close. That makes us feel special.

I have only gone to this school for the last two years. My experiences here have opened up to me a whole new world. I have learned to openly express my love for family and friends. I have learned to care about a wide variety of people, whether I have met them or not. This has made my whole outlook on life much more positive because I know that I am loved and that I've got a lot of love to give.

[St. Martin's] has a feeling of friendliness. No matter what I wear, what I look like, what my grades or athletic abilities are, I am a welcomed part of this family. I feel it also applies to others from the way my teachers, classmates, and family have taught me. I love it.

*Personal Growth.* The vocabulary of growth psychology was quite familiar to many seniors, with themes of self-respect, personal direction, and positive outlook characterizing their answers.

I think many graduates of [St. Martin's] have a sense of themselves, whereas many other graduates I know from elsewhere are confused as to where they're heading and who they are.

Having attended a small school has helped me to get closer to people and given me a better self-image because I didn't feel lost and unimportant, as many people who attend a public high school feel.

I have learned to respect authority more and to accept rules and regulations that have been set down to follow. I have learned to discipline myself in academics, sports, etc., and to always persevere. I have also strengthened my ambition, and my views of the Church and morals have been upheld.

I see the world as a better place in which I can make a difference. I also know that there is more to life than money or success. I am more aware of the deeper success of spiritual peace. This may sound dumb, but in the end, it is all that really matters.

*Religion and Theology Program.* Many seniors showed explicit awareness of the religious and spiritual teaching and guidance they had received. Some wrote about learning through questioning.

I've learned not to accept something at face value but to probe and question it and form my own opinion, using my conscience and moral guidelines provided by the Church. I also think I have a better understanding and acceptance of other religions.

Theology classes have helped my to understand my religion and myself more and have helped make me a more caring and understanding person. I've become more concerned with others around me and have been taught to form my own opinions and conscience and not let others control me.

At [St. Martin's] we are informed of other religions and their beliefs. We also learn more about our own Catholic beliefs so that they are clearer for us to understand. The teachers tell us what the Catholic side is about some issues but do not say we must agree with them. Therefore, with the learning about other religions, I think [St. Martin's] graduates are able to be more open-minded when other religions do something or we meet a person that has different beliefs from our own. We can listen to them and not say they are wrong.

I think I have a better grasp for deciding how to make religious and moral decisions, as well as understanding all of the issues involved. Through the years, I have learned how to make an objective decision, not just an emotional or hurried decision. I am also aware that I am not alone in my thoughts and beliefs but that others share those with me. I think possibly one of the most important things I've learned, strange as it is, is to question authority and don't accept things blindly. Also, to have respect for others' beliefs as they disagree, at least in part, with a few of my own.

*School Discipline.* While seniors often chafe under school rules, many acknowledge at graduation that the school's enforced discipline has its virtues. Unfavorable comparisons are made with other schools.

I think perhaps I have had a better education than I would have at a public school. Since I'm a lazy person, I would have slacked off much more in my studies than I already did. There was more motivation to do the work because I had to.

Since in public school there is rarely any emphasis on studying or behaving, the kids don't learn discipline through their actions. Having a brother who attends public school, I see the laid-back attitude of all the kinds; none of them think about college (rarely); and they are a lot more rebellious. I think their attitudes are due to lack of discipline in the system.

My mother insisted I come here. I am glad I attended because from what I hear from my friends from public schools, I would also be ditching classes all the time since you can get away with it.

If anything emerges from these responses, it is the very high regard the seniors have for St. Martin's. Though they do complain about restrictive dress and behavior codes, and a few feel they are overly "sheltered" from problems in the surrounding world, very few graduate resentful of the school (in 1988, for example, only eight out of 194 graduates were clearly negative, complaining about excessive discipline or, in two cases, that religion was "forced" on them). If Catholic high school principals hold that forming a community is their primary task, St. Martin's seems to have achieved that goal remarkably well. Seniors obviously set high store on the sense of knowing well and caring for one another, often ascribing these advantages to the small size of the school.

Several comments on the theology program stand out: first, simply the fact that values were imparted. Many seniors contrasted the absence of value formation at other schools, public or private. Secondly, the *kind* of instruction received, particularly in senior year. Phrases like listening to other students, preparing us to make decisions, given us choices, and so on strongly suggest the give-and-take characteristic of class discussions. Almost no comments indicated that doctrine or norms were "forced" on them. They also appreciated the wide range of problems discussed in class, often in contrast with the comparative ignorance of world problems shown by friends attending other schools.

It is clear, then, that the *authority* of their teachers comes over to seniors as respecting them and leaving room for their own ideas and experiences. Let us explore this in further detail.

### *Authority*

In the halls and classrooms of St. Martin's, the individual autonomy of judgment cherished by the seniors constituted a cultural meaning by no means taken for granted by their theology instructors. The latter inevitably represented part of a larger authority structure expressed in the disciplinary rules of the school as enforced by the principal and his assistants, and in the doctrinal and moral teachings of the Catholic Church as taught by these instructors. Both these symbolic forms of authority were part of the very fabric of the school and were literally inescapable: one risked expulsion if one consistently violated the rules; all Catholic students were required to take the four years of theology courses.

An insightful discussion of authority as experienced by high school students is provided by Gary Schwartz in his recent *Beyond Conformity or*

*Rebellion: Youth and Authority in America*. An ethnographic study of six communities in a midwestern state, his book portrays adult-adolescent relationships in varying local cultures. Each community is distinct: a small town in an economically depressed region; another in a rich agricultural setting; a working-class community in an urban setting; a suburban working-class community, and a relatively affluent suburb ("Glenbar") similar to those from which most St. Martin's students come. Authority relations form a central motif as Schwartz shows not only their variation from setting to setting, but how authority is negotiated and "settled upon" somewhat differently in each community. In a school context, authority is not just school officials exacting compliance to codes of conduct. Authority must be analyzed within a particular tradition. It "embodies what a community feels is valuable or worthwhile about its past regardless of whether that experience in intelligible in terms of universal laws."[2] As Schwartz points out, how students regard authority depends on whether it comes across to them as both *rational* and *reasonable*. Rational means that authority constitutes a means to ends meaningful to young people. At St. Martin's, seniors chafe under discipline but admit it has a worthwhile purpose in their lives; having a class in moral and spiritual values is good, since without them many young people lead confused lives. Reasonable means that "authority must be exercised in ways that respect the dignity of those subject to it."[3] More concretely, Schwartz remarks that youth find authority unreasonable and thus illegitimate when either (1) it puts them in a humiliating position, causing shame and embarrassment or (2) they experience authority as "an arbitrary intrusion into their own affairs or as excessive coercion."[4] "You can't tell us how to run our lives." Both approaches strike teenagers as an assault on their personal dignity, upon their self-conceptions as autonomous individuals making their own judgments even if the judgments are mistaken.

Parental expectations carry some weight as well. As Schwartz tells us about the one high-SES school in his study, parents struck a consensus on the following point: getting good grades so that daughter or son can launch herself or himself into a good college and a professional career is all-important.[5] Like the students in Schwartz's Glenbar High School, St. Martin's students come from homes in which matters are discussed critically; they are no less encouraged by their teachers to think critically, to ask questions and to probe beyond the "given" of their textbooks (as some of their comments above suggest). One popular senior English teacher assigns Camus, Joyce, and Kafka, explicitly challenging his students to take a critical view of their own values and those of the surrounding American culture. Seniors do not leave this attitude at the door on entering their theology classrooms. In earlier years (freshman and sophomore), teachers presented such themes as Scripture and Liturgy quite straightforwardly, stating what they believed to be "the Church's teaching." Seniors looking back resent some of these courses largely because they seem to have been taught in a you-must-accept-this mode, in contrast to courses in junior and senior years where theology teachers encourage the critical questioning seniors expect in English or Social Studies.

Junior and senior theology teachers, in taking this approach, come across to the students as acknowledging their autonomy and self-direction. In taking the opinions of their students seriously, they neither shame nor embarrass them; they avoid "excessive coercion" by tacitly letting the students know they are not trying to "run their lives." The teachers know, as their comments will illustrate, that juniors and seniors will challenge some of the doctrinal and moral teaching presented. Yet student challenge does not come across to them as "rebellious teenage antagonism" or readiness just to do battle for battle's sake. As Schwartz remarks of a Catholic all-girl high school in his study, St. Martin's is, in a sense, "an extension of the home, a place where parents have absolute faith that their children are in good hands—its policies and practices have their support and approval."[6] Thus, the teachers are aware that students will rarely "take them on" antagonistically, since students know parents approve of the theology curriculum and expect them to take it seriously. Thus, teachers note that objections raised in class are not proposed out of belligerent defiance. In fact, as the previous chapter make clear, with the exception of premarital sex, the seniors are basically in alignment with official Catholic teaching. It is difficult, then, to resist the impression that even when seniors do voice objections, they are not expressing some "final rejection of the legitimacy of the moral authority of church and community."[7] Lively questioning, one infers, is regarded as part and parcel of the normal adolescent process of growing up that commonly brings with it some testing and challenging of authority figures.

But there *are* important differences between St. Martin's students and their well-off counterparts in Schwartz's Glenbar High School. These differences are an important key to understanding the effectiveness of St. Martin's theology teachers and their classes. Schwartz points to the sharp separation of students' expressive lives from time spent in the classrooms. Seldom do their assignments or discussion touch on their personal lives; teachers who attempt to do so meet little enthusiasm from the students. The latter make

a radical separation between . . . private enthusiasms which are communicated to friends and . . . public involvements in the formal culture of the school. . . . The classroom is not the appropriate place to share one's insights into the world with one's peers.[8]

Such is *not* the case at St. Martin's. The three junior and senior theology instructors invite students explicitly to talk about expressive areas of their lives. Having listened to these discussions myself in visits to the classrooms, I can testify to the open and frank self-revelation of students and instructors. Seniors often supply telling examples from their own lives and those of friends. All the issues—and more—represented by the senior survey items come into play, particularly in the fourth-year courses, "Man and Woman" and "Moral Issues." Instructors show respect for students' views even while inviting them to question their own opinions, which are frequently at odds with official Church teaching, and use their questions to further discussion without "putting down" student viewpoints. They present Catholic teaching in both historical and psychological context, attempting to show the teaching as "making sense" in terms, for example, of respect for life and for another person in matters of abortion and premarital sex, respectively. Students feel free to disagree, knowing they will not be scolded or abruptly corrected.

The upshot of this mode of interaction and communication is that the vast majority of seniors do not see Catholic teaching and the authority it represents as "unreasonable" in the sense Schwartz indicates, i.e., as violating their personal dignity or autonomy. They do take issue with their teachers, of course. Lively debates often ensue in class, but the give-and-take, from my own observations, seems good-natured and rarely antagonistic—nor do seniors' comments indicate a classroom atmosphere of combative tension.

None of this should be interpreted, however, as indicating some form of tension-free harmony or consensus. The religious or theological individualism of the students *is* problematic for the teachers. They do not always find it easy to deal with. So far, however, this individualism has been broadly stated and alluded to without discussion of its origin or large context in American religious culture. I offer the following "excursus" as a way of clarifying the meaning of this concept before presenting seniors' concrete expressions of it.

### *Religious Individualism: An Excursus*

Let us return to the post–Vatican II ascendancy of the "individual conscience" over what one believes and practices. This selectivity is mainly apparent in areas of sexual teaching and practice, in birth control, remarriage following divorce, and in abortion under some circumstances. It also extends into regularity of Mass attendance on Sundays and on holy days of obligation such as The Feast of the Assumption and Immaculate Conception and Ascension Thursday.

Receiving less commentary is that the very process of conscience formation has been individualized. The Vatican II document, *The Declaration on Religious Freedom* explicitly invoked the principle of individual human dignity to undergird its assertion that "all men are to be immune from coercion on the part of individuals . . . and of any human power, in such wise that in matters religious no one is to be forced to act in a manner contrary to his own beliefs."[9] The commentator's footnote in the edition from which I quote cautions against overextending this principle:

> It is worth nothing that the Declaration does not base the right to the free exercise of religion on "freedom of conscience." Nowhere does this phrase occur. And the Declaration nowhere lends its authority to the theory for which the phrase frequently stands, namely that I have the right to do what my conscience tells me to do, simply because my conscience tells me to do it. That is a perilous theory. Its particular peril is subjectivism—the notion that, in the end, it is my conscience, and not the objective truth which determines what is right or wrong, true or false.[10]

Selective Catholicism has come to mean, for all practical purposes, something akin to the subjectivism deplored in the above quotation, a kind of "tuning in" to oneself and one's experiences, legitimated religiously by the assumption that God expects us to follow our own consciences and that these promptings transcend the rules and regulations of any institution, including one's church.

This subjectivizing of conscience reflects a broader American pattern, one termed by Roof and McKinney "the new voluntarism." The latter has its roots in the autonomous individual of Reformation theology. But there it meant individual responsibility for a relationship with God and with Jesus Christ inside the boundaries set by the institutional church, i.e., no institutional norms could substitute for the individual act of adherence to what one believed and practiced. The American religious trend, particularly in this century with its competing denominations, has spawned an emphasis on individual choice of denomination and with this trend, an implicit relativizing of what each denomination stands for in terms of beliefs and practices. The outcome spells supremacy of individual authority:

> Dominant patterns of the secular culture shape religious norms. For Americans, religious authority lies in the believer, not in the church, not in the Bible, despite occasional claims of infallibility and inerrancy on the part of some.[11]

Cultural influences abetting this trend are not difficult to identify. The young people who are the subjects of this book are scarcely immune from the various "quests for self-fulfillment" arising out of the cultural shifts of the late 1960s and early 1970s and from the disenchantment with (or at least suspicion of) major institutions of our society.[12] No parent raising teenagers within the past two decades in unaware of the appeals to self-enhancement, self-indulgence, and pleasure-seeking put forth in the popular media—music videos, song lyrics, the easy accessibility of films in theaters and in homes through VCRs. Further, when one keeps in mind that many parents of today's teenagers were themselves in young adulthood during the mid- to late 1960s, it is hard to believe that their own "quests" have not influenced the attitudes and emotional resonances of their daughters and sons.

Whatever be the case, by the late 1970s, the principle of religious individualism seemed well woven into American culture. In 1978, 81 percent of the American population (and 76 percent of those belonging to a church) agreed that "an individual should arrive at his or her own religious beliefs independent of any churches or synagogues," and 78 percent (70 percent of church members), believed that one can be a "good" Christian without attending a church or synagogue.[13]

Students in Catholic high schools enjoy no insulation from these trends and influences. Indeed, the 1983 research of McAuley and Mathieson shows considerable confusion and misunderstanding of some basic planks of Catholic teaching, including the role of the Church in the lives of these high school students. "Many students believed that they could more or less design their own 'Catholicism';" others entertained the notion that "an institutional church was not necessary." In general, "there was a widespread sense that the church was too authoritarian."[14] Let us look now at St. Martin's seniors' personal expressions of this principle of individual conscience reflected in their comments on a key survey item.

### Formation of Conscience: Comments of St. Martin's Seniors

Once again, the question asked from 1983 through 1989 on formation of conscience found seniors selecting the second response by an overwhelming extent (78 percent): "As a Catholic, I should listen respectfully to the Church's teachings on religious beliefs and moral behavior, but then make up my mind according to my own conscience."

The survey invited seniors to comment on this question. Responses typical of the second choice displayed unmistakably the sovereignty of individual choice and decision-making, with the Church as a kind of well-informed resource rather than a compelling authority.

I think the Church's job is to make sure we are well informed. Its opinion carries a lot of weight, but in the end we have to choose for ourselves the way we want to live. (Anglo male)

I believe that religion is a private thing between the individual and God and that the Church only serves as a guide to help when things seem unclear. (Hispanic female)

Being brought up a Catholic, my conscience has mainly been formed on the Church's beliefs, because that's all I knew, but I feel that one's conscience should be formed by one's experience and informed opinions, because your conscience is part of yourself and you must live with your decisions. (Anglo-Hispanic female)

Some seniors expressed a degree of doubt or even antagonism toward the Church as they chose this response. Coming through is a firm sense of reliance upon one's "inner voice."

I really don't believe that any religious group has the right to tell people how to run their lives. They are there to offer advice and set guidelines. God gave us free will in order to choose for ourselves. (Anglo female)

There are just too many things that are too hard to accept as far as Church teachings go. If I honestly feel I'm right, then God, I'm sure, accepts my actions. (Anglo-Hispanic male)

The Church has disappointed me throughout my years of Catholic schooling. I am aware of many teachings, but I feel I must be myself and follow what I truly believe. (Anglo-Hispanic male)

No matter how hard they (the theology department) try to force the Catholic faith upon me, it has to come from within myself, so I wish they'd stop pushing. (Anglo female)

Eleven percent of the seniors chose the third response, "I don't believe any authority has the right to influence the formation of anyone's conscience. That's strictly up to each individual." They were expectedly forthright and blunt in their comments, and for the most part reject Church authority and rules altogether.

I was a Catholic before I came to St. Martin's, but have since abandoned my belief. (Anglo male)

The Catholic Church is an anachronistic, dried out medieval society in the twentieth and on to the twenty-first centuries. To preach it in modern society is difficult, humiliating, and rarely well done, St. Martin's being no exception. (Anglo male)

I think God is very important in my life, but I don't think it's right to have rules about how to live with God. I think God will love us no matter, just as long as we are doing our best to please Him and not the Church. (Anglo female)

Few, too, were the seniors (10 percent) who chose to grant the Church a preeminent role in conscience formation: "As a Catholic, I should form my conscience according to the Church's teaching on religious beliefs and moral behavior." These disgruntled young traditionalists betray resentment against the way in which religious and moral teaching is presented. The risk of theological individualism and moral relativism are not lost on this small group of seniors.

In general, they teach in a way to make you feel that there are no wrong answers in what you believe. So, in other words, the Catholic religion is each individual's own view. They lead many students astray. Here they teach that the Pope is not necessarily infallible, but you should listen and then make your decision. But that is not the Catholic faith, if that's the situation. The Church teaches us what is right and wrong and we must follow. (Anglo female)

If God had wanted us to form our own opinions, He wouldn't have created the Church. (Anglo male)

The Church is there to guide us because we don't know everything. God would never have intended the Church to exist if He wanted us to be with no guidance. (Hispanic female)

If you belong to any group, you should follow the rules. If you don't like things the group does, get out of it. The same goes for religion. If you don't want to believe what the Church teaches and follow the rules, you should not be a Catholic. (Anglo-Hispanic female)

I think that if we let our conscience interfere with our religion, there is a good possibility of rationalization, so we won't have to give up—or not do—certain things we enjoy because the Church says it is wrong. (Anglo male)

Clear, then, is the pervasive character of religious or theological individualism, apparent in responses of both "liberal" and "conservative" seniors. We now ask how their theology teachers cope with this mentality.

### The Theology Teachers

Each of the four theology teachers had been on the faculty during the entire time of the study, that is, at least eleven years. During that period, I had many occasions to talk with them, and twice, in 1978 and again in 1981, presented senior survey findings to them. I participated in the ensuing discussions. In the spring of 1987, I interviewed each of them for approximately half an hour, probing four areas: (1) their perception of student attitudes toward religious teaching and whether student attitudes had changed during their tenure at the school; (2) how the curriculum developed along with the division of labor they had worked out, i.e., who taught what; (3) areas of maximum difficulty in conveying religious teaching to students, i.e., areas of student resistance and how they addressed them; (4) what continuing problems they perceived in their basic charge of student religious formation—what was needed; what, if anything, ought to be changed. Three of the teachers were junior and senior theology instructors; the fourth was department chair and taught freshman and sophomores.

Before presenting the interview findings, let me say that the theology department in the late 1970s was the target of criticism by a small group of parents belonging to "Catholics United for the Faith" (CUF). A national organization of Catholics, CUF members believe that orthodox Catholic doctrine has been severely diluted and distorted in post–Vatican II Catholicism. Even core teachings have been relativized and watered down. At St. Martin's, two members of the school board who belonged to CUF protested to the school principal that religious teaching at St. Martin's was "too liberal," deviating from Catholic teaching concerning the authority of the pope, sexual morality, and abortion, and in effect, permitting students to "make up their own minds about what they believe," in the words of one school board member. The board asked the principal to investigate. After meeting with theology department members, he concluded the charges were unfounded; the department was teaching nothing he considered deviant from official Catholic doctrine. The controversy melted away in the 1980s as children of the protesting CUF parents graduated and their terms of membership on the school board expired. Nevertheless, as one theology teacher remarked,

> It put us on our guard because it was annoying to have to be accountable to people who did not understand what we were trying to do. We knew we were not distorting Catholic doctrine. We were just trying to present it in ways that wouldn't alienate our students. But I think the CUF parents thought we were heretics trying to destroy the faith of their kinds or something. At least we had a principal who understood what we were trying to do and backed us up.

In the interviews set forth below, there appears a kind of dialectic of resistance and response. The teachers exhibit a keen awareness of "where their students are," and what they believed they had to do in order to "reach" them. Coming across clearly is their simultaneous concern with both maturational and ideological factors as elements requiring carefully thought-out adaptive strategies on their part as they presented Catholic teaching in the classroom.

*Interview Findings.* All four teachers agreed that students seem to progress from relative open-mindedness in freshman and sophomore years to a resistive stance by junior year. The combination of maturational and ideological concerns is strikingly evident.

A kind of pseudo-sophistication sets in around junior year. The kids don't seem as reachable, simple and open. You often feel close bonding with many freshmen and sophomores; they're willing to plan liturgies with you. But not when they come back in junior year. It's like they're going through a phase of casting off institutions or something. And for the boys, there's this macho thing that sets in about this time. I see a definite gender difference, too. Boys are harder to get through to in class.

Adolescents these days question *all sources* of authority. This generation of kids, especially in the last few years, really has knowledgeable parents, so the kinds are more sophisticated. They get it from their parents. So by all means, yes, the tendency is toward questioning and not swallowing something just because you're told to. You know, it's like they're saying, "Anytime an authority figure asks me to do something, I'll ask why. You prove it to me." Our job as theology teachers is not just to present but to persuade these days. We're selling more than telling.

There's so much resistance to discipline and to teaching these days. "Why the hell are we doing this?" is the impression you get. By junior year, questioning really sets in. The Church is viewed as saying "no" to so much. As one senior said, "It's like a lot of old men are trying to set up rules for us and they don't know anything about us. They think we're bad, so they set up all these rules." But you can make a more favorable impression when you help them see that the Church does favor stands considered liberal, for instance, civil disobedience in certain situations.

Three out of the four called attention to the recent (since the early 1980s) higher socioeconomic status of the student body.

It's hard to get through to them nowadays. More focus on "things." They get their status from externals, how they dress, especially. I think this status-consciousness is the weakness of St. Martins as a family.

The dress code (no jeans; shirts and blouses neatly tucked in) increases competition about "how I look."

Kids transferring from other schools feel the competition and the preppy look. They seem these days less tolerant of the poor. It's almost like there's an attitude that you can buy anything, including happiness.

No, I think the school has always been upper-middle class. But I have noticed over the last few years less reverence for religion, church, and priesthood. Less urgency about what the Church has to say. In general, they are harder to teach, being less disciplined. Many have just gotten their way with their parents, that's all. They're used to manipulating them. And in some cases, they are simply spoiled brats, though I'd have to say I notice this somewhat less among the Hispanic kids and the few black kids we have.

Curriculum development stemmed from theology department meetings in the early 1970s. Revisions followed themes of the *Catechetical Directory* published by the National Conference of Catholic Bishops in 1973. Each faculty member chose a subject matter and the class (freshmen, sophomore, etc.) he or she felt most comfortable teaching. The first two years of the curriculum focus on liturgy, scripture, and social gospel (social teaching of the church). In junior year, a comparative religion course exposes the students to the teachings of Buddhism, Hinduism, Islam, and Judaism in comparison with Roman Catholicism. Senior year features two courses, Man and Woman (Christian marriage) and Moral Issues, dealing with contemporary issues such as abortion, business ethics, capital punishment, and sexual morality.

I think we've worked out a pretty good curriculum, but you still have some problems. I teach Social Gospel, and I do encounter resistance to the teachings of the Church. Mostly it's from their parents. They lean to the conservative side; they support a kind of patriotic view of "America first," and are suspicious of the social teaching. It doesn't help that many priests on the faculty and in the administration don't seem very interested in the social teaching. I'm not sure that any one of them has yet read the pastoral letter on the economy.

Well, you take the Comparative Religion course. This course is really a way of getting them to look at Catholic doctrine. It's what used to be called apologetics. But it would turn the kids off if you labeled it like that or just came at them with doctrine. But you know, when you show them what other religions believe—and they're really interested in them—it's a lot easier to show them that what the Church says makes sense. They're surprised when they come to understand the Church's reliance on scholarship in coming to various positions, that the Church does take scholarship seriously.

In presenting moral issues, I think you have to begin with society's views on a given issue, and what prominent authors say—what are people saying about this. [My question: why not start with the Church's view?] Because the best pedagogical strategy is to find out where the kids are and listen to them. Don't start with what the Church says or teaches. They will feel you are trying to preach to them; "you're shackling us; you don't care what we really think." Often after presenting conflicting views from society, etc., the church's teaching makes good sense to them. Comes across as rational, except for birth control. But any direct "this is it" approach will not work.

Clearly, teachers felt the urgency, particularly in regard to junior and senior classes, of "reaching" students through strategies of presentation that make religious teachings, both doctrinal and moral, plausible—approaches that invite the students to take the teachings seriously. The teachers show themselves deeply aware of the cultural shifts that have rendered the principle of individual conscience formation central to Catholic teenagers, a principle shared not only by seniors' non-Catholic peers but, as one might suppose from Greeley's notion of "communal Catholics," by many of the seniors' parents. The teachers are equally aware of the resistance to theology teaching stemming from the high-SES backgrounds of their students, a resistance especially evident to the teacher responsible for the Social Gospel course explaining the Church's social teaching. The teachers' contribution to the "dialectic" appears most evidently in the following two strategies they have devised for reaching their students:

1. Steps in conscience formation: Students are presented in junior year with "steps in conscience formation," a scheme worked out by junior and senior theology teachers. A discussion on abortion, for example, would follow this sequence: (1) your experience—what is it? What does it say? (2) Church teaching along with relevant New Testament passages bearing on the issues(s); (3) society's attitudes—what are the various currents of public opinion on the issue in question? (4) teacher and students pray together about the issue; (5) students are asked to "develop their own judgments on the matter."

2. Weights assigned to Catholic teachings: The senior moral issues teacher draws upon a traditional Catholic theological scheme for

assigning degrees of certainty to Catholic teachings: (1) *De fide definita:* infallible teaching, e.g., the divinity of Christ and the Immaculate Conception; (2) official Catholic doctrine, e.g., teachings of the Second Vatican Council along with most moral teaching; (3) teachings commonly considered revealed, e.g., prayers for the souls in Purgatory; and (4) teachings only probably revealed, e.g., existence of the state of Limbo and of personal Guardian Angels. The teacher introduces this scheme during that part of the Comparative Religion course dealing with Roman Catholicism.

I asked each teacher whether these two approaches might lead to the promotion of individual judgment as paramount and thus afford legitimation to the very individualism they found problematic. They were indeed aware of the risk-taking involved in the strategy but also saw a payoff, i.e., reaching the students.

> OK, let's really deal with that one. Let's say you're a bishop and you asked me that question about conscience formation. I'd say to you that at least I can get them to *listen* to you. Any approach from sheer authority is wasted. It turns them off. At least this way, they are amenable to listening and I think that's a lot.

> Well, to that kind of objection, I just say, what's the alternative? Even the Archbishop when he visits St. Martin's talks to the kids using the same technique. He questions and suggests. He never says, OK, this is it—you have to believe it or do it. Besides, when I use this approach in distinguishing different levels of church teaching, so often they say, why weren't we taught this before (that some doctrines are not as weighty as others)? Once you show them this gradation, then they aren't as likely later on to reject everything because they assume all Catholic teaching is on the same level.

These teachers, then appreciate the risks involved in presenting these schemes to their students: that teachings will seem simply one alternative among many in our culture and that each individual can decide for herself or himself how seriously to take each doctrine presented. As they see it, divesting the students of their misunderstanding that "you have to believe all that stuff" is important enough to run these risks—which, of course, they believe they can offset in the classroom and in personal conversation outside class.

Classroom teaching of religion ought to be supplemented, the teachers believed, by religious experiences outside the classroom. Too few such experiences were available to students. Three of the four teachers lamented the absence of mandatory closed retreats off campus. Such retreats were regularly scheduled in the mid-1970s, but a new principal in 1979, hearing of "disciplinary problems" on one overnight retreat, abolished them. A more recent substitute is a half day of recollection held separately for each of the four years, sometimes at a parish near the school, at other times on the campus itself. All teachers believed them to be much less effective than a closed off-campus overnight retreat. "It all depends on the particular priest who gives the half-day of recollection, and we've had some who are not satisfactory in recent years." Three teachers strongly affirmed the lack of any "religious experiences" for the students, regretting the restriction of religious formation, for all practical purposes, to the classroom. "It's all too intellectual, and when we do have Masses for the students, they're too large, involving the whole student body, and the students have little or no participation in the planning of these Masses."

When I asked the school's principal about retreats, noting that the theology teachers favored them, he replied, "Retreats are fine and I favor them, but the kids are out of school for so many things as it is, sports for example. How would you find time for a retreat? In a spread-out state like this, they spend much more travel time to play other teams than a school in a big metropolitan area would. And co-ed retreats don't work; they're too hard to manage. Besides, once a semester, each student is assigned to a small group that plans a Mass just for that group. They pick the readings, and so on. That works out pretty well."

The theology teachers, then, operated on the assumption that whatever religious formation the students received would be almost entirely through the classroom. This situation is not, of course, true of Catholic high schools everywhere. But in this case, the burden lay mainly on the shoulders of the theology staff.

## *Commentary*

Certainly the interactive dynamics between students and teachers we have just seen bears out Giddens's structuration perspective, i.e., social actors not constrained by a web of norms and values, but taking initiatives within a given social structure. Convinced that by sophomore (and certainly by junior) year, both male and female students are ready to question authority and submit the latter to the bar of individual conscience, St. Martin's theology teachers sat down to devise strategies aimed at making Catholic teaching plausible to "this generation." Explicitly aware of competitive cultural definitions (Swidler's phrase) of what is OK, right, wrong, "cool," makes sense, etc., teachers deliberately adopted a method that asks students to deal explicitly with these competitive meanings, thus enabling teachers to discern patterns of resistance shared by the majority of students. Exercise of arbitrary authority ("this is what you must believe") would only sharpen resistance. Their strategies stem from full awareness of the cultural ascendancy of doctrinal and moral individualism among the students. They counter by trying to persuade students that the teachings both "make sense" when compared to other choices offered in American society and form part of an age-old tradition deserving of the students' respect. Compare Schwartz's depiction of "the rebellious girls of St. Irene's," whose "response was one of incredulity and laughter" when a written set of "traditional rules for sexual behavior" was handed to them, without benefit of discussion or an attempt to solicit their own views on these issues.[15]

But the teachers are also sensitive to misconceptions they believe students have picked up in elementary and middle-school years (whether or not they attended Catholic schools). Chief among these is the notion that *all* Catholic teachings are to be taken with equal seriousness or gravity; that if you are a Catholic, you must, in one teacher's phrase, "believe all that stuff." Their response, as we have seen, was to dust off an old and orthodox theological model in use mainly in schools of Catholic theology and make it a linchpin of presentation to juniors and seniors. Church doctrines can be arrayed in order of certainty or infallibility, beginning with those that are *de fide definita* and progressing through less certain rungs or niches. Skeptical students can then be shown that Catholics do not have to "believe all that stuff" but can consider distinctions wherein the most certain levels of teaching constitute what is essential to defining yourself as Catholic; the less certain can, if one so chooses, be taken less seriously in one's personal pantheon of beliefs. Making this key distinction allows the teachers to entertain seriously the skepticism of their students and discuss their doubts more openly without appearing judgmental. Put aside is the role of a doctrinal or moral authority figure saying you *must* believe "or else" — a not uncommon posture in earlier decades. Teachers thus assume the task of convincing by persuasion or, in the pregnant phrase uttered by one teacher cited above, of "selling rather than telling."

But how do students react to this approach? Do they see themselves as manipulated by their teachers into "believing" and "accepting"? Seniors' reflections set down in this chapter suggest the answer is no. But researchers embracing a critical pedagogical approach might well counter that just because seniors don't perceive themselves as victims of a "hidden curriculum" doesn't mean they are uninfluenced by the power of the classroom's "ritual performances." Peter McLaren's study of a Catholic middle school in Toronto is a potent reminder of how teachers, in trying to exercise surveillance over and manage the behavior of students, engaged in ritualized activities that mask the arbitrary nature of classroom conventions even if those conventions proved to be objectionable to the students. . . . What seemed to transpire frequently through enactment in the rituals of instruction was the wielding of power for its own sake.[16]

In this light, do the preceding accounts smack of a shallow analysis oblivious of processes such as the falsification of consciousness, deprivation of alternative views of social structure and institution, and what McLaren calls "oversanctification" or absolutizing of rules, routines, and (more importantly) the content of teaching itself?

I don't see it this way. In the first place, St. Martin's students and teachers alike come from middle- and upper-middle-class backgrounds including, for the most part, the Hispanic seniors. McLaren's study featured middle-class teachers and lower income students from Portuguese-speaking families recently arrived from the Azores. The cultural gaps were striking, as McLaren tells us, resulting in daily conflicts of perception, goals, and procedures between students and teachers. If one adds the younger ages of the student body, the teachers' emphasis on discipline and order—indeed, the central role of the teacher—is hardly surprising. Yet McLaren himself notes that religion classes were settings

> where prevailing societal norms were often questioned, and individual values were relativized in terms of what could benefit humanity as a whole. Religion classes constituted the only occasions during which students were encouraged to adopt a critical stance towards the dominant culture.[17]

As I have indicated, St. Martin's theology teachers did attempt to spell out the implications of Catholic social teaching with its challenges to self-satisfaction and sheer material accumulation as life goals. How well they succeeded, only the future lives of the students will truly reveal, although chapter 5 provides some initial indications. Certainly, no teacher at St. Martin's unequivocally identified the role of "hard worker" (or skilled professional) with being a "good Catholic," as McLaren found in the school he studied.[18] On the other hand, no teacher that I know of simply condemned the capitalist state or depicted it as "the coagulation of oppression and despair" postulated by McLaren.[19] I sense that St. Martin's theology teachers felt they were pushing the students as far as they could in a reflective direction; given the students' comparatively affluent background, any further pushing in a critical vein could easily have alienated them. In fact, one religion teacher of freshmen and sophomores noted for her socially "liberal" stances, e.g., explicitly criticizing U.S. policy in Central America, was viewed by many seniors, looking back on their four years, as simply "too radical"—though a few whose outlook matched hers were eloquent in praising her.

I do, however, find myself in agreement with McLaren and most critical theorists when they underscore the enormous formative power of classroom and liturgical *rituals*. Teachers and administrators would indeed do well to try to understand and appreciate the transactions of power and influence taking place through ritual and symbol. Are the messages that they intend and would want to impart the ones students are receiving? The most striking deficiency in St. Martin's religious education, in my opinion, was that carefully thought-out and constructed liturgies, ranging from student body Masses to off-campus retreats, were seriously undervalued. The school principal certainly did not see them as high priorities. Arranging Masses, retreats, and so on was usually left to the school chaplains and counselors. Though skilled in counseling and helpful to students, chaplains seemed to share in the generalized lack of appreciation for the power of thoughtful ritual performance and participation.

When students *do* participate in and creatively contribute to a Mass liturgy, the effects can be nothing short of electric. In her study of an American Catholic high school, Nancy Lesko describes a "pantomime Mass" in which students dramatized the Gospel message, "the last shall be first and the first last."

> While the priest read the brief passage, students portrayed a big car greedily pushing its way to a gas pump and guzzling almost all the fuel, so that little was left for the unassuming small car that had been pushed aside. Another scene depicted a power-monger ruthlessly eliminating people who obstructed his rise to absolute control.[20]

Comments of the students after the Mass left no doubt that they expected to be engaged in the ritual and that it held their attention both mentally and emotionally.

In brief, my own impression was that the preponderance of religious formation at St. Martin's was of an intellectual character—the process of developing convictions—and in this respect, I believe the teachers enjoyed considerable success.

But let us return to the seniors themselves, who were anything but silent partners in the dialectic of teaching and response initiated by their teachers. Seniors become active agents interpreting, distinguishing, appropriating, or discarding what they are taught. Everything is filtered through the screen of personal experience and subjected to "checking out" with peers. Cultural values of individual autonomy and the supremacy of individual conscience are palpably evident throughout their responses. Though the latter are but "one-shot" answers to an open-ended survey question, few are the voices making the careful distinctions advocated by their teachers concerning gravity or seriousness of doctrine. An overwhelming majority indicate that while they "take into consideration" the Church's teaching, "my conscience" remains the ultimate arbiter of what they will appropriate or set aside. Giddens's emphasis on unintended consequences highlights the irony of students seizing upon the very principle the teachers had relied on to make Catholic teaching plausible—the theological scheme of gradation of doctrine—and using it to establish a blanket principle of individual supremacy in deciding what to believe and practice. A kind of "sorcerer's apprentice" scenario emerges: a distinction designed to help students remain Catholic "in essentials" seems to have put into their hands the very broom some need to sweep their doctrinal and moral arsenals clean of everything but what they "feel" and "believe" makes sense to them. Given this situation it is perhaps all the more remarkable that the seniors seem so well-disposed toward some teachings; certainly indicators of social consciousness have shown the seniors as positive toward ideals of sharing with others in need and of combating injustices in society. Only in the area of sexual morality do the seniors bear out Gallup and Castelli's remark that in this area, Catholic leadership finds a laity that is "not listening."

\* \* \* \*

Still missing, however, is a portrait of how seniors, in a more global sense, see themselves as Catholics—given their cherished autonomy of judgment and caution about accepting "authority as such"—in comparison with their parents. Do they exhibit a distinct sense of identity as Catholics when compared with their parents? Do they consider *themselves* as different? If Catholic tradition, expressed in the self-conceptions of these young Catholics, has shifted in their lives, are they aware of this shift? How do they express it? The next section explores this issue. I set forth some of the responses to a question asked only of the senior classes of 1987 through 1989. I formulated it on the belief that it would highlight the differences, as seniors see them, between an older Catholicism characteristic of their parents and grandparents and their own "versions."

### Seniors' Views of "Being Catholic": Portraits of Identity

I asked seniors from the graduating classes of 1987 through 1989 about their religious identity through an open-ended question appended to the survey:

Obviously, "being a Catholic" has different meanings for different people, and sons and daughters may differ in this respect from their parents. In your case, how would you say "being a Catholic" differs in meaning for you—if at all—comparing yourself to your parents?

In wording the question this way, I hoped to capture what seniors thought was distinctive about their own religious convictions compared to their parents. The theology teachers had warned that any question asked "too directly," particularly after seniors had answered a series of religiosity questions in the survey, risked "skips" or flippant answers. Thus, inviting comparison with parental religiosity seemed a sensible way to proceed, suggesting that the question be given some measure of respect. All but three Catholic seniors responded and apparently regarded the question seriously. Some answered at considerable length.

### Response Categories

I coded the responses as follows:

1. No difference between my parents and myself (30 percent).

2. I differ from my parents' beliefs in that I take some teachings less seriously than they do (35 percent).

3. I differ because I view religion mainly as something that makes me a better person and/or has made my faith even more important to me than to my parents (10 percent).

4. What's important is a personal conversion experience I have had (14 percent).

5. I have serious doubts about Catholic teaching and/or moral precepts (7 percent).

6. Expressions of alienation and hostility toward the Church and its teachings (5 percent).

As table 4.1 shows, important differences appear when controls for ethnic background and gender are introduced. Anglo seniors are more than twice as likely as Hispanics or Anglo-Hispanics to fall into the doubter or alienated categories. A fifth of the Anglo seniors claim their outlooks are the same as their parents'; somewhat over a third of Hispanics and Anglo-Hispanics chose that answer. Gender differences are smaller and, unlike ethnic controls, are not statistically significant. Fourteen percent of male seniors and 11 percent of female seniors fall into the doubter and

Table 4.1

**Responses of Seniors from 1987 to 1989 to "Being a Catholic," by Gender and
Ethnic Background**

| Gender | Same as Parents | Less Strict | Better Person | Conversion | Doubter | Alienated |
|---|---|---|---|---|---|---|
| | | Response Categories | | | | |
| Male | 27% | 34% | 11% | 14% | 8% | 6% |
| Female | 32% | 36% | 9% | 13% | 6% | 5% |
| | | | | | | Sig/ = n.s. |
| *Ethnic Background* | | | | | | |
| Anglo | 21% | 28% | 19% | 4% | 12% | 16% |
| Anglo-Hispanic | 36% | 43% | 7% | 7% | 4% | 4% |
| Hispanic | 32% | 37% | 6% | 19% | 5% | 1% |
| | | | | | | p = .0000 |

alienated groups. Female seniors are slightly more likely to say their Catholicism is the same as their parents'.

Setting aside the traditional student whose Catholicism is the same as their parents, I have selected below student comments that seem representative of departure, at least to some extent, from the devotional Catholicism of the past.

### *The Alienated*

Variations appear in responses of the 5 percent of seniors one could describe as alienated. Some affirm their own religiosity, divorcing it from what they ascribe to the Catholic Church; others make sharp contrast with their parents. Some are quite angry.

"Being a Catholic" doesn't mean a thing to me. I differ from my parents because they're involved with the Church. I don't agree with some of the teachings (Confession) and hate to attend Mass. My parents make me go and that's the only reasons I am there. I don't believe in religion. It's just there so people can feel secure and have someone else tell them how to behave because they can't do it on their own. . . . Religion is just around because there are too many insecure people around. (Hispanic female)

My mother has a deep faith in her religion and supports the Church. Personally I have faith in my religion, but *despise* the Church for what it has done. In my educated opinion, the Church is not better than Jim Baker or those other con artists. (Anglo-Hispanic male)

I have to pretend to go to Church so that my parents don't have a mental breakdown thinking I'm possessed by unclean spirits. (Anglo male)

To me, "being a Catholic" means turning over your conscience to a bunch of old men who don't know what in the hell is going on. "Being a Catholic" is just an excuse to not make any hard choices but to blindly follow the words of someone else. I think of Catholicism as mental slavery for immature people. They can't disagree without punishment or try to escape because they are held against their will. Therefore I see "being a Catholic" as something to avoid. (Anglo male)

### The Doubters

Seven percent given evidence of struggling with either their entire religious background or with particular teachings. Occasionally, doubters indicate they differ little from their parents:

My view differs only slightly from my parents' concerning the Catholic Church. They feel that going to Church is enough. Participation in other activities in not needed. They feel the Catholic Church is a bunch of B.S. The faith and teachings are all right, but the Church hierarchy and supporters are demented. This view I share with my parents, but on participation, I feel more spirituality is needed. I attend non-Catholic Christian services twice a week and Catholic service once a week. More is needed but not from a decadent Church. (Anglo male)

Because of the theology classes at [St. Martin's,] I've learned to doubt my Catholic faith more and more. I got into existentialism during Man and Woman and Moral Issues [two senior courses] and really subconsciously came up with some great stuff. I believe in God. I don't believe in Hell really. I don't believe in the Pope. No man and his crew at the round table in their little white robes should take such decisions into their hands and expect to have people abide by them. That's our conscience's job. We'll do fine if we do what *we* believe is correct, not what an old man in Rome thinks. . . . Meditation about yourself and world or even a self-confession type deal is much better. While in Church, you feel better but also guilty, or at least I do. Once again, doubting like this, there's the flashback of my faith. All I can really say is that I'm not through learning and never will be. I hope I'm a Catholic. I just don't believe anybody will go to Hell for what they believe. (Anglo male)

I do not really consider myself a Catholic. I feel right now I am confused on religion and that I won't make a decision upon my religion until later in my life. I think I feel this way because I disagree with *some* of the teachings of the Catholic Church. So at this point I can just say that I'm a Christian. (Anglo female)

My parents are Catholics, but don't express it a lot. They go to Church but don't act "holy" all the time. They brought me up as Catholic but through CCD and [St. Martin's] religious courses I have heard a lot I don't agree with. At the present time I am in a very confused state since I disagree with so much that the Church teaches. I have often thought at times I should not be considered a Catholic. Friends are trying to convince me that through Church I may gain faith—who knows, we'll see. (Hispanic female)

God, where do I begin? To me, "being a Catholic"—well, it really doesn't matter so much to me as my parents, especially my mother. I really resent the Church for its politics, and in my opinion, it seems like it's taken a lot of money to Rome and not done much good with it. Now the Church is bankrupt, and we're supposed to dig in our pockets and give some more. . . . Women can't be priests. Birth control? Married priests? When is the Church going to stop being so archaic? I think my parents (Mom) are more prone to following the Church's teaching about it. "The Church says no so I say no." I don't feel that way. I'm going to decide what *I* want to do, and if it goes against the Church, c'est la vie. I'm also not really "into" organized religion. My faith is much more personal, so going to Church is not so important to me as it is to my parents. (Anglo female)

### The Selectors

The principle of individual judgment is evident above in several responses of the doubters. But it is etched even more clearly in the 35 percent of seniors seeing see themselves as Catholics but nevertheless practicing "selective Catholicism." Neither the Church nor Catholicism is subjected to serious doubt or rejection, but the supremacy of individual judgment means that not everything in tradition is acceptable.

Being a Catholic to me means respecting and listening to what the Church teaches and then deciding what we believe and living that out. I think my parents go along with a lot more of the Church's teachings and rituals than I do. (Anglo-Hispanic female)

I try to think of myself as more open. I respect the Catholic Church, all of its requirements and such, but I also respect myself. I want to be able to make my own decisions on my own. I think my parents blindly accepted a lot more than this generation. (Anglo male)

Being a Catholic to my parents, since they were both raised in a strict Catholic environment, one *has* to do certain duties: Church on Sunday, Baptism, Confirmation, etc. With me, it is more like I do something because I *want* to. (Anglo-Hispanic male)

Being a Catholic is very important. My parents pretty much stay with the traditional teachings of the Church. I, on the other hand, take and use only what I feel is right for me. (Hispanic male)

I don't see "being a Catholic" by just following what the Church says. I feel that being a Catholic means doing what you feel is right while keeping in consideration the Church's teachings. I don't agree with everything it says; therefore, I should be able to form my own opinion and still be considered a good Catholic. (Anglo female)

"Being a Catholic" for me means that I could go to the Church for guidance, help, and understanding. For me the Catholic Church is not the basis for *my* religion—my relationship with God is. I won't let the Catholic Church get in between what I feel is right or wrong, but I will take its teachings into serious consideration. (Hispanic male)

In some cases seniors explicitly cite their theology classes as contributing to their views, at times alluding to the "levels" of certainty assigned by their instructors to various teachings.

At [St. Martin's] . . . we learn more about our own Catholic beliefs so that they are clearer for us to understand. The teachers tell us what the Catholic teachings are about some issues but do not say we must agree with them. . . . "Being a Catholic" to me is to know of the Church's teachings and accept the ones I agree with, but also to not accept the ones I disagree with. I do not accept the teachings if I feel they are not right. (Anglo-Hispanic female)

To my parents a "Catholic" means following all the rules and doing whatever the Church or the priest says. I disagree with this "blind faith" attitude and realize the Church may be wrong on teachings that aren't on Level I. This [my theology courses at St. Martin's] has led me to be more critical of the Church. (Hispanic male)

Being a Catholic to me means respecting and listening to what the Church teaches and then deciding what we believe and living that out. . . . We still have our own minds and our own opinions. The best thing

our teachers could do is make us aware of these morals and then leave
it up to us, and they have. (Anglo-Hispanic female)

An occasional senior contrasts ways of "living out" one's religious
tradition, e.g., a ritualized approach versus a more personalized one.

My parents sometimes seem to be going through the motions in their
religion. Going to Mass on all the right days is more important than
really living the faith. I'm sure they don't realize it because they were
raised that way, but I have difficulty going through the motions of
anything. I find it hard to be Catholic and believe in the death penalty,
for instance. Or go to Mass if you are truly needed by a friend instead.
It's hard for me to believe this openly in my house, but I don't want to
change how I feel. (Anglo female)

Others take a kind of global approach, viewing themselves as members
of a generation possessing a distinctive outlook and one communicated from
peer to peer.

My parents' views are very old-fashioned. Mine are more liberal than
theirs, probably because of the different views of friends and peers. I
find myself questioning the Church more often than before because I
have talked to friends who feel differently than myself and their
opinions have made sense to me. I accept the faith, but I feel I have not
made a solid decision in accepting all of it. (Hispanic female)

I feel that in my generation the Church will change a lot. I know my
parents have very different religious views than I do. Most of my
friends seem to share my views, so it seems to me that some of them
will make changes in the Church. It is my belief that if the Church
doesn't make some changes, then it is likely they will end up losing a
lot of the people from my generation. I know when my parents try to
pressure me into believing their views, it causes me to turn away from
them even more. Hopefully, the Catholic Church will not put as much
pressure on us. (Hispanic female)

### Personal Growth

Approximately 10 percent of seniors fell into a category closely related
to the above—religion as means of personal growth. Religious beliefs and
practices are auxiliary to leading a good life, a viewpoint that dovetails easily
with the principle of individual judgment. For if a particular doctrine or

moral precept fails to further one's personal growth, what reason remains to retain it?

> Being a Catholic is a way to become a better person. By this I mean a way to help others, help yourself but with meaning, not just going through actions. (Hispanic male)

> My idea of being a Catholic is not so much forcing someone to go to Church on Sunday, but rather being a good person—how you treat yourself and others. That's what is important first—you can't get anything out of Mass if you don't do that first. (Anglo female)

> My father and I are Catholic in name, but do not practice the faith. When in fact we do go to Church, it is a time for meditation—getting a psychological grip on the past and future weeks of our lives. So perhaps "being a Catholic" means having the strength to think and cope, not to mention form opinions and philosophies. (Hispanic female)

> You could go to Church seven days a week and still be a "bad" person. Being kind, using your potential, and living life to better yourself is what seems to matter to me. Being a hypocrite is one of the worst things to be. Live your life as a "good Catholic" would and you don't necessarily need to be one. (Hispanic female)

## Conclusion

Young men and women graduating from high school are still searching for their identities as persons, a quest that may well extend into adulthood. Tentative as their statements may be, however, some themes seem evident. Recalling Phillip Hammond's distinction (see Introduction) between a "collective-expressive" identity and an "individual-expressive" one, a good proportion of seniors appear free (as far as young people still living at home can be) from "mandatory" involvement in their Church that an identity rooted in devotional Catholicism would prescribe. Few have "overlapping memberships" that would act to reinforce a Catholic identity: less than one in five seniors belongs to a religious group or organization in either school or parish. In the case of seniors for whom "being a Catholic" means the same to them as it does to their parents, the "collective-expressive" mode of identity may well be an accurate designation. At the opposite pole, one may exclude the "alienated" seniors who have forsaken a Catholic identity.

Leaving aside these two "extreme" categories, however, the remaining 58 percent of seniors reach for the vocabulary of "individual-expressive" identities. The doubters admit confusion but state disagreement with some teachings as they search for a faith not yet firmly possessed. The selectors emphasize choice: "I want to, not have to . . . ," "I want to do what I feel is right . . . ," "consider teachings, but I do the deciding," and so on. Some refer to thinking through the teachings as opposed to accepting them "blindly" (as some parents are said to do). For others, "going through the motions" is unacceptable; one should consider deeply and then make one's own choices.

The impression remains that a majority of the seniors do see the Church as an important resource for forming one's religious and moral stances; it is not an "enveloping" institution, as it was for their parents, that projects a compelling moral authority. But the authority of the Church is nonetheless present to these seniors, mediated through adult teachers representing its doctrines. How the students *regard* their teachers is a critical issue affecting students' receptivity to teachings presented. An instructive contrast arises if one compares student-teacher relations at St. Martin's with those at Schwartz's Glenbar High School, which, like St. Martin's, serves students from comfortable middle- and upper-middle-class homes. At Glenbar, teachers went out of their way to make their subject matter interesting and their classroom climates informal and relaxing. Yet their students were unresponsive largely, as Schwartz tells us, because of the absence of moral bonds between the generations in the community. Genuinely attached to their parents, Glenbar's students seemed incapable of seeing in "nonfamilial" adults qualities of sensitivity, caring, and concern they sought and could only discern in peer relationships. Students therefore avoided engaging their teachers in other than routine ways enabling them to perform well enough to get the grades needed for admission to college.[21]

At St. Martin's, while it is probably true that certain moral, especially sexual, attitudes are formed largely through peer interaction, it is clear from seniors' comments that their theology teachers, along with certain other faculty members, evoke a good deal of admiration and respect. Furthermore, seniors feel free to discuss aspects of their expressive lives with their teachers and with one another in the theology classrooms. Moral bonds between the generations are implicitly present; for all the reservations the seniors may entertain about some Catholic teachings, they acknowledge membership, unlike Glenbar's students, in a common community of belief and worship with their teachers.

At this point, St. Martin's seniors may seem more like the Catholic students from St. Irene's and Mother of God high schools in Schwartz's "Parson's Park" community. But teachers in those schools projected an authority students considered unreasonable: "there is a joyless quality to the way authority insures that its voice is hear and removes whatever warmth it feels for those for whom it is responsible."[22] St. Martin's teachers, by contrast, made carefully thought-out efforts to reach their students in ways that respected them as thinking persons. Seniors were aware that in working out such presentational schemes as the steps in conscience formation and weight assigned to Catholic teachings, teachers were exhibiting reasonable authority: a respect for their students, an understanding that students deserve an approach to doctrine that takes into account their cultural situation, their experiences, and the importance of their personal judgments. The weighting scheme of doctrine conveys the notion that no arbitrary burden of belief is being laid on them, but rather one that supports a commonsense view that not all teaching is of equal gravity. These approaches embody the reasonableness of authority to the seniors. The theology faculty, for their part, seemed to take some comfort from the perception that their presentations, while not cutting substantial inroads into the students' well-entrenched theological and moral individualism, at least create an openness to Church teaching that may come to a fuller flowering at later stages in their students' lives. Teachers are aware that students have other resources at hand, sometimes mentioned explicitly: one's peers, one's own learning experiences, trusted friends, and of course, one's parents and family—not all of whom, including parents, may reinforce Catholic teaching. In any case, the vocabulary of individual choice abounds, reflecting familiar themes in students' everyday conversations as well as cultural assumptions projected daily in the media.

In the face of this basic individualist orientation shared by a majority of seniors, the teaching strategies of their instructors are understandable (whatever other judgment one might make about them): "give them the information" as persuasively as you can, show them the "reasonableness" of the teachings and their graduation of solemnity, indicate the respect for life and personhood inherent in traditional doctrine, and the rest is up to them. Doctrinal and moral choices are to be personally appropriated, not inculcated by bearers of authority.

We are returned to the theoretical notion that social structure is not simply—or even mainly—constraining. Persons as social actors maintain and continue social structures over time and space. But as actors knowledgeable about the social systems they "inhabit," students and teachers at St. Martin's creatively respond to one another in ways that "transform" a system while at the same time reproducing it. St. Martin's teachers succeed, for the most part, in transmitting elements of a tradition so that seniors generally accept it. But in this process, both parties understand the structures in which they are interacting and how those structures might permit change. The students are aware that they live in a Catholic world their parents did not know, one where former certitudes and "absolutes" no longer hold sway but are called before the bar of individual conscience. They thus feel free to challenge and, in some cases, withhold assent to elements of this tradition. The theology teachers respond not by trying to impose teachings in a "this is it" mode; instead, they adapt the tradition they represent in ways that render it more acceptable to the young Catholics sitting in their classrooms. In this process, a tradition is maintained even as it is changed; as the principle of conscience supremacy emerges intact for the seniors, some traditional beliefs and ways are successfully imparted. If the system is "reproduced," it is also changed, As many observers have pointed out, the American Catholic Church comes to resemble in the post–Vatican II era, a characteristically American denomination whose members freely bestow their consent to its teaching, worship, and practice. If boundaries emerge, they do so, as the St. Martin's case suggests, through a negotiatory process in which each party emerges with not as much as each might like but with a compromise each party seems able to live with. Not all segments of the Catholic community will be pleased, of course. The CUF parents cited previously are a case in point, but they remain a transient minority posing no threat to the faculty or school administration. Nevertheless, no matter how one views the developments above, they are inherently changeful of a tradition that was formerly top-down only in its channels of authority.

In the final data chapter to follow, I ask what a group of St. Martin's graduates might look like some years later as they move out into the world beyond high school. Does the individualism remain, and if so, how does it show itself in terms of adherence to or casting off elements of Catholic tradition? What is their self-conception as young Catholics—in this case, Catholics in their late twenties?

# 5 "People Nowadays Put Religion on the Back Burner": St. Martin's Graduates in Their Late Twenties

Given the profile of graduating seniors revealed in the preceding chapter, how do they appear some years later? Does "individual conscience" reign supreme? Have beliefs and practices changes, and if so, how? The senior theology teacher agreed to my suggestion that volunteers be sought from the graduating classes of 1978 and 1979 who, after completing a survey as seniors, would consent to be resurveyed some years later. I asked those volunteering to append their names and parental addresses to the questionnaires. The survey instrument was similar to the one given to all seniors, save for the addition of a few social and moral issues (such as attitudes toward homosexuals and toward cohabitation before marriage). Fifty-five seniors volunteered, twenty-three from the class of 1978 and thirty-two from the class of 1979.

I was able in the spring of 1987 to recontact fifty-four out of the original fifty-five, sending each a copy of his or her original questionnaire with a request to review each answer, noting any change from senior year to 1987. I also requested current background data (e.g., marital status, educational attainments) and posed additional attitudinal and behavioral questions.

Are these volunteers a representative sample of the senior classes of 1978 and 1979? Table 5.1 compares volunteers with all seniors from the combined classes of 1978 and 1979 in terms of sex, ethnic background, and father's occupation. While the two groups are closely matched by ethnic distribution, the volunteers include notably more females (63 percent to all seniors' 56 percent) and are weighted toward the upper end of the socioeconomic scale by father's occupation. Fully 91 percent of the volunteers' fathers fall into the business manager or owner and professional categories as compared to 72 percent of all seniors' fathers for 1978 and 1979. The volunteers, then, by comparison with all seniors graduating in those years, are disproportionately from high-status families. They are also less devout than their classmates. Three-quarters of seniors in 1978 and 1979 reported weekly church attendance; slightly over half the volunteers attended that regularly in senior year. In this respect, then, they are not typical of their

127

**Table 5.1**

**Volunteer Sample Compared with Entire Classes, 1978 and 1979,
by Demographic Characteristics**

|  | Volunteer Sample (N = 54) | Combined Seniors Classes 1978 and 1979 (N = 371) |
|---|---|---|
| Female | 63% | 56% |
| Male | 37% | 44% |
| Hispanic | 26% | 22% |
| Anglo-Hispanic | 7% | 8% |
| Anglo | 67% | 70% |
| *Father's Occupation* | | |
| Blue-Collar | 0% | 9% |
| White-collar | 9% | 17% |
| Owner-manager | 30% | 23% |
| Lower professional | 26% | 26% |
| Upper professional | 35% | 23% |

high school classmates. When it comes to social sensitivity, however, volunteers are *more* likely than their classmates to affirm sharing with others and opposing injustice (98 percent and 96 percent, respectively, in contrast to slightly under 90 percent for all seniors).

The volunteers themselves generally mirror the high status of their families of origin. When recontacted in 1987, three were medical doctors beginning residency; ten had master's degrees; twenty-five had bachelor's degrees, with four of these having two such degrees and three currently in law school; four were registered nurses; two had associate of arts degrees; and fourteen had no college degree, though four were currently enrolled in a degree program. By almost any comparison, then, this group of fifty-four St. Martin's graduates can be characterized as high achievers.

What does contemporary research tell us about religious practices and views of young adults? Let us return to survey findings reported by Fee and colleagues in *Young Catholics,* and more recently by Gallup and Castelli in *The American Catholic People.* After age 22, Catholics exhibit a sharp decline in religious practices, a decline bottoming out at ages 26 to 28, exactly the ages of the volunteers in 1987. A "rebound" effect occurs as they approach age 30. Women, more devout than men, also decline in practice during these years, but less so than Catholic men.[1] The present sample of 27- and 28-year-old Catholic graduates of St. Martin's, then, "should" have declined, compared with their senior year of high school, in religious devotion and practice. Gallup and Castelli note that among Catholics under age 30 surveyed in 1985, 37 percent attended church in the past seven days; among the subgroup 25 to 29 years old, the figure climbs two points to 39 percent. These figures are lower than the overall U.S. attendance figure of 53 percent and lower than the 30 to 49-year old attendance rate of 54 percent.[2]

A recent Minnesota study of young adults ages 19 to 34, in which the biggest proportion (40 percent) were Catholic, found that Catholics showed less interest in church involvement and in nonworship church activities than either mainline or nonmainline Protestants of the same age. Unlike the hypothesis suggested above, "marrying or becoming a parent seemed to have little effect on Catholics' church interest and involvement." They remained low on these measures whether single or married.[3]

How people develop and change the ways in which they believe and hold convictions as they move through stages of the life-cycle, is the subject of considerable research and theorizing. Work by Fowler and more recently, by Parks, suggests that adults in their twenties may experience changes in their lives that move beyond what Fowler calls the "stage of synthetic-conventional faith," typically generated in adolescence. Here the teenager's religious faith may be quite firmly held, but it is intertwined with the expectations and judgments of significant others—family, peers, and neighbors. Many persons never move beyond this faith stage, in which autonomy of judgment and action are barely operative. Little, if any, critical reflection on one's faith takes place. Stage 4, "individuative-reflective faith," usually begins when events break one's reliance upon conventional sources of authority and guidance. Fowler's inventory is helpful:

> Factors contributing to the breakdown of Stage 3 and to readiness for transition may include serious clashes or contradictions between valued authority sources; marked changes, by officially sanctioned leaders, or policies or practices previously deemed sacred and unbreachable (for example, in the Catholic Church changing the Mass from Latin to the vernacular, or no longer requiring abstinence from meat on Friday); the encounter with experiences or perspectives that lead to critical reflection on how one's beliefs and values have formed and changed, and on how "relative" they are to one's particular group or background. Frequently the experience of "leaving home"— emotionally or physically or both—precipitates the kind of examination of self, background, and life-guiding values that gives rise to stage transition at this point.[4]

The transition Fowler describes is easier for young adults in their early to mid-twenties. When it occurs during one's thirties or forties it is often more painful—triggered by a divorce, death of a parent, children growing up and leaving home, etc.

Sharon Parks has proposed another stage in between Fowler's two: "young adult faith," a concept inspired by the work of Kenneth Kenniston.

This stage is part of Fowler's "individuative-reflective faith" but is held prior to its full possession by the individual believer. Unsettled for the young adult is the relationship between emerging not-quite-adult self and how one may integrate or fit into society itself. Young people in this postulated stage are apt to engage in "probing commitments," "trying on" various stances, exploring them and sorting them out in terms of what they themselves are becoming as persons. These probings have a tentative, ambiguous character. Often a mentor or a mentoring community is critical at this stage as the young person gropes toward firmer meaning and seeks a community that embodies his or her emerging values. Fowler's stage, the full flowering of this process, would then come out as one of "tested commitment." Until arriving at this fullness of personal meaning and social commitment, however, the young adult may entertain a keen awareness that all stances are relative and find himself or herself struggling for personally appropriated meaning and a community that supports and sustains his or her growing commitments.[5]

Let us look first at the religious practice and attitude profiles of these young adults eight and nine years after graduating from high school. What do the volunteers look like in 1987? Table 5.2 presents a profile of thirteen measures of religious practices and attitudes plus sociomoral viewpoints, comparing their senior-year percentages (in 1978 and 1979) with those of 1987. The following commentary also alludes to variations, not shown on the table, by gender, ethnicity, and type of elementary school attended (all Catholic, both Catholic and non-Catholic, or non-Catholic only).

## Religious Practices

### Church Attendance

The volunteers are no different from other young Catholic adults surveyed nationally. Whereas 54 percent attended church weekly or several times per month as high school seniors, just one out of five reported attending church that often in 1987. A third say they go monthly, but almost half (48 percent) said they went a few times per year or not at all (17 percent indicated they never attend—not shown on table).

Hispanics continue, as they did in senior year, to "out-attend" Anglos on a frequent basis, but are considerably more likely to say in 1987 that they attend a few times a year or not at all. Among the biggest surprises is the 1987 discrepancy between males and females in a pattern opposite to national data. As seniors, girls expectedly attended church more regularly than boys. As young adults, however, women had dropped their attendance more sharply than men. In fact, the volunteer men are 4 percentage points *more*

## Table 5.2
## Graduates of 1978 and 1979 Resurveyed in 1987
### (N = 54)

| | All Volunteers | | | Women only | | | Men only | | |
|---|---|---|---|---|---|---|---|---|---|
| | 1978–79 % | 1987 % | Percent change | 1978–79 % | 1987 % | Percent change | 1978–79 % | 1987 % | Percent change |
| 1. Mass attendance | | | | | | | | | |
| Weekly to Several times per month | 54 | 22 | −32 | 56 | 21 | −35 | 50 | 25 | −25 |
| Monthly | 39 | 30 | −9 | 38 | 35 | −3 | 40 | 20 | −20 |
| Few tmes a year or never | 7 | 40 | +41 | 6 | 44 | +38 | 10 | 55 | +45 |
| 2. Frequency of prayer | | | | | | | | | |
| Daily | 59 | 50 | −7 | 56 | 47 | −9 | 65 | 55 | −10 |
| Weekly | 24 | 24 | 0 | 29 | 35 | +6 | 15 | 5 | −10 |
| Monthly | 28 | 22 | −6 | 12 | 12 | 0 | 10 | 30 | +20 |
| Never | 6 | 7 | +1 | 3 | 6 | +3 | 10 | 10 | 0 |
| 3. Frequency of confession | | | | | | | | | |
| Monthly | 9 | 2 | −7 | 9 | 3 | −6 | 10 | 0 | −10 |
| Few times a year | 41 | 22 | −19 | 38 | 24 | −14 | 45 | 20 | −25 |
| Never | 50 | 76 | +26 | 53 | 74 | +21 | 45 | 80 | +35 |
| 4. Importance of religion | | | | | | | | | |
| Important but no more so than other aspects of my life | 59 | 44 | −15 | 59 | 50 | −9 | 60 | 35 | −25 |
| Of minor importance compared to other aspects of my life | 7 | 15 | +8 | 6 | 12 | +6 | 10 | 20 | +10 |
| Of central importance and comes before all other aspects | 33 | 41 | +8 | 35 | 38 | +3 | 30 | 45 | +15 |
| 5. How sure of religious beliefs | | | | | | | | | |
| Very sure | 28 | 41 | +13 | 21 | 35 | +14 | 40 | 50 | +10 |
| Pretty sure | 61 | 50 | −11 | 71 | 59 | −12 | 45 | 35 | −10 |
| Not too sure or unsure | 11 | 9 | −2 | 9 | 6 | −3 | 15 | 15 | 0 |
| 6. Spiritual experience that lifted you out of yourself | | | | | | | | | |
| Once or twice | 35 | 30 | −5 | 38 | 41 | +3 | 30 | 11 | −19 |
| Several times or often | 28 | 32 | +4 | 26 | 24 | −2 | 30 | 47 | +17 |
| Never in my life | 37 | 38 | +1 | 35 | 35 | 0 | 40 | 42 | +2 |

*(Continued)*

## Table 5.2 (Continued)

| | All Volunteers | | | Women only | | | Men only | | |
|---|---|---|---|---|---|---|---|---|---|
| | 1978–79 % | 1987 % | Percent change | 1978–79 % | 1987 % | Percent change | 1978–79 % | 1987 % | Percent change |
| 7. It is my responsibility to share what I have with those who have less | | | | | | | | | |
| Basically agree | 98 | 91 | −7 | 100 | 88 | −12 | 94 | 95 | +1 |
| Basically disagree | 2 | 9 | +7 | 0 | 12 | +12 | 6 | 5 | −1 |
| 8. Unjust practice in society: if I do nothing to oppose it I share responsibility | | | | | | | | | |
| Basically agree | 96 | 86 | −10 | 94 | 84 | −10 | 100 | 89 | −11 |
| Basically disagree | 4 | 14 | +10 | 6 | 16 | +10 | 0 | 11 | +11 |
| 9. Premarital Sexual relations* | | | | | | | | | |
| Always or almost always wrong | 52 | 32 | −20 | 56 | 35 | −21 | 45 | 25 | −20 |
| Wrong only sometimes or not at all | 39 | 63 | +34 | 35 | 56 | +21 | 45 | 75 | +30 |
| 10. Cohabitation with Person of Opposite Sex | | | | | | | | | |
| Simply wrong and can't see myself doing it | 37 | 26 | −11 | 35 | 27 | −8 | 40 | 25 | −15 |
| In doubt but open to possibility | 50 | 43 | −7 | 56 | 41 | −17 | 40 | 45 | +5 |
| See nothing wrong and could do it | 13 | 32 | +19 | 9 | 32 | +23 | 20 | 31 | +11 |
| 11. Abortion is acceptable to me for reason of possible birth defects | | | | | | | | | |
| Basically Agree | 13 | 27 | +14 | 15 | 27 | +12 | 10 | 26 | +16 |
| Basically Disagree | 87 | 73 | −14 | 85 | 73 | −12 | 90 | 74 | −16 |
| 12. Abortion acceptable to me should child be unwanted | | | | | | | | | |
| Basically Agree | 7 | 14 | +7 | 9 | 21 | +12 | 5 | 0 | −5 |
| Basically Disagree | 93 | 86 | −7 | 91 | 79 | −12 | 95 | 100 | +5 |
| 13. Support city ordinance prohibiting discrimination against homosexuals | | | | | | | | | |
| Support it | 44 | 52 | +8 | 50 | 53 | +3 | 35 | 50 | +15 |
| Be against it | 30 | 41 | +11 | 24 | 41 | +17 | 35 | 40 | +5 |
| Don't know | 26 | 7 | −19 | 27 | 6 | −21 | 25 | 10 | −15 |

* Don't know responses (under 10 percent) excluded

likely to attend than women. However, men are *less* likely to attend monthly than women and are 10 percentage points more likely than women to go to church a few times a year or never.

The impact of previous Catholic schooling evokes the findings of *Young Catholics,* especially chapter 6 ("Catholic Education and the Life Cycle").[6] Eight years of Catholic education is the point at which differences begin to appear in religious behavior and attitudes. The present data permit no direct comparisons, reporting only those who, as seniors had (1) attended Catholic elementary schools only (twelve years in all of Catholic education, including high school); (2) attended both (a minimum of five years altogether); of (3) no prior Catholic elementary schooling (four years of high school religion classes only). As seniors, volunteers clearly showed the positive devotional effect of all-Catholic elementary schooling; in fact, the relationship between type of school attended and church attendance or communion reception is virtually linear, i.e., the more pre–high school Catholic schooling, the stronger the religious behavior as seniors. By 1987, the effects of all-Catholic elementary school education are even more striking. Whereas the all-Catholic subgroup is slightly less likely to attend frequently, 70 percent attend at least monthly, compared to 42 and 27 percent among those with some or no Catholic elementary schooling, respectively. It is true that the proportion of all-Catholics saying they attend a few times a year or never jumped dramatically in the intervening years; nevertheless, those with some or no Catholic elementary schooling are strikingly more likely to appear on the low-attendance end of the scale. Patterns of receiving Holy Communion follow closely those of church attendance.

### Prayer

While overall practice of prayer changed relatively little from senior year to 1987, women continue in 1987 to pray weekly or monthly much as they did as seniors; the men, however, dropped by 10 and 20 percent, respectively, in these two categories. Other controls are of little impact, save for all–non-Catholic elementary schooling in which the dropoff in weekly prayer and the increase in few times a year or never is enormous (46 percent). In this devotional area, then, Catholic education (at least some years before high school) seems an important buffer against erosion in the practice of prayer.

### Confession

The practice of confession has fallen sharply among all Catholics, particularly younger ones, in the last two decades. Half the volunteers, even as seniors, said they never went. By 1987 three-quarters had abandoned the practice. Dropoff among Hispanics and women was less severe. Previous Catholic schooling made little difference, with strong attrition characterizing all three educational groups.

### Spiritual Experience

Volunteer seniors were asked about their experience of spiritual state(s) which lifted them out of themselves. Very little change is visible overall among the volunteers from senior year to 1987. Respondents are distributed almost evenly by thirds among the three responses (once or twice, several times or often, and never). Hispanics, however, are less likely to report such experiences. But gender differences emerge as most striking: whereas female showed very little change in such experiences over the years, male respondents reported a notable increase (17 percent) in those saying several times or often. The impact of religious education is minimal, but those with *no* Catholic education are markedly *more* likely to shift from once or twice to several times or often.

## Religious Attitudes

### Importance of Religion

This item was worded somewhat differently for the volunteers, allowing them to compare religion to "other aspects of life." Fifteen percent *fewer* volunteers in 1987 said religion was "important but no more so than other aspects of my life." Half of those who shifted went to "of minor importance" and half to "of central importance." Ethnic background controls show Anglo volunteers accounted for most of this shift. Again, some differences stand out: while women changed little over the eight- or nine-year period, men shifted dramatically in proportions of those switching from "important but no more so" to the other two categories with the biggest gainer being "of central importance" (45 percent chose this response in 1987). In terms of prior religious education, an all-Catholic elementary education meant almost no shift over the years in importance assigned to religion. Not so with "mixed" or no previous Catholic schooling, where the shift from "important but no more so . . ." is evenly divided between "of minor importance" and "of central importance" for those with *some* Catholic schooling, but heavily toward "minor importance" for those without any Catholic elementary school education. Once more, early religious education has a marked impact.

### Sureness of Religious Beliefs

Patterns here are similar to importance of religion. The overall shift from senior year to 1987 is toward more respondents "very sure" of their beliefs—a result unsurprising from young adults who have had almost a decade to reflect on what they adhere to. Men continue, as was the case in senior year, to say "very sure" more often than women; in fact, both groups increased their proportions of "very sures" over the eight- to nine-year period, with 50 percent of the men now (1987) saying they were very sure. Hispanics experienced the same shift to "very sure," but less strongly than Anglos; unlike the latter, too, Hispanics had experienced a slight shift toward "not too sure" by 1987. Religious educational background seems to make little difference in shift patterns—those who had a completely non-Catholic elementary education being the "surest" of all. Whatever the changes they have gone through in eight or nine years, these young adults exhibit little doubt about their religious beliefs.

## Sociomoral Attitudes

*Responsibility to Share.* Overall, the years brought little change in responses to this survey item with the sharp exception of women and Hispanics who are *less* likely to say in 1987 that they have a responsibility to share. Prior religious education carries relatively little weight in attitude change.

*Opposing Unjust Practices.* Commitment to oppose injustices in society diminishes by 10 percent for the whole group from 1978–79 through 1987. Hispanics experience a much bigger drop than Anglos; women and men differ little. Peculiarly, those with an all-Catholic elementary education, beginning at a lower level of commitment as seniors, continue to be notably less likely as young adults to evince commitment.

*Morality of Premarital Sex.* A 20 percent drop over the eight or nine years is evident among those saying intercourse is always or almost always wrong. This findings aligns the volunteers with Catholics nationally in 1985 (33 percent saying it is wrong).[7] Anglo and Hispanic graduates, far apart as seniors on this issue (28 percent of Anglo seniors saying "wrong only sometimes" or "not at all," compared to 61 percent of Hispanic volunteers) differ by only 6 percentage points in 1987. Women are expectedly more conservative on this issue than men, but an all-Catholic elementary schooling provided little cushion against the erosion of an orthodox position as these graduates became young adults; in fact, by 1987 they were virtually identical to those with no Catholic elementary schooling.

*Cohabitation with Persons of the Opposite Sex.* Like the previous sexual morality item, shifts occur in the expected "liberal" direction over the years. Hispanics, though, are less likely to see "nothing wrong with it," but more likely to see themselves open to the possibility. Quite striking is the "flattening out" of gender differences from senior year to 1987. From opinions markedly more conservative than men, women shifted to views closer to their male counterparts (9 percent of the women, not shown on the table, chose "don't know" in both 1978–79 and in 1987). The most striking change, perhaps, occurs in those with all-Catholic elementary schooling, who show the biggest single increase across any category in terms of "see nothing wrong with it" (the other two show but minor shifts). Catholic elementary schooling, it seems, is no bulwark against the powerful cultural currents of sexual freedom.

*Abortion.* Two items are reported in table 5.2. Abortion for reasons of birth defects was more acceptable to the group in 1987 than in 1978–79, though only a quarter showed agreement. Men and women are nearly alike in attitude shifts over the years. Ethnic background is another matter: Hispanic seniors in 1978–79 were much most likely than Anglos to indicate acceptance of abortion for this reason. Those differences continue in 1987, even widening a bit: by 1987, almost half the Hispanic volunteers stated their agreement. In terms of elementary school religious education, no changes took place among the mixed schooling respondents. All-Catholic elementary school education proved, again, no buffer in shifting of attitudes toward more acceptability, but having no religious education prior to high school left these young women and men wide open to a marked shift toward abortion.

Abortion should the child be unwanted finds agreement from few volunteers, though the percentage indicating agreement doubled over the years (from 7 to 14 percent). Hispanic-Anglo differences occur here, too, but are much less pronounced than above. Outstanding are gender differences: by 1987, one-fifth of the volunteer women were open to abortion for an unwanted pregnancy, while no men were. No shifts occurred among those having attended mixed or totally non-Catholic schooling. But volunteers with an all-Catholic schooling did shift to a more open attitude.

*Homosexual Ordinance.* Volunteers were asked whether they would support a city ordinance banning discrimination against homosexuals. While a slight shift toward a more tolerant position is visible by 1987, the biggest change is from "don't know" in the senior year to being against such an ordinance by 1987. Hispanics are much more likely to support the ordinance than Anglos; men and women differ very little by 1987, but men "got there" by moving from a more conservative to a more "liberal" position over the years, whereas women moved mainly from "don't know" to being against the ordinance. Catholic-only elementary school volunteers underwent the biggest shift, i.e., in a more liberal direction. Those with a completely non-Catholic elementary schooling background are the only group to show change in a *less* tolerant direction over the years since graduation.

\*   \*   \*   \*

In summary, these young adults indeed share the sharp decline in religious practices characteristic of their age group across the nation. In fact, going back to the Gallup and Castelli figure stated above, the volunteers are 17 percentage points less likely to attend church regularly than Catholics 25 to 29 years old (22 versus 39 percent), a fact doubtless reflecting their lower regular attendance as seniors. However, (in data not shown in the tables), two-thirds of the volunteers attending *weekly* as seniors continued to attend regularly (weekly or almost weekly). Only 21 percent attend a few times a year or less as adults. The opposite is the case with those attending *almost weekly* as seniors: 70 percent of this group now attends a few times a year or never; and the four volunteers in senior year saying they attended monthly now turn up in the few times a year or never category. Being female and having attended Catholic elementary school cushion the drop a little (except for Confession—everyone drops a good deal), but being Hispanic means an even bigger drop: somewhat more likely to attend frequently, but *more* likely than Anglos to have shifted toward the few times or never category. Looking at marriage patterns, graduating from a Catholic high school is no guarantee of marrying a Catholic: only five of the seventeen married volunteers have Catholic spouses (of these five, two attend church a few times a year, one monthly, and two weekly). Twelve attended a Catholic university; five of those (42 percent) attend church a few times a year or never, four monthly, and three weekly. Slightly less than half (twenty-four or 48 percent) of the whole group say they belong to a parish, defined in the survey as attending at least twice monthly.

But religiosity is not defined sheerly by external observance. By other criteria, the volunteers assume a different profile. Only 15 percent say religion is of minor importance in their lives; more in 1987 than in 1978–79 say it is of central importance. Spiritual experiences have not diminished over the years, and whatever their beliefs, fewer are unsure by 1987. When one looks at the two social sensitivity questions—sharing with others in need and opposing unjust practices—volunteers continue to be "caring" in 1987, even if the youthful idealism of senior year has faded a bit, particularly among Hispanics and those with an all-Catholic education and, to a lesser extent, among women. Nor is abortion favored (though why Hispanic volunteers are more tolerant of abortion in case of birth defects is puzzling).

A liberal shift in sexual views is simply to be expected. Women continue to be more cautious than men, though a majority of them say premarital sex is wrong only sometimes or not at all. No gender differences emerge when it comes to cohabitation; in fact, women account for most of the liberal change from senior year to 1987.

Does all-Catholic schooling make a difference by the time of young adulthood? Yes, it does—but not always in the expected direction. Church attendance, frequency of prayer, reception of Holy Communion are all in positive alignment with years in Catholic schools. But on issues of social morality, of sexual and abortion attitudes, it provides no "protection" from the liberalizing trends visible in this group. In fact, on social sensitivity and on cohabitation, all-Catholic schooling renders one *less* likely than graduates with fewer years of religious education to state a position consonant with Catholic tradition. Catholic institutions, then, if one judges from this group of young adults, seem positively reinforcing of religious observance (attendance), a finding familiar from previous research. But they apparently fail to render young Catholic adults distinctive on questions of personal morality and social sensitivity.

None of the above factors, however, necessarily speaks to the issue of a Catholic sense of identity that would tell us something about continuity or discontinuity in relation to their parents' sense of "being Catholic." As we explore this issue through their own self-portraits, we can expect to see "selective Catholicism" once more at work, but in forms somewhat different from seniors due to volunteers' later stage of young adulthood.

### Catholic Identity: Volunteer Self-Portraits

Let me repeat the open-ended question I used both with 1987 to 1989 seniors and with volunteers in the 1987 follow-up study:

Obviously, being a Catholic has different meanings for different people, and daughters and sons may differ in this respect from their parents. In your case, how would you say "being Catholic" differs in meaning for you, if at all, comparing yourself to your parents?

Asking this question of your persons in their mid-twenties, it seemed to me, would reveal not only their degree of "conscience individualization" and invite comparison with seniors from 1987 to 1989, but also the quality of struggle—or more settled sense of "having arrived"—whether that arrival reflects the "synthetic conventional" stage of Fowler's, or the later mature "individuative-reflective" faith. But it would also, in asking respondents to compare themselves with their parents, reveal whether these young adults reflect the "individual-expressive" identity already visible in many of the 1987–89 seniors. In the process, I probe whether, as Catholics, they are cut of a different cloth than their parents. I hoped the question would elicit both their present stances and the journeys taken to arrive at them. I wished to rely on their own words, uncramped by the boundaries of neatly worded survey items.

### "Volunteer" Faith Descriptions

Volunteer responses fell into six categories similar to those characterizing the senior classes of 1987 and 1988. Table 5.3 lists each

**Table 5.3**

**Categories of Volunteers' Self-Descriptions of "Being Catholic"**

| Category | No. of Respondents (N = 54) |
|---|---|
| 1. Beliefs and outlooks basically the same as parents, though practice may differ | 16 |
| 2. Explicit citation of differences with parents on beliefs but still considers oneself a practicing Catholic | 12 |
| 3. Differs from parents in that spiritual quest more important | 3 |
| 4. Adherence to Catholicism not as important as being a Christian (includes converts to other Christian denominations) | 8 |
| 5. Considers oneself as Catholic, but practices not at all or very seldom | 6 |
| 6. Does not consider oneself as Catholic any longer | 8 |
| Total | 53* |

\* One respondent did not answer question

category and the number of replies in each. Slightly over half fell into the first two, self-described practicing Catholics. The first group saw themselves as closer to parents' practice than did the second, who emphasized (like the seniors) their own choices of doctrine and moral norms. Category 2 respondents not unexpectedly cited teachings on birth control, divorce, and premarital sex as issues dividing them from their parents. But the one-third comprising category 1 respondents are scarcely uncritical imitators of their parents. Here they differ from high school seniors in reflecting more deeply on their parents' faith in comparison with their own. While admiring their parents' faith and devotion, some are critical of what they regard as "automatic" practice of the faith; yet they often admit that their own practice falls short of mother's and dad's.

The remaining categories (47 percent altogether) embrace comparatively few respondents each. The three persons in category 3 view themselves as Catholic, but clearly felt that a personal quest for faith and sensitivity to the promptings of the Spirit transcended the requirements of "organized religion." Category 4 respondents see a "Catholic identity" as subordinate to a "Christian" identity and includes three persons who have converted to other denominations, in each case citing an experience of "finding Christ" in their present church. The last two comprise those either seldom or no longer practicing: category 5 respondents continue to retain a Catholic identity, whereas the eight persons in category 6 explicitly reject it, considering themselves no longer Catholic.

I turn now to that 30 percent of all volunteers who fall into category 1: basically the same as their parents in believing and practicing. I have chosen the following responses as typical of the sixteen persons in this category. Each exhibits a basic sense of continuity with their parents' religious perspective, but some leave room for departure from the "strict Catholicism" of their mothers and fathers. Missing from their accounts are elements of "crisis" or what Fowler terms the "break" from reliance upon conventional sources of authority and guidance. Some, however, seem to have arrived at what appears to be a personally appropriated faith stance. A fairly uneventful transition accompanied their shift from youthful taken-for-granted to adult reflective faith, at times involving some critical distance from the parental mode.

I close each statement with respondent's gender and ethnic identity and level of religious attendance. Revealing any more personal information would risk possible identification of the respondent.

I don't know that there's much of a difference between my parents' perspectives and mine on being a Catholic. I was raised more on the basis of what is right or wrong, not on strict Catholic teaching. (Hispanic male, attends a few times a year)

I really don't think my "being a Catholic" differs in meaning from my parents in any drastic ways. I do feel that I am more open to discussion of the issues the Church is facing. I think our "faiths" differed greatly back in the 1970s when the Church took on a "youthful" air with guitar groups and laymen. However, as the Church has changed, my parents and I have changed with it. We are, shall we say, liberated. (Anglo female, attends weekly)

"Being a Catholic" to me is not as much a way of life as it is for my parents. I view Catholicism as an important guide and aid through our existence. Some of the rituals, however, seem outdated and somewhat silly. I appreciate Catholicism, as do my parents, and plan to remain a Catholic. (Anglo female, attends almost weekly)

According to my parents, being Catholic means going to Mass every week, remembering that it is through the Lord that we have what we have today and we should be thankful to Him. I, too, realize that it is through the Lord that I have what I have today and am most thankful for it . . . but I also feel that if we become more aware of the beauty that is in all that surrounds us, if we become more attuned to the realization that there is good in all things . . . then we can have this interaction with God without the structure of the Mass. I still find myself having conflicting emotions about this. I realize . . . the celebration of the Mass is a very central part of the Catholic religion, but there is so much more to our faith than simply going to Mass because that's the way it's always been done, a ritual. . . . What we do for the other sixteen hours of our awake time, how we conduct ourselves, how we interact with others, how we view our surroundings, if we can see God throughout all our activities, if we can pause and say, look at those mountains, they're beautiful, thanks Lord . . . then I feel we are putting our Catholic religion into practice. I imagine that as I grow older, I will return to attending Mass regularly, just as my parents do; after all, it is because of them, and I am most thankful, that I am a part of the Catholic faith. (Hispanic male, attends Church a few times a year)

To my mother, being a Catholic means following any and all directives of practically any member of the Church. She draws a line sometimes, though. My father is slightly more liberal, and although he's pretty much hard line, he's very educated and thinks carefully about what he's told by members of the Church (I really mean priests, bishops, etc.). I take many of the things I'm told very skeptically, depending on who says them. Some priests I believe far less than others and only after serious consideration will I either assimilate or accommodate what I've been told. I think the only reasons I go to Mass anymore are that sometimes I get some sleep there and sometimes I can find a little time to ponder and consider some of the issues put before me at Mass. (Anglo male, attends weekly)

I don't feel the way I and the way my parents feel about "being a Catholic" differs in meaning. My parents are not of the old school which taught that you believe and do what the Church (priests, nuns, etc.) tells you just because. They listen, they read, they learn, they ask questions and then they form their beliefs. That's what they do and that's what they raised my sister and brother and me to do. (Hispanic female, attends weekly)

I would say I am not as strict a practicing Catholic as my parents are. People, including myself nowadays, tend to put religion on the back burner and only seem to get interested when we are faced with a crisis situation. We tend to just believe in religion and not practice it as much as our parents did and still do. We realize that God does exist, but there are too many religions in the world today, and sometimes we tend to doubt our faith, but I think that is the only way we can learn more about it. (Hispanic male, attends weekly)

Category 2 volunteers draw a sharper contrast between their own practice and beliefs about Catholicism when making comparisons with their parents. They come closest to Andrew Greeley's "communal Catholics," and developmentally, to "individuative-reflective faith." Many make it clear that they are still, as Sharon Parks would indicate, working through their personal stances. Explicit reflection on their beliefs has clearly led several to differentiate themselves from a parental belief system they may respect but that no longer serves them adequately. Important is selecting beliefs and moral stances that "make sense" to them and involve a quality of concrete concern for people that goes beyond institutional prescriptions. In fact, accepting beliefs because an institution prescribes them is contrary to this cherished autonomy of conscience and belief.

Both my parents adhere to the rituals of the Church far more than I do. I tend to look at Church teachings on a far more academic level. I believe that I question many of the teachings more, but my conclusions are often very similar in result. My attitude toward organized religion is probably somewhat more negative, and I tend to be somewhat more existential in my outlooks. (Hispanic male, attend a few times/year)

To me, "being a Catholic" has two meanings: a cultural and an ethical one. Catholicism has provided me with a sense of belonging and identity with a very rich culture. It not only gives me an identification with the past, but more importantly, provides me with an ethical code for living in the present. To me, Catholicism gives its members thoughtful, consistent moral teachings. To my parents, "being a Catholic" means something different. For instance, my father is a Catholic mainly because during Mass he feels Christ is truly present during Communion, and that no other Church can provide that. (Anglo female, attends monthly)

When I compare myself to my parents, the meanings of being a Catholic are definitely different . . . modern-day influences from friends, media, and literature have all changed the Catholic in me. Today's influences focus *not* on reiteration of prayers, songs, etc., but on the needs of individuals and how prayers, programs, etc., are being developed for the "specialty groups" of the community. One example is support groups for divorced Catholics (in my parents' thinking, divorced Catholics should be refused acceptance as part of the community). But God is a God of support, forgiveness, and love. God is all-forgiving and loves us even when we sin and are truly sorry for our downfall. (Anglo female, attends almost weekly)

My parents go strictly "by the book." They believe in every traditional aspect of the Church. They follow whatever the Pope says. I, however, believe in birth control, not attending Confession, and premarital sex. If the Church were to separate into two different Churches, Roman

Catholic and American Catholic, I would believe more in the American Church because the values fit my own beliefs. (Anglo female, attends weekly)

Being a Catholic provides me with a foundation of religion and spiritual beliefs. But being a Catholic is not the be-all and end-all. My parents, particularly my mother, are devout Catholics. It really is a *religion* for them. For me it's merely a foundation. I enjoy attending Mass merely because I enjoy community prayer. But if I don't feel up to Mass on a given Sunday I'll skip it. Thus, I do not follow religiously the teachings and practices of the Catholic faith. But yet, it has provided me a good foundation upon which to view the world. (Hispanic female, attends monthly)

In "being a Catholic," I am a conscientious observer of practices and rituals that aid me in my day-to-day life. I differ from my parents in that I am conscientious: I do not unquestioningly take the word of the Vatican as truth; I take the basic teachings of Jesus and adapt/apply them to my life. (Anglo female, attends a few times a year)

I practice my religion and I attend Mass not only because there is an obligation, but because I want to. But I believe my parents, especially my mother, are more devout than I am. Our views on several issues differ greatly, such as birth control or divorce or becoming pregnant and not being married. The latter is taken very personally as if done on purpose to hurt the parents. I find myself not taking such issues as seriously as my parents. (Anglo female, attends almost every week)

Three of the volunteers saw themselves as having embarked on spiritual quests that led them outside the conventional boundaries of Catholicism, though in one case, the respondent saw no incompatibility with frequent church attendance. Here spiritual insights have given rise to an "individual-reflective faith" that goes beyond conventional adherence and broadens or diffuses one's identity as Catholic.

Unlike my parents, I have been raised in a generation in which every issue can be openly discussed, questioned, analyzed, and criticized with the possible result of altering what is believed or held as a truth. In spite of my tendencies to be rigid and ritualistic, I seldom accept a teaching, or "truth" unless I can justify this with my own truths—reason and values. I, for instance, am willing to accept alternatives to the traditional performances of the sacraments, i.e., Mass, wedding, Confession, etc., and my parents are not. I am also open to new ideas on the nature of God, an afterlife and heaven, etc.

Actually I'm not so sure that some of these (heaven, hell) are of any significance to me at this point in my life. I think that these thoughts would be totally unacceptable to my parents. I think I am seeking a level of spirituality quite different from my parents. I have a need to understand my own beliefs about God and who or what God is. It must make sense to me; I must be able to justify it with my conception of the world and the reason for my existence. I believe my parents were content with a religious faith in which everything was determined for them and they simply believed and practiced as told. (Anglo female, attends almost every week)

I'm not sure I can any longer say "as a Catholic . . ." the formation of a given individual's conscience is inevitably influenced by an external authority, outside factors, etc., and is not a question of rights. The will of someone who really wants to strengthen himself—and strength in the truest sense is spiritual, I think—eventually comes of its own and directs one to turn away from the endlessly contradictory external influences to heed an inner, perhaps divine voice or influence (I really don't pretend to be so wise, but I really want this to be my creed). To me there is nothing mild about Catholicism. Its intent is not to make people "feel better" spiritually. Its depth and passion, its extreme yet simple demands (Christ's commands, love one another as I have loved you, and follow me) are those of great art as well. I think Catholicism as practiced today is too often made insipid—and that is not the fault of ritual per se, for I think ritual can be quite the opposite. I think that being raised with Catholicism has made me a catholic (with a lower case "c") thinker, and I want my mind always to be Catholic. (Anglo male, attends a few times a year)

"Being a Catholic" *was* (as it still is for my parents) attending Mass daily and on holy days, saying my prayers at night, receiving Communions (I've never believed in Confession). Now I still hold a lot of respect for my parents and their beliefs, and I am still thankful for my upbringing as a Catholic and will never regret this. But now I feel it's not organized religion that will teach me about me and my own spirit. It's me—my beliefs, my spirit, it's all in me. Looking back in high school shows me that I was closed-minded. Catholicism was the *only* religion, and I couldn't and/or didn't understand why or how others were not Catholic. . . . Now I'm beginning to feel that everyone has his or her own Spirit. Getting in touch with our Spirit (mine, at least) is a difficult task. But once we get in touch and keep in touch, I feel this is what brings happiness and peace, and this is what God is about—the finding of oneself. I feel this is that higher power. Being born and raised Catholic, this new way of thinking is different and at times difficult. I was taught and always have believed God to be someone who watches over us. I still have some faith in this, but maybe I'm feeling that in order to get and keep faith, one has to discover that higher power, the Spirit that's within us all individually. (Hispanic female, attends a few times a year)

The fourth category of eight volunteers see themselves as trying to be "good Christians" rather than "good Catholics." Explicit mention is made of conversion experiences that marked, in some cases, a relatively dramatic shift in religious identity. For others, personal experiences have led to an identity away from being conventionally Catholic; more important is being "Christian."

There are still many such stipulations in today's Church, but it seems as if the Church is not as overpowering or controlling as it once was. Personally being a Catholic is important to me, but being a Christian is more important. (Hispanic male, attends weekly)

I must admit that I am *not* a very good Catholic, but I would like to think that I am a very good Christian and that is what is most important to my husband and myself. I would have to say that being a Catholic is very different for me versus my parents. My parents think they have failed as parents because I'm not a great Catholic like they are. For this reason, I have some animosity toward the Catholic Church for making my parents feel this way. My Mom and Dad have been the most wonderful parents in the world, and it makes me angry that they have allowed the Church to make them feel guilty for my not turning out to be a wonderfully devout Catholic. I know I will raise my children to be exposed to the Catholic religion, but I will certainly not enforce it on them or tell them they will never get into heaven if they are not "good Catholics." (Hispanic female, attends a few times a year)

I feel I am not as strict with myself about my Catholic beliefs as my parents were with themselves and their children. I am proud to be a Catholic, but I am more proud of being a Christian, and I do not look down on other Christian faiths just because they are not Catholic. I am involved with my parish and very happy with it, but I don't punish myself if I don't make it to Church every single week or attend every holy day of obligation. I am involving my boyfriend and his two children in my parish and hope that one day we will get married and raise our family in the Catholic Church—and, if able to afford it, in Catholic schools. I believe my Catholic upbringing is a lot of the reason why I am the person I am today. I hope my children have that same opportunity because I love myself and I love my God very, very much. (Anglo female, attends almost every week)

My parents are "very Catholic" and would always side with the Church just because they feel they should. They are very narrow-minded and to them being a Christian is a lot different than being a Catholic; and even though they know nothing about services or beliefs taught at a nondenominational Christian church, they won't give it a chance, even to listen. My mom, for example, thought when I started going to Salvation Chapel that it was a "cult." When I explained that a Christian and a Catholic are similar in many ways and to come check out a service, she said, "Oh, no, I'm very happy with our Church," and acted like I was trying to convert her. Being Catholic versus Christian to me is just certain beliefs (saints, pope, etc.) are different, but we all believe in God as our creator and savior. (Anglo female, attends weekly)

I accepted Christ about five years ago and have begun to learn what God is really all about. I have tried to maintain myself as a Catholic, but there are a few areas of teachings of the Catholic Church that I cannot accept; this is where my parents and I differ. To my parents, Catholicism is the chosen religion and the one right way; I don't [believe this]. I believe that Jesus needs to be a part of your life and asks to be a part. I don't believe that any human being is infallible, including the pope, and I am unsure of his function in the Catholic Church. I believe that the Blessed Mother Mary was a great woman and would hope to be more like her, but I do not believe in praying to her. The Bible states that only Jesus can intercede for us. I want my children to be raised with Jesus as the center of our lives, but never just accepting everything without question. (Anglo female, attends weekly)

To me, it's like being an American—I don't always agree with what the hierarchy says or does or teaches, but it's part of my identity. I really believe that "the Church" *is* the people who make it up, and as in any organization the personality, values, goals, etc., are changed and influenced by the people who make it up. I think my parents really changed along with the Church, so their attitudes and mine aren't so different. One difference that I can think of is that it seems more important to them that the Catholic faith be "right" or "the best way." For me, that's not so crucial. I think most religions are meaningful and that the people who practice them are "doing the right thing" in trying to be closer to God. There are many parts of the Catholic religion that I think are stifling and hurtful (especially the "guilt-inducing" teachings), and so I don't think it's the "best" for everyone. I think my parents and I are basically similar in attitudes toward "being a Catholic" — it is the source of faith, of hope and community, but also a source of challenge to implement the "Christian" way of life in our lives as best we can. Sometimes that means not agreeing with what the hierarchy teaches. I would like to stay involved in the Church, but I want to make sure my kids (and husband) can have an experience like the one I had — I'm not sure how to do it, though. (Anglo female, attends monthly)

I can look back at the last ten years or so and see the slow, consistent process I feel God used to draw me into a personal relationship with Jesus Christ. It is my belief that without His death on the Cross, His resurrection from the dead, and my acceptance of and dependence on that saving work, I would spend eternity separated from God. I thought it was interesting, looking over my questionnaire I filled out in 1978, that I would write that "I would follow anything that God wanted me to do." As I look back reflectively, I would say that my senior year was the beginning of a process that God would use to cultivate in me a heart and desire to follow Him, that He included a decision to accept Him as my Lord and Savior in the spring of 1980. Since then, my life has been rewarding, satisfying, and fruitful, for as my knowledge of God and His plan for my life has grown, I have become more fully convinced of the "worthwhileness" of a life devoted to Christ. (Anglo male, attends weekly)

Before Campus Crusade in college, I was not very close to God and did not even consider myself a Christian. Well, I learned how to accept Jesus as my Lord and Savior. Countless Bible studies and a few conferences have brought me even closer to the Lord. The main concern, I believe, is being a Christian and growing closer to the Lord. On the other hand, my parents think more highly of the word "Catholic" than "Christian." They feel it's more important to be a Catholic. Needless to say, we don't see eye to eye. We discuss religion and agree on many "Christian" aspects of the Catholic religion. It's only on Catholic principles such as the pope is infallible or hosts being the true body of Christ where we disagree. (Anglo male, attends weekly)

The six category 5 respondents, while stating a Catholic identity at least nominally, attend Church a few times a year. Only one points to an event — not being able to marry in the Catholic Church — that apparently accounts for her alienation. The others seem to have "drifted away." In four of the six cases, at least one parent did not practice (or did so weakly) and/or was not Catholic.

In answering the above questions on your survey, it is obvious that I am Catholic "in name only." In this I closely resemble my father's viewpoint—I believe in God, but not the Catholic Church's viewpoints. I strongly oppose the teachings on divorce, birth control, remarriage, and the role of women in the Church. I find the Church's rituals occasionally enjoyable and/or comforting, but they have no real significance for me; my father feels the same. My mother, while she doesn't attend Church often, is deeply religious and what I would term a "strict Catholic" in many ways. On the issues in which she does disagree with the Church, like birth control and women's roles, she has some guilt feeling about it; while I respect her beliefs, I do not, for the most part, share them. I do not follow the various "rules" (attending Mass on days of obligation, not eating meat on Fridays during Lent), and I have, indeed, for the most part, forgotten a good deal of my religious obligations. My mother is disappointed with this, but she also respects my beliefs. My sisters and brothers also share my feelings. I would not, however, change my faith; while I definitely cannot be termed "Catholic," the rites and rituals of another faith would be alien to me. (Anglo female, attends a few times a year)

My mother is a devout Catholic attending services regularly, very involved in charity work, church programs, serving Communion, confession, abstaining from items on holy days, and all that goes along with being "all-out" Catholic. Myself, I very rarely attend or am involved with any of the above, but somehow I still consider myself Catholic in the sense that I was brought up as a Catholic, and even though I do not practice the religion, it is still part of me. What I learned through twelve years of Catholic school and obligations remains with me and my decisions and way of life today. (Anglo male, almost never)

My parents were not "strong Catholics," but I think that being Catholic means believing in and closely following the rules of the Church. Although I don't consider myself a practicing Catholic, I feel closer to it than any other religion because of my upbringing. I have never really felt the need to explore other religions. My daughter was baptized in the Catholic Church more for my husband and his family's sake than mine (his family is very strict Catholic). Even though I don't agree with all of the Catholic Church's rules like birth control, premarital sex, Confession, etc., I would consider myself more Catholic than any other religion. I realize most Catholics probably believe in following these guidelines in order to be Catholic. And I suppose I feel a bit hypocritical in saying I am Catholic. I feel that God/Jesus was not sent for the benefit of a "Catholic" or any other religion. My belief and relationship with God does not have to "go through" the Church. I do not believe that the Church rules were set up by God, but rather by its members and founders. (Anglo female, attends a few times per year)

I would say I am a changed Catholic—meaning I really respect the Catholic Church, but not being able to get married in the Church, I found myself drifting away from going to Mass. But I would like my little girl (2½) to be a Catholic until she can decide what is best for her. She has been baptized and taken to a few services. I would like for her to go to a Catholic school or CCD classes. My parents still go to Sunday services and light candles. They don't preach to me anymore, but I know what they would like and I try to keep them in mind when I go (alone). I just feel the Church let me down. But like I said, I still go to a few services, and my husband will go if I ask. When I was in school, I didn't think I was a "real" Catholic because I didn't belong to any of the "Catholic" clubs. I didn't go to all the morning services, and I didn't hold hands with anyone and sing all day long. But I know now that I didn't have to have a grade to know what I believe. I still have the same beliefs, just changed feelings about people. I would like to go to Church more often, but I feel respect for my husband also, so I need to find a religion we can both share. That scares me, but I know it will work out. I think I will always consider myself a Catholic. (Hispanic female, attends a few times a year)

The last group of eight volunteers no longer consider themselves Catholic. Several of the same types of dropouts noted by Dean Hoge in *Converts, Dropouts, Returnees* are visible in these accounts.[8] "Family tensions" appear in some; certainly life-style dropouts who find the Church's teaching objectionable in some (or most) respects are present, as are the "spiritual-need" persons for whom Catholicism provided little inspiration. But also distinguishable are some Hoge did not catalogue as such: persons convinced that Catholicism is (or was) incompatible with or irrelevant to world problems or "pragmatic issues," as one respondent phrased it. Finally, in five of the eight cases, a parental divorce and/or a nonpracticing parent is part of the narrative.

For my parents, being Catholic is a way of explaining their existence. It's rituals, it gives them "God." I believe it offers them guidelines—a way of life for them. Being Catholic has taught my parents the importance of family, love, and God. My parents in turn have shown us these things. I don't consider myself Catholic. I believe there are other "guidelines"—love over fear, and universal laws which offer me solutions in daily life. There are a lot of things about "being Catholic" that I don't agree with, so I choose to not live with them. My parents, though, even if they don't agree, would try to include them into their lives. (Anglo female, attends once a month)

I'll never forget the day I decided "being Catholic" just didn't make sense, especially to an intelligent, mature adult. It was in a theology class at St. Martin's. We were discussing what it was to be Catholic—what you *had* to believe. The priest said you had to believe the pope is infallible. I asked him exactly what that meant; he told me and I just couldn't buy it. The man (pope) is human just like you and me, and as far as I'm concerned, no better or worse. That's my feeling about anyone. I do *not* believe in organized religion. I believe the Bible is just a book to read and learn from like any other—*not* to be memorized and worshipped. I believe there is a Superior Being. I believe Jesus was a wise and great man, but the "Son of God"—I don't know. I believe we are all part of "God"; he is in each of us and we are all connected. I do not believe in heaven, hell, limbo or that babies have original sins weighing heavily on their souls. I feel "being Catholic" means believing all of this and much more that I absolutely cannot believe. I do not consider myself a Catholic and have not for twelve years. My husband was also born and raised Catholic (schools and all), and he believes and feels as I do about religion. My father was not Catholic and did not attend Church. My mother was (and still is) very Catholic. Being Catholic to her is believing in *everything* the Church tells her to believe and feel. It's an easy way out, "being Catholic," no questions, only answers. (Anglo female, does not attend)

My mom is what I refer to as a conventional Catholic. By this I mean she is a firm believer and regular practitioner of the conventional, institutional things that one is supposed to do as a Catholic. To my mind, all religion is good for is to provide some advice and counsel, some contribution to society as to what are good, true, honest, humane, socially productive ways to live and to organize life and society (things like the Bishops' letter on the economy). The other things like prayer, lighting candles, saying rosaries are symbolic things that I find hollow. But I want to stress that I also don't find them benign. In a sense, I find the emphasis on the importance of such religious conventions detrimental because it detracts from people's attention to the pragmatic issues in life (like poverty, funding an arms race, formulating a tax code that is generous to the most wealthy). In short, I have rejected the conventional (and symbolic—that which my mom seems devoted to) and now focus on pragmatic issues and social problems in this life, this world, something my mom doesn't seem as attuned to. As for my dad, my parents have been divorced for about ten years, and he and I haven't been on speaking terms for about 9½ years. My view is that he is neither a symbolic practitioner of things religious nor one who tries to put religious principles into practice. He lives by the rule of self-interest and self-glorification. The differences between this approach and mine should be obvious. (Hispanic-Anglo male, does not attend)

"Being Catholic" is enormously different for me than for my parents. Basically, I've become quite cynical about Catholicism and Christianity in general. I view Catholicism as a doctrine which promotes ethnocentricity among its believers—that is, they think *their* God is the "right" God. I feel that my parents believe this to a large extent. "Being Catholic" to them is something they don't really *think* about—they just follow, blindly believing what is set before them by the clergy. I, on the other hand, believe that "being Catholic" is exactly that—blindly following doctrine written by people across the world who seem to have no sense of their followers or of their hypocrisy in maintaining such a large *expensive* organization when people are starving on this planet. (Anglo female, does not attend)

First of all, I no longer consider myself Catholic. Over the years since high school, I have grown extremely weary of denominational labels. In high school all I knew were Catholics—hence my view of Christianity was very ethnocentric. However, after high school I've seen other denominations and faiths, and I have realized that being Catholic is not at all important. Rather, it is important to follow Christian ethics—whether one attends a Mass, a Protestant service, or merely discusses values with friends. As far as my parents are concerned, neither has ever instilled any sense of "Catholic loyalty" in me. They never seemed to think that "being Catholic" meant anything more or less than being a Christian. (Anglo male, does not attend)

Both of my parents' Catholic views and beliefs are very different. They both claim they're strict Catholics, but their morals and values are very different. My parents are divorced and their life-styles are very different. My mother is very involved in Church, including administering Communion in the hospitals. She goes to Church at least every Sunday and to retreats several times a year. My father attends Church once a week (he just recently started). He participates in the Beginning Experience group for Catholic (I think) families. My father objects to anyone who is different from him and his views. Many times what he says and what he does are two different things. Sometimes I think he is confused in life and tries to find the answers in his Catholic religion. My religious views could not be considered Catholic anymore, and this bothers both my parents. My beliefs are not in any major organized religion, but are my own. I strongly believe in God and the Word of the Bible. I'm not a reborn Christian, but I do believe that man through his indifference to God and His laws is in great trouble. I believe God should be first in a life, others second, and yourself third. However, I live my life for others first, myself second, and God third. I keep trying to change this and put God first again. (Anglo female, does not attend)

Being Catholic is a code of ethics and morality for my parents. They judge right or wrong by their conscience and by the Church. My father is a lay minister who is deeply hurt by the fact that my brother is living with his girlfriend (both are over 25 years old). They do not put down other Christian denominations but are Catholic to core and observe feast days, Lent, and "never skip a Sunday." Being Catholic is only an issue to me when I hear bigots putting down a faith they have no experience with. To me it is no better or worse than the other thirty-one flavors of Christianity. I do not identify with Catholicism. In fact, I see no need to have any children we may have baptized. However, I would probably do so because my parents wouldn't have a decent night's sleep if I didn't. While I don't identify with Catholicism, I am pleased I attended St. Martin's High School. The liberal theology department gave me roots in a traditional religion from which I am able to branch into my personal spiritual quest. I never doubted the existence of God. And God was always personal and real. Those roots are liberal Catholic. I do not practice Catholicism because it seems to stop short of where my heart wants to go. Sermons, rules and rituals seem to hit the same deferential, petty themes. God is so alive and present in the world and creation that I see a need for inner communion, not petition and supplication. (Anglo female, does not attend)

I really don't consider myself a Catholic due to the fact I don't practice that or any particular faith. Therefore, I don't feel I can answer this question. I will say my Mom used to tell us to go to Church, but she didn't attend herself. (Anglo female, does not attend)

### Summary

Recontacted eight and nine years after graduation, the volunteer respondents from the classes of 1978 and 1979 show a survey profile not unlike well-educated young Americans nationally, whether Catholic or mainline Protestant. Once again, except for abortion, they are expectedly "liberal" on issues of personal and social morality. A little over half attend church at least monthly; the others show up a few times a year or not at all.

Less than half attend a parish regularly; nine out of ten belong to no parish organizations.

If one looks beyond "institutional" religiosity, however, three-quarters pray at least weekly (half do so daily), 40 percent say religion is "of central importance and comes before all other aspects" of their lives, 62 percent have had a spiritual experience that "lifted them out of themselves;" almost nine out of ten agree they have a personal responsibility to share what they have with those who have less and to oppose unjust practices in society; and over half would support a city ordinance prohibiting discrimination against homosexuals. All in all, this is a group that seems spiritually alive, if not conventionally religious. They show concern for human rights and for bettering the human situation.

Those who have "fallen away" from practice are, to some extent, influenced by the familiar factors of parental religiosity (or lack of it), but in some cases are "turned off" by ritualism, hypocrisy, or too much focus on the supernatural at the expense of the everyday world and its pressing needs.

What *is* important to note, given the "selective Catholicism" of younger Catholics, is that even category 1 and 2 Catholics, who see themselves as quite firmly rooted in their religious faith, often explicitly base their stances upon a "personally selected" religious identity reflecting specific beliefs or practices embraced or discarded. Little seems inherited as a traditional possession "handed down" from one generation to another. Nor does any sense of guilt come through in these responses. A ready impression from these accounts is that whatever the content of the theology courses at St. Martin's, these classes did not implant a "sense of transgression" that left residues of guilt and remorse in those who have strayed from the tradition. Whether Catholic identity is affirmed with some changes, retained tentatively, or discarded, choices are apparently made freely and deliberately.

Little comes through of what Fowler calls "conventional" faith. Almost all volunteers seem to have undergone, by the time they reached their mid-twenties, some kind of confrontation with previously held beliefs, values, and moral stances. They were ready to state where they were in these respects. Their faith had become Fowler's "individuative-reflective" type. At the same time, few manifested what Parks refers to as "young adult Faith"; almost no one seems to have been engaged in "probing commitments;" perhaps most had already passed through that stage. Little "tentative relativity" comes across in any of these accounts.

The religious faith of these young adults, in historical perspective, is a far cry from pre–Vatican II devotional Catholicism. The centrality of ritual regularity, and the sense of sin, authority, and the miraculous, have yielded to the tentative, to exploring and testing, to the passing of judgment upon what seems irrelevant, senseless, or even harmful on the one hand, and to what is liberating, fulfilling, and comforting on the other. Many have obviously decided that the world of Catholic ritual, belief, and moral norms passes these tests solidly and can thus be given personal allegiance. But if they do not, they are set aside; in a few cases, new faiths are embraced as meaningful substitutes.

From the profile in chapter 4 of St. Martin's theology teachers and their students, one can see that style of presentation and teacher-student interaction in those classes prepared the way for the personal searching and sifting evident in the responses above. Religious adherence as the outcome of a quest in which personal experience is an important element, *along with* a sense that some teachings continue to be valid today, seem to have combined to motivate these graduates to find standpoints that are personally meaningful and fulfilling as adults. Tradition is not simply discarded in this search; these graduates consider it, weigh it, and modify it in ways their accounts reveal. Some traditional elements seem firmly dismissed by most (sexual morality); other are affirmed (abortion). Social commitments apparently remain strong—many of these accounts mirror back to us socially sensitive and responsible young women and men.

Absent from many accounts is any sense of owing loyalty to an institution as such. None per se deserves allegiance. One can look to institutions for guidance and favorably regard them only insofar as they support the "humanistic" values many of these young men and women embrace. The "individual-expressive" identity of which Hammond speaks is clearly evident; many of these young Catholic adults exemplify it. Even those aligning themselves with their parents' faith have managed to "step back" a bit from the Church as an institution, noting those features that they have chosen as meaningful to themselves, and observing that they feel freer to select those features than their parents did (or still do). Voluntary allegiance, with some thought given to reasons for so choosing, seems the order of the day. This shift, noted by other observers, and confirmed once more in the words of these young Catholics, is perhaps the most important change in the tradition that once defined Roman Catholicism in this country.

# Conclusion

I began this book with the idea of tradition. I noted the struggles and quandaries we adults experience in our concern to pass on to our children that "something solid" inherent in a long-standing tradition we have found meaningful for ourselves. Chapter 1 reflected on Catholic tradition in its pre–Vatican II form, pointing to its apparent solidity and seeming unchangeableness, and to the assurances that devotional Catholicism bestowed upon its largely immigrant population. They could find security in this anchor to the past within a strange environment often unpredictable and at times hostile.

As American Catholics quickly found their paths to middle-class status following World War II, devotional Catholicism became, in Herberg's phrase, one version of the American way of life. This way helped to provide a double identity as Catholics and as Americans. Catholics gained respect and felt at home in an American cultural bestowing "the good life" in an era of tranquility and affluence.

It had been tempting to think of this mid-twentieth-century Catholicism—and of American society itself—as virtually changeless, fixed firmly in its bearings. This was not the case, of course. The Catholic Church is an international system, and all systems are subject to continuous change unless they are wholly isolated and can remain "perfectly traditional." Even before Vatican II, as Catholicism stretched across "time-space paths," it could not, in the increasingly modernizing world of the twentieth century, avoid contact with social movements and worldwide developments that, in effect, raised questions about its traditional stances and policies. Through this century—one could go back further, of course—both individual and collective social actors within the Church were trying to build bridges from church to world: priest workers in factories, theologians in ecumenical dialogue, laity asking for meaningful worship in a revived liturgy. As modern communications linked people together and opened social systems to increasing critical scrutiny, it became difficult to maintain the "information control" that administrators resort to in any bureaucratic system to retain the

155

status quo, keep alive "sacred traditions," and for some, protect their privileged positions.

But structuration theory insists that change does not occur because "the system" can no longer remain in some kind of equilibrium and therefore "must take action" to adapt or lose its identity. A system does not act; people within it do. Functionalist perspectives overlook the central role of system actors, knowledgeable about the organization and what is going on in its environment to affect it. Knowledgeable actors—Pope John XXIII, for example—aware of the pressures on the Church brought about by other social actors, made a decision to hold an ecumenical council, the first in a century. The changes I have reviewed are, in Giddens's terms, "conjunctural," i.e., occurring in a situation with other factors that operate to affect the outcomes of the original decision or activity. A Pope knowledgeable about the Church and its historical situation, and "reflectively monitoring" its environment, had the explicit intention of bringing the Church up to date; he intended nothing by way of far-reaching change. But human history always escapes the intentions of the people who make it. Every instance of social change, then, has to be studied in its historical and situational contexts to tease out the linkages of human choice and policy decisions with other social actors (both individual and collective), to discern the consequences those interactions actually have. The consequences may not be immediately evident.

We saw in the United States the impact of one such decision—Pope Paul VI's encyclical letter *Humanae Vitae*. The Pope's intention was to restore a solemn teaching by proclamation of Church doctrine. The ensuing unintended consequence took shape through clergy, who in counseling or interpreting the teaching, stated or inferred that this "solemn norm" could be subject to modification through one's "personal conscience." Few foresaw the major breach in the traditional lines of authority. No longer could Church officials "make their accounts 'count,' " nor could they any longer "draw upon modes of domination structured into" a particular social system.[1] Eventually, Catholic lay persons, especially the younger cohorts following the Council, put forth their own "interpretive schemes" reflecting the individualism and experienced-based judgments becoming deeply embedded in American youth culture at the time. The result was that much of the traditional Catholic normative structure was no longer "sustained and reproduced" in everyday encounters between laity and clergy. The claims of authority figures no longer seemed as persuasive, or even as valid.

In other words, actions and decisions of one set of actors triggered reactions and changed viewpoints in others. Changed in the years following the Council was the sense of reverence and deference to authority that undergirded devotional Catholicism. That system no longer seemed as real for many Catholics when so many changes seemed to call its "four pillars" into question. Church authorities as actors could no longer mobilize obligations successfully through the medium of other actors' responses.[2]

As the breakdown in the security system of devotional Catholicism was occurring in the lives of many Catholics, the time-space situation of American Catholics was shifting, as well. Ascendancy to middle- and upper-middle-class status by millions of Catholic families carried with it worldviews containing independence of thought and of self-direction—characteristics of well-educated women and men. The two contexts—breakdown of authority relations and the dynamic of upward mobility—worked hand in hand to alter the "rules and resources" that had formerly governed relationships between church authority figures (in this volume, both clergy and teachers of religion), and lay Catholics. Reproduction of the older system proved practically impossible and would have met with resistance from many Catholics anyway, especially younger ones. Older practices could no longer be reproduced.

But to stop here would do little justice to the full range of reactions following the Council. The seniors, graduates, and theology teachers of St. Martin's are a case in point. They are obviously knowledgeable social actors within the system they inhabit, creative in adapting and working out new modes of behavior. As communicators, the theology teachers at St. Martin's came up with new elements to sustain their roles as teachers of norms and values, fresh approaches to their students to make the content of their courses more plausible in classroom encounters. They drew upon resources in the older tradition (theological models) and sharpened their sensitivities to the larger culture and the strong influence it exercised over their students. "We're selling more than telling." Just as importantly, St. Martin's teachers seemed to realize, unlike the teachers Schwartz portrays in his study, that "one cannot encourage young people to develop habits of mind that go along with being good students at an elite institution without also promoting autonomy."[3] The ensuring "moral Protestantism," as Schwartz describes it, indeed carries with it an emphasis on primacy of personal conscience. In fact, many of the seniors comprising the classes of 1983 through 1989 may well have been schooled in independence of thought in their homes prior to entering St. Martin's.

The seniors contributed their dialectical response, as well. Finding the exercise of authority in their theology classes "reasonable," they responded more favorably than they would have otherwise to doctrines and norms capable of generating considerable resistance. By the same token, seniors were not prepared to acquiesce in traditional teaching on sexual morality. Their own experiences and insights, as they interpreted and discussed them in peer contexts, effectively rule out for most any favorable consideration of the Church's traditional teachings. The theology teachers, then, constitute an excellent example of social actors' creative responses in a context providing few guidelines as tradition shifted in the views and behavior of their students. Yet there remains the possibility that this very adaptation on the teachers' part may have reinforced as an unintended consequence the very selective Catholicism the teachers hoped to counter.

Personal identity as Catholics forms a central theme in the chapters comprising Part II. The changes just discussed above meant a severe undercutting of a "collective-expressive" identity formerly bestowed merely by being born and raised a Catholic. In their identity stories, the seniors of 1987, 1988, and 1989 and the volunteers often acknowledged such an identity in their parents' Catholicism but denied it of their own. "Individual-expressive" better fits the younger Catholics' versions of "being Catholic" today. The theological individualism or selective Catholicism we have witnessed among these young Catholics effectively severed a sense of "collective-expressive" identity and deprived them of an enveloping sense of "ontological security" characteristic of an older traditional Catholicism— save, of course, for that one-third of both seniors and volunteers who said their Catholicism was basically the same as their parents'.

For the remaining two-thirds, "being Catholic" was simply a matter of choice, sometimes coming across as choosing specific teachings while rejecting others. This mode of choosing lies at the heart of the contemporary form, for younger Catholics, of Catholic self-identification. The outcomes of choice comprised, as we have seen, a spectrum ranging from selection of teachings and norms to outright rejection of the religious heritage itself. For a few, the security of an alternative belief system is appealing; for others, being Catholic is a form of moral stance, of "acting right," a conviction that this is more important than a set of practices. The volunteers of chapter 5 match other young Americans in proportions of the alienated, the indifferent, and those rejecting Catholic identity altogether.

I believe it is this attenuated sense of identity operative in the two-thirds not identifying with their parents' Catholicism that is reflected in Gallup and Castelli's diverse findings grouped under Catholics' "lesser intensity" of religious feelings and viewpoints when compared to Protestants (see chapter 3). For many Catholics, as the preceding pages demonstrate, being Catholic is not that compelling or formative of ideals or viewpoints. The Catholic sensibility portrayed in the literary passages of chapter 1 seems to have undergone, as Catholics assimilate into a likeness of other Americans of similar social standing, a kind of "fadeout."

But how negative for American Catholicism is an attenuated sense of identity as Catholics? The findings in this volume give pause to any notion that these "elite" young Catholic men and women have abandoned beliefs and values central to Catholic tradition. For among these central themes are ones shared with the broader Judaeo-Christian heritage. As Bellah and colleagues put the matter, "the litmus test that both the biblical and republican traditions give us for assaying the health of a society is how it deals with the problem of wealth and poverty."[4] In supporting their Church as teacher on issues of racism, world hunger, nuclear disarmament, and economic decision-making, and in indicating their own sense of responsibility for involvement with these issues, St. Martin's seniors generally show support for core elements of their religious tradition. They falter somewhat, especially in the later 1980s as classes come to be composed increasingly of sons and daughters of professional families; particularly attenuated is a sense of being responsible for the correction of injustices in society. Fully assimilated young Americans, they fall under the spell of culturally dominant assumptions. As Bellah trenchantly observes,

> What American does not believe somewhere in his or her heart that anyone with self-discipline and hard work can make it and that poverty is essentially the fault of the poor? Such assumptions have not only shaped our welfare system for over two hundred years, they have also shaped our ideas of what a good and successful person is. It is these assumptions that the bishops' letter calls into question. No wonder there is resistance.[5]

True, these young women and men are by no means fully formed adults; their views may well shift as the years go by. Catholic educators may find encouragement in the portrait of the volunteers, who as adults maintain a readiness to say they are responsible for others in need and for opposing injustices as a moral obligation. Perhaps they will yet "buy into" the individualism and success ideology of which Bellah and colleagues speak; perhaps it is too early to tell whether they are yet willing to "give up our dream of private success for a more genuinely integrated societal community."[6] But at least St. Martin's seems to have given them an initial sense of community and of membership in a long tradition of moral discourse that includes responsibility for one's neighbor as well as for oneself. One could argue that these outcomes are among the most significant registered in these pages.

But if this sense of community is to be translated into a responsiveness as young adults to the recent social initiatives of American Catholic leadership, more is required than positive sentiments toward racial justice, alleviation of hunger, etc. As their classroom experiences demonstrate (chapter 4), young Catholics must encounter teaching authority that is both "rational" and "reasonable." Little doubt emerges on the score of reasonableness. These young men and women find congenial the respectful approach of their teachers that acknowledges their own thinking and experiences. But it is clear that the overall rationality of the Church's teaching, as it touches the area of sexuality, is questionable to many, very much including young women. The old double standard is in retreat. An arresting finding of this study is that many young women have "caught up" with men in their views of sexual morality and find the Church's teaching irrelevant. As long as this is so, a minority of students will resist Church leaders' attempts to guide, counsel, and form consciences in *any* area, personal or sociomoral. Lack of credibility in the area of sexual teaching, then, makes more difficult the task of persuasive teaching on sociomoral issues. What the data of this study show as well is that this resistance is particularly evident in recent years among St. Martin's seniors. The school's shifts in admission policy may have introduced students from "less devout" Catholic families, as I suggested earlier, manifested in the decline of church attendance and in other religiosity indicators. But seniors in the late 1980s may also represent age cohorts who are themselves less devout and more privatized in terms of personal belief and moral stances, holding on even more unshakably than their predecessors to theological and moral individualism. Should further research confirm that this is indeed the case, Catholic high school teachers and administrators are likely to encounter increasing resistance to orthodox Catholic doctrine and insistence upon the primacy of "personal conscience."

None of the above is intended to downplay the potential effectiveness of the Catholic high school in socializing young Catholics positively toward their Church's teachings. But key issues go beyond the school itself. The structural changes embodied in American Catholics' socioeconomic ascendancy have meant a significant shift in relationship to Church authority. Astute commentators like psychologist Eugene Kennedy speak of a "new Church" that, rather than claiming authority, "receives it as a gift from the listeners who recognize that they make sense." Bearers of authority receive a respectful hearing to the extent they are perceived to be tuned in to human experience, "motivated by a desire to understand rather than an urge to control."[7] St. Martin's theology teachers aptly fit this description, for in listening to their students and attempting to understand their values, attitudes, and moral quandaries, they became, in effect, cultural co-constructors with their students of a moral universe that, without offering solutions for every situation, at least provided moral categories and guidelines that their students could ponder. The preceding pages suggest which teachings survived this pondering intact, which remained problematic, and which were rejected.

To the extent that St. Martin's is representative of the more flourishing Catholic high schools in the 1980s, it seems evident that the characterization of Catholic schools made over a decade ago by a leading scholar of parochial education needs revising. James Sanders, viewing the Chicago parochial school system in the mid-1970s, ended his study by concluding that "the Catholic school as powerful cultural agent had ceased to exist."[8] The milieu of which Sanders wrote had indeed ceased to exist in which Catholic schools shaped the children and grandchildren of immigrants into a Catholicism recognizable as that of their forebears. But a new cultural agency seems at work in today's Catholic schools: an environment of doctrinal and moral individualism. As this study has emphasized, this development has stimulated a new approach to value formation that is inevitably dialectical and negotiatory. The portrait of the volunteers from the classes of 1978 and 1979 suggests that this mode of socialization has been, on the whole, reasonably successful.

But the preceding chapters give pause when one considers the dilemma facing the American Catholic Church: as its school system becomes increasingly expensive—particularly Catholic high schools—with little support for tuition scholarships, schools remaining economically viable draw students from precisely those socioeconomic strata that show resistance to an ethic of social justice as promoted by American Church leadership. In attempting to make teachings relevant and specific to a complex society, Church leaders risk the by now familiar charge that they have no business suggesting principles and solutions for the problems they bring up. The reactions of St. Martin's seniors show that the more controversial an issue, the less inclined they are to acknowledge that the Church has any business teaching about it. As the controls for religiosity indicate, young men and women who are "good Catholics" by these measures are more likely to affirm the Church's role in economic decision-making—but even here, between a quarter and a third of 1987–89 seniors for whom religion is very important and who are very sure of their convictions disagree that the Church has a legitimate role in these matters.

The young women of the study are worth explicit reiteration in a Catholic Church under pressure to recognize their potential contributions to spiritual renewal and to leadership. Social justice themes currently advocated by Catholic leadership are a case in point: the senior girls of the late 1980s were twice as likely as their male classmates to agree strongly they had responsibilities to share with the less fortunate and to combat social injustice. They assigned more importance to religion in their lives; although they drew nearer to the boys' norms on premarital sex, they were markedly more inclined to doubt that more sexual freedom would be a good thing. The volunteer women in their late twenties, though institutionally no more involved than the men, were much more likely to pray frequently, to be sure of their religious beliefs, and to report rather frequent spiritual experiences. These findings certainly indicate no deep alienation, but rather an openness the Church might well call upon.

Finally, Hoge's "assimilation model" receives indirect support from this study. The seniors and especially the volunteers do seem to exhibit "a convergence to Protestant attitudes about sexuality and individualism."[9] As "educated young adults," the volunteers as a group feel little loyalty to the institutional Church, with fewer than half active in a Catholic parish or attending Church with any regularity. As westerners living in "middle-class urban areas far from ports of entry," they fulfill Hoge's portrait of those most likely to resemble other young Americans of non-Catholic religious identity.[10] Ethnic identity as Hispanics per se is not strong enough, as we have seen, to override these factors and set them apart as a distinct and "more devout" subgroup. In most respects they are indistinguishable from their Anglo classmates. Again, a dilemma arises: as young Hispanics move away from familiarity with their language, a key cultural support of alignment with Church teaching disappears. Yet the history of non–English-speaking Catholic ethnic groups in this country demonstrates that loss of language is almost inevitable by the third or fourth generation. Today's Catholic high schools are no less "assimilative" in effect than those of yesterday. Indeed, the present study supports Hoge's contention that "probably the situation in the Catholic future will resemble that in Protestantism today—the more affluent and educated the group, the less success in transmitting church commitment to the young."[11]

But "church commitment" in itself is not the primary goal of Catholic religious formation. Catholic educators can scarcely ignore such commitment, but declining institutional practice may lie more with "a youth culture demanding more freedom in life-style" than in a fault of institutional leadership.[12] Hoge appears correct here. But that very leadership can also look to a reservoir of social idealism not far below the surface in these educated and assimilated young Catholics. If American Catholic leadership wishes to tap this potential source of commitment, it would do well to look to Catholic educational institutions and particularly to those teachers and administrators who know how to combine a sensitive and caring classroom approach to students with closed retreats and "renewal weekends" that harness this social idealism to spiritually and intellectually resonant experiences expressed in meaningful symbolic and liturgical forms. This twofold strategy might well prove "counter-assimilative," yielding a generation of Catholic laity open and responsive to seeing, in the words of *Economic Justice for All,* "economic questions . . . as part of a larger vision of the human person and the human family, the value of this created earth, and the duties and responsibilities that all have toward each other and toward this universe."[13]

# Appendix 1

## Variables, Coding, and Frequencies

### Case Study: St. Martin's High School

| Variable (1977 to 1989) | Coding | N | Distribution Percent |
|---|---|---|---|
| *Dependent* | | | |
| Church attendance [RELATTND] | 1 = weekly | 1209 | 68 |
| | 2 = 2 or 3 times/month | 315 | 18 |
| | 3 = few times a year/less | 250 | 14 |
| Membership in Religious | 1 = do not belong | 1429 | 81 |
| group [RELIGGRP] | 2 = belong | 334 | 19 |
| Importance of religion | 1 = very important | 746 | 42 |
| [RELIGIMP] | 2 = fairly important | 845 | 48 |
| | 3 = unimportant | 188 | 11 |
| Convinced of teachings of | 1 = very | 499 | 28 |
| Catholic Church [RELGCONV] | 2 = fairly | 942 | 53 |
| | 3 = don't know | 32 | 2 |
| | 4 = not convinced | 306 | 17 |
| Future involvement in | 1 = take active part | 427 | 24 |
| parich [PARISH] | 2 = attend, not active | 714 | 40 |
| | 3 = don't know | 436 | 25 |
| | 4 = nothing to do with | 202 | 12 |
| Responsibility to share with those | 1 = strongly agree | 632 | 36 |
| who have less [RESPSHR] | 2 = agree | 885 | 50 |
| | 3 = don't know | 87 | 5 |
| | 4 = disagree | 178 | 10 |
| Responsibility to oppose unjust | 1 = strongly agree | 564 | 32 |
| practices in society [RESPUNJS] | 2 = agree | 737 | 42 |
| | 3 = don't know | 113 | 6 |
| | 4 = disagree | 366 | 21 |
| Premarital sexual relations are | 1 = strongly agree/agree | 621 | 35 |
| immoral [PREMSEX] | 2 = don't know | 242 | 14 |
| | 3 = disagree | 524 | 30 |
| | 4 = strongly disagree | 392 | 22 |

**163**

| Variable (1977 to 1989) | Coding | N | Distribution Percent |
|---|---|---|---|
| More sexual freedom is a good thing [SEXFREED] | 1 = strongly agree/agree | 619 | 35 |
| | 2 = don't know | 394 | 22 |
| | 3 = disagree | 550 | 31 |
| | 4 = strongly disagree | 215 | 12 |
| Abortion is acceptable if baby likely to have serious birth defects [ABORDEF] | 1 = strongly agree | 200 | 11 |
| | 2 = agree | 296 | 17 |
| | 2 = don't know | 169 | 10 |
| | 4 = disagree | 494 | 28 |
| | 5 = strongly disagree | 600 | 34 |
| Parents' political views [PARNTPOL] | 1 = conservative | 603 | 35 |
| | 2 = in middle | 599 | 34 |
| | 3 = liberal | 426 | 24 |
| | 4 = don't know | 116 | 7 |
| Sex [SEX] | 0 = male | 830 | 46.5 |
| | 1 = female | 955 | 53.5 |
| Grade point average [GPA] | 1 = 3.5 to 4.0 | 472 | 27 |
| | 2 = 3.0 to 3.4 | 696 | 39 |
| | 3 = 2.5 to 2.9 | 503 | 28 |
| | 4 = below 2.5 | 109 | 6 |
| Ethnic background [ETHNCTY] | 1 = Anglo | 1063 | 60 |
| | 2 = mixed Anglo/Hispanic | 491 | 12 |
| | 3 = Hispanic | 217 | 28 |
| Importance of ethnic background to respondent [IMPETH] | 1 = very important | 473 | 27 |
| | 2 = somewhat important | 630 | 36 |
| | 3 = not important | 670 | 38 |
| Language spoken at home other than English [HOMELNG] | 1 = English only | 1083 | 64 |
| | 2 = Spanish | 603 | 36 |
| Father's occupation [FATHOCCP] | 1 = blue collar | 118 | 7 |
| | 2 = white collar | 330 | 20 |
| | 3 = owner/manager | 333 | 20 |
| | 4 = lower professional | 448 | 27 |
| | 5 = upper professional | 446 | 27 |
| Father in military eight years or more [FATHMIL] | 1 = yes | 417 | 24 |
| | 2 = no | 1348 | 76 |
| Mother's occupation [MOTHOCCP] | 1 = housewife | 568 | 33 |
| | 2 = white collar | 537 | 31 |
| | 3 = owner/manager | 158 | 9 |
| | 4 = professional | 481 | 28 |
| Religious education prior to high school [RELCLASS] | 1 = in Catholic school | 845 | 48 |
| | 2 = in CCD classes | 614 | 35 |
| | 3 = no religious classes | 290 | 17 |

| Variable (1977 to 1989) | Coding | N | Distribution Percent |
|---|---|---|---|
| (1983 to 1987 only) | | | |
| Father's education | 1 = some high | | |
| [FATHEDUC] | school only | 46 | 6 |
| | 2 = high school graduate | 107 | 13 |
| | 3 = some college | 122 | 15 |
| | 4 = college degree | 173 | 22 |
| | 5 = graduate degree | 350 | 44 |
| | 1 = some high | | |
| Mother's education | school only | 21 | 3 |
| [MOTHEDUC] | 2 = high school graduate | 245 | 31 |
| | 3 = some college | 228 | 28 |
| | 4 = college degree | 142 | 18 |
| | 5 = graduate degree | 166 | 21 |
| Church's business to be | 1 = high (positive) | 183 | 23 |
| involved with social issues | 2 = moderate | 333 | 42 |
| (see Appendix 2) | 3 = low (negative) | | |
| [CHRCHTCH] | | 288 | 36 |
| Personal responsibility to be | 1 = high (positive) | 176 | 22 |
| involved with social issues | 2 = moderate | 360 | 45 |
| (see Appendix 2) [MEINVOLV] | 3 = low (negative) | 368 | 33 |
| Viewpoint on conscience | 1 = form according to | | |
| formation [CONSCNCE] | Church's teaching | 88 | 11 |
| | 2 = listen to Church's | | |
| | teaching but make | | |
| | up own mind | 632 | 78 |
| | 3 = no authority has | | |
| | right to influence | | |
| | formation of | | |
| | anyone's | | |
| | conscience | 89 | 11 |
| (1987 to 1989 only) | | | |
| Church's business to help | 1 = strongly agree | 52 | 10 |
| Catholics form consciences | 2 = agree | 233 | 45 |
| on moral dimensions of | 3 = don't know | 52 | 10 |
| economic decision-making | 4 = disagree/str. | | |
| [ECONBISH] | disagree | 175 | 34 |
| My responsibility to be | | | |
| involved with solutions to | 1 = strongly agree | 124 | 24 |
| unemployment, poverty, | 2 = agree | 253 | 49 |
| immigration, national | 3 = don't know | 67 | 13 |
| spending priorities | 4 = disagree/str. | | |
| etc. [ECONPERS] | disagree | 78 | 15 |

# Appendix 2

## Independent Variable Impact on Two Social Sensitivity Measures by Two Time Periods (N = 1750)

"It is my responsibility to share what I have with those who have less"

"If some practice in society is unjustly harmful to people and I do nothing to oppose that practice, then I share responsibility for the harm done"

## Appendix 2
### Independent Variable Impact on Two Social Sensitivity Measures by Two Time Periods (N = 1750)

| Independent Variables | Percentages | | | | | | Percentages | | | | | |
|---|---|---|---|---|---|---|---|---|---|---|---|---|
| | 1977 to 1982 | | | 1983 to 1989 | | | 1977 to 1982 | | | 1983 to 1989 | | |
| | St. Ag.[1] | Ag.[2] | Dis[3] | St. Ag. | Ag. | Dis. | St. Ag. | Ag. | Dis. | St. Ag. | Ag. | Dis. |
| *Gender* | | | | | | | | | | | | |
| Male | 39* | 50 | 11 | 23* | 60 | 17 | 42 | 41 | 17 | 14* | 48 | 38 |
| Female | 47 | 46 | 6 | 34 | 56 | 10 | 46 | 41 | 14 | 27 | 49 | 23 |
| *Ethnic Background* | | | | | | | | | | | | |
| Hispanic | 45 | 48 | 6 | 32 | 60 | 8 | 42 | 42 | 15 | 21 | 49 | 30 |
| Mixed Hispanic | 46 | 44 | 10 | 34 | 49 | 17 | 49 | 37 | 14 | 22 | 49 | 30 |
| Anglo | 43 | 49 | 9 | 27 | 58 | 15 | 43 | 41 | 16 | 21 | 49 | 30 |
| *Importance of Ethnic Background* | | | | | | | | | | | | |
| Very important | 52* | 42 | 6 | 40* | 51 | 10 | 42 | 42 | 15 | 25 | 46 | 28 |
| Somewhat important | 37 | 54 | 10 | 28 | 60 | 11 | 39 | 45 | 16 | 19 | 53 | 27 |
| Not very important | 44 | 47 | 9 | 23 | 60 | 17 | 49 | 36 | 15 | 20 | 46 | 35 |
| *Language at home* | | | | | | | | | | | | |
| English | 42 | 49 | 10 | 27 | 57 | 15 | 44 | 41 | 15 | 21 | 48 | 31 |
| Spanish | 47 | 47 | 6 | 32 | 60 | 9 | 46 | 40 | 15 | 21 | 50 | 29 |
| *Grade point average* | | | | | | | | | | | | |
| 3.5 or better | 52* | 43 | 5 | 35 | 55 | 10 | 54* | 39 | 7 | 25* | 54 | 22 |
| 3.0 to 3.4 | 40 | 50 | 10 | 32 | 55 | 13 | 42 | 40 | 18 | 21 | 51 | 28 |
| 2.5 to 2.9 | 40 | 52 | 8 | 24 | 62 | 15 | 36 | 47 | 17 | 21 | 41 | 38 |
| below 2.5 | 42 | 42 | 16 | 20 | 60 | 20 | 42 | 26 | 32 | 15 | 46 | 39 |
| *Father's occupation* | | | | | | | | | | | | |
| Blue-collar/white collar | 42 | 49 | 9 | 25 | 59 | 16 | 40 | 44 | 16 | 20 | 42 | 38 |
| Business owner/Manager | 43 | 47 | 11 | 32 | 57 | 11 | 41 | 46 | 13 | 21 | 48 | 30 |

*(Continued)*

**Appendix 2**
*(Continued)*

| Independent Variables | Percentages | | | | | | Percentages | | | | | |
|---|---|---|---|---|---|---|---|---|---|---|---|---|
| | 1977 to 1982 | | | 1983 to 1989 | | | 1977 to 1982 | | | 1983 to 1989 | | |
| | St. Ag.[1] | Ag.[2] | Dis.[3] | St. Ag. | Ag. | Dis. | St. Ag. | Ag. | Dis. | St. Ag. | Ag. | Dis. |
| Professional | 46 | 47 | 8 | 29 | 59 | 13 | 46 | 39 | 16 | 22 | 51 | 27 |
| *Mother's occupation* | | | | | | | | | | | | |
| Housewife | 43 | 50 | 8 | 32 | 54 | 14 | 49 | 38 | 13 | 21 | 48 | 32 |
| Clerical | 43 | 49 | 8 | 28 | 62 | 11 | 43 | 49 | 8 | 28 | 62 | 11 |
| Owner/Manager | 41 | 48 | 11 | 30 | 58 | 13 | 39 | 42 | 19 | 23 | 46 | 31 |
| Professional | 46 | 46 | 9 | 28 | 56 | 15 | 43 | 44 | 13 | 20 | 52 | 28 |
| *Church attendance* | | | | | | | | | | | | |
| Weekly | 48* | 45 | 7 | 33* | 58 | 9 | 46 | 40 | 14 | 23* | 52 | 25 |
| 2 to 3 times/month | 34 | 56 | 10 | 25 | 57 | 18 | 39 | 43 | 18 | 18 | 43 | 38 |
| Few times/year | 29 | 57 | 14 | 21 | 57 | 23 | 37 | 40 | 22 | 18 | 42 | 40 |
| *Religious education* | | | | | | | | | | | | |
| Catholic elementary | 41 | 51 | 8 | 34* | 55 | 11 | 44 | 42 | 15 | 21 | 50 | 29 |
| Catechism (CCD) | 49 | 44 | 7 | 29 | 58 | 13 | 48 | 39 | 13 | 21 | 48 | 32 |
| No catechism | 43 | 45 | 12 | 19 | 62 | 19 | 38 | 41 | 21 | 17 | 49 | 33 |
| *Religious group membership* | | | | | | | | | | | | |
| Belongs | 41* | 50 | 10 | 26* | 58 | 15 | 42* | 42 | 16 | 19* | 49 | 32 |
| Does not belong | 57 | 40 | 4 | 39 | 55 | 6 | 55 | 34 | 11 | 28 | 49 | 22 |
| *Importance of religion* | | | | | | | | | | | | |
| Very important | 56* | 37 | 7 | 42* | 52 | 5 | 51* | 37 | 13 | 28* | 47 | 24 |
| Somewhat important | 34 | 58 | 8 | 23 | 63 | 14 | 38 | 45 | 17 | 18 | 52 | 30 |
| Unimportant | 28 | 50 | 22 | 13 | 56 | 31 | 37 | 37 | 27 | 12 | 42 | 46 |

*(Continued)*

**Appendix 2**
*(Continued)*

| Independent Variables | Percentages | | | | | | Percentages | | | | | |
|---|---|---|---|---|---|---|---|---|---|---|---|---|
| | 1977 to 1982 | | | 1983 to 1989 | | | 1977 to 1982 | | | 1983 to 1989 | | |
| | St. Ag.[1] | Ag.[2] | Dis[3] | St. Ag. | Ag. | Dis. | St. Ag. | Ag. | Dis. | St. Ag. | Ag. | Dis. |
| *Sure of religious beliefs* | | | | | | | | | | | | |
| Very sure | 54* | 39 | 7 | 45* | 51 | 4 | 52* | 36 | 12 | 28* | 52 | 20 |
| Fairly sure | 40 | 52 | 8 | 25 | 65 | 11 | 42 | 43 | 15 | 18 | 52 | 30 |
| Not too sure | 35 | 53 | 13 | 19 | 52 | 29 | 33 | 41 | 26 | 18 | 39 | 43 |
| *Credibility of church teaching through theology classes* | | | | | | | | | | | | |
| More credible | 46 | 47 | 7 | 32* | 58 | 10 | 46 | 42 | 12 | 22* | 52 | 26 |
| Less credible | 46 | 38 | 16 | 24 | 56 | 21 | 43 | 32 | 24 | 17 | 46 | 37 |
| *Rate theology program* | | | | | | | | | | | | |
| Excellent | 48 | 46 | 7 | 35* | 55 | 10 | 48 | 38 | 14 | 25* | 50 | 25 |
| Good | 43 | 49 | 8 | 26 | 62 | 13 | 43 | 42 | 15 | 19 | 49 | 32 |
| Fair or poor | 41 | 49 | 10 | 27 | 53 | 20 | 41 | 42 | 17 | 21 | 44 | 35 |

* $p \leq = .05$.

[1] Strongly agree.

[2] Agree.

[3] Disagree & strongly disagree (combined due to small $N$ of strongly disagree).

# Appendix 3

## Crosstabluation Tables for Bivariate Analysis

### Table 1

#### Index of Personal Involvement by Church Attendance

| | My Business to be Involved | | | | | | | |
| | Hi | | Mod | | Low | | Total | |
| Church Attend | No. | % | No. | % | No. | % | No. | % |
|---|---|---|---|---|---|---|---|---|
| Weekly | 116 | 23.5 | 236 | 47.9 | 141 | 28.6 | 493 | 100.0 |
| 2–3 Mo | 32 | 19.9 | 71 | 44.1 | 58 | 36.0 | 161 | 100.0 |
| Few–Year | 26 | 18.1 | 51 | 35.4 | 67 | 46.5 | 144 | 100.0 |

p = 0.0526

### Table 2

#### Index of Personal Involvement by Importance of Religion

| | My Business to be Involved | | | | | | | |
| | Hi | | Mod | | Low | | Total | |
| Import of Religion | No. | % | No. | % | No. | % | No. | % |
|---|---|---|---|---|---|---|---|---|
| Very | 82 | 27.1 | 151 | 49.8 | 70 | 23.1 | 303 | 100.0 |
| Fairly | 72 | 19.6 | 158 | 43.1 | 137 | 37.3 | 367 | 100.0 |
| Unimp. | 20 | 15.4 | 50 | 38.5 | 60 | 46.2 | 130 | 100.0 |

p = 0.0190

## Index to Tables:
### Major Dependent Variables by Background Factors

171

**Table 3**

**Index of Personal Involvement by Sureness of Belief**

| Sure of Belief | My Business to be Involved | | | | | | | |
|---|---|---|---|---|---|---|---|---|
| | Hi | | Mod | | Low | | Total | |
| | No. | % | No. | % | No. | % | No. | % |
| Very | 56 | 26.7 | 88 | 41.9 | 66 | 31.4 | 210 | 100.0 |
| Fairly | 79 | 20.8 | 191 | 50.4 | 109 | 28.8 | 379 | 100.0 |
| DK | 6 | 19.4 | 11 | 35.5 | 14 | 45.2 | 31 | 100.0 |
| Not Too | 33 | 18.3 | 69 | 38.3 | 78 | 43.3 | 180 | 100.0 |

p = 0.0148

**Table 4**

**Index of Personal Involvement by Religious Group Membership**

| Belong to Relig. Group | My Business to be Involved | | | | | | | |
|---|---|---|---|---|---|---|---|---|
| | Hi | | Mod | | Low | | Total | |
| | No. | % | No. | % | No. | % | No. | % |
| Not Belong | 124 | 20.0 | 277 | 44.6 | 220 | 35.4 | 621 | 100.0 |
| Belong | 47 | 28.0 | 76 | 45.2 | 45 | 26.8 | 168 | 100.0 |

p = 0.0455

**Table 5**

**Index of Personal Involvement by Gender**

| Sex | My Business to be Involved | | | | | | | |
|---|---|---|---|---|---|---|---|---|
| | Hi | | Mod | | Low | | Total | |
| | No. | % | No. | % | No. | % | No. | % |
| Male | 68 | 18.3 | 168 | 45.3 | 135 | 36.4 | 371 | 100.0 |
| Female | 108 | 24.9 | 192 | 44.3 | 133 | 30.7 | 433 | 100.0 |

p = 0.0198

**Table 6**

**Index of Personal Involvement by Home Language**

| Home Language | My Business to be Involved | | | | | | | |
|---|---|---|---|---|---|---|---|---|
| | Hi | | Mod | | Low | | Total | |
| | No. | % | No. | % | No. | % | No. | % |
| None | 124 | 24.3 | 220 | 43.1 | 166 | 32.5 | 510 | 100.0 |
| Spanish | 45 | 17.4 | 125 | 48.3 | 89 | 34.4 | 259 | 100.0 |

p = 0.0365

**Table 7**

**Index of Personal Involvement by Father in Military**

| Father in Military | My Business to be Involved | | | | | | | |
|---|---|---|---|---|---|---|---|---|
| | Hi | | Mod | | Low | | Total | |
| | No. | % | No. | % | No. | % | No. | % |
| Yes | 49 | 27.2 | 61 | 33.9 | 70 | 38.9 | 180 | 100.0 |
| No | 126 | 20.2 | 299 | 48.0 | 198 | 31.8 | 623 | 100.0 |

p = 0.0029

**Table 8**

**Index of Personal Involvement by Grade Point Average**

| Grad. Pt. Average | My Business to be Involved | | | | | | | |
|---|---|---|---|---|---|---|---|---|
| | Hi | | Mod | | Low | | Total | |
| | No. | % | No. | % | No. | % | No. | % |
| 3.5+ | 54 | 29.2 | 85 | 45.9 | 46 | 24.9 | 185 | 100.0 |
| 3.0–3.4 | 69 | 21.6 | 140 | 43.9 | 110 | 34.5 | 319 | 100.0 |
| 2.5–2.9 | 42 | 17.1 | 118 | 48.0 | 86 | 35.0 | 246 | 100.0 |
| Below 2.5 | 10 | 20.0 | 16 | 32.0 | 24 | 48.0 | 50 | 100.0 |

p = 0.0163

**Table 9**

**Church Business to Teach by Ethnic Background**

| | Church Business to Teach | | | | | | | |
| | Hi | | Mod | | Low | | Total | |
| Ethnicity | No. | % | No. | % | No. | % | No. | % |
|---|---|---|---|---|---|---|---|---|
| Hispanic | 62 | 24.8 | 113 | 45.2 | 75 | 30.0 | 250 | 100.0 |
| Mixed | 24 | 28.2 | 29 | 34.1 | 32 | 37.6 | 85 | 100.0 |
| Anglo | 96 | 20.6 | 189 | 40.6 | 181 | 38.8 | 466 | 100.0 |

$p = 0.0323$

**Table 10**

**Church Business to Teach by Language Spoken at Home**

| | Church Business to Teach | | | | | | | |
| Home | Hi | | Mod | | Low | | Total | |
| Language | No. | % | No. | % | No. | % | No. | % |
|---|---|---|---|---|---|---|---|---|
| None | 119 | 23.4 | 198 | 38.9 | 292 | 37.7 | 509 | 100.0 |
| Spanish | 58 | 22.3 | 122 | 46.9 | 80 | 30.8 | 260 | 100.0 |

$p = 0.0193$

**Table 11**

**Church Business to Teach by Church Attendance**

| | Church Business to Teach | | | | | | | |
| | Hi | | Mod | | Low | | Total | |
| Church Attend | No. | % | No. | % | No. | % | No. | % |
|---|---|---|---|---|---|---|---|---|
| Weekly | 125 | 25.4 | 210 | 42.7 | 257 | 31.9 | 492 | 100.0 |
| 2–3 Mo. | 33 | 20.5 | 67 | 41.6 | 61 | 37.9 | 161 | 100.0 |
| Few–Year | 23 | 16.0 | 55 | 38.2 | 66 | 45.8 | 144 | 100.0 |

$p = 0.0055$

**Table 12**

**Church Business to Teach by Importance of Religion**

| Imp. of Religion | Church Business to Teach | | | | | | | |
| | Hi | | Mod | | Low | | Total | |
| | No. | % | No. | % | No. | % | No. | % |
|---|---|---|---|---|---|---|---|---|
| Very | 94 | 30.9 | 120 | 39.5 | 90 | 29.6 | 304 | 100.0 |
| Fairly | 69 | 18.9 | 165 | 45.1 | 132 | 36.1 | 366 | 100.0 |
| Unimportant | 18 | 13.8 | 47 | 36.2 | 65 | 50.0 | 130 | 100.0 |

p = 0.0000

**Table 13**

**Business of Church to Teach by Religious Conviction**

| Religious Conviction | Church Business to Teach? | | | | | | | |
| | Hi | | Mod | | Low | | Total | |
| | No. | % | No. | % | No. | % | No. | % |
|---|---|---|---|---|---|---|---|---|
| Very | 68 | 32.2 | 78 | 37.0 | 65 | 30.8 | 211 | 100.0 |
| Fairly | 86 | 22.7 | 178 | 47.0 | 115 | 30.3 | 379 | 100.0 |
| DK | 5 | 16.7 | 8 | 26.7 | 17 | 56.7 | 30 | 100.0 |
| Not Too | 22 | 12.2 | 68 | 37.8 | 90 | 50.0 | 180 | 100.0 |

p = 0.0000

**Table 14**

**Business of Church to Teach by Membership in Religious Group**

| Religious Group | Church Business to Teach? | | | | | | | |
| | Hi | | Mod | | Low | | Total | |
| | No. | % | No. | % | No. | % | No. | % |
|---|---|---|---|---|---|---|---|---|
| Not Belong | 126 | 20.3 | 266 | 42.8 | 229 | 36.9 | 621 | 100.0 |
| Belong | 50 | 29.8 | 63 | 37.5 | 55 | 32.7 | 168 | 100.0 |

p = 0.0085

**Table 15**

**Church Business to Teach by Credibility of Teachings**

| Credibility of Church Teachings | Church Business to Teach | | | | | | | |
|---|---|---|---|---|---|---|---|---|
| | Hi | | Mod | | Low | | Total | |
| | No. | % | No. | % | No. | % | No. | % |
| More | 143 | 27.4 | 233 | 44.7 | 145 | 27.8 | 521 | 100.0 |
| DK | 22 | 12.1 | 68 | 37.4 | 92 | 50.5 | 182 | 100.0 |
| Less | 17 | 17.3 | 31 | 31.6 | 50 | 51.0 | 98 | 100.0 |

$p = 0.0000$

**Table 16**

**Church Business to Teach by Rating of Theo Program**

| Rating of Theology Programs | Church Business to Teach | | | | | | | |
|---|---|---|---|---|---|---|---|---|
| | Hi | | Mod | | Low | | Total | |
| | No. | % | No. | % | No. | % | No. | % |
| Excellent | 74 | 28.5 | 124 | 47.7 | 62 | 23.8 | 260 | 100.0 |
| Good | 79 | 20.6 | 161 | 42.0 | 143 | 37.3 | 383 | 100.0 |
| Fair | 30 | 18.8 | 48 | 30.0 | 82 | 51.2 | 160 | 100.0 |

$p = 0.0000$

**Table 17**

**Conscience Formation by Church Attendance**

| Church Attendance | Conscious Formation | | | | | | | |
|---|---|---|---|---|---|---|---|---|
| | Chrch Tch | | Listn-Me | | No Auth | | Total | |
| | No. | % | No. | % | No. | % | No. | % |
| Weekly | 76 | 15.4 | 396 | 80.3 | 21 | 4.3 | 493 | 100.0 |
| 2–3 Mo. | 9 | 5.6 | 122 | 75.8 | 30 | 18.6 | 161 | 100.0 |
| Few–Year | 3 | 2.0 | 109 | 73.6 | 36 | 24.3 | 148 | 100.0 |

$p = 0.0000$

## Table 18
### Conscience Formation by Membership in Religious Group

| Religious Group | Conscious Formation | | | | | | | |
| | Chrch Tch | | Listn-Me | | No Auth | | Total | |
| | No. | % | No. | % | No. | % | No. | % |
|---|---|---|---|---|---|---|---|---|
| Not Belong | 52 | 8.3 | 494 | 78.9 | 80 | 12.8 | 626 | 100.0 |
| Belong | 34 | 20.2 | 126 | 75.0 | 8 | 4.8 | 168 | 100.0 |

p = 0.0000

## Table 19
### Conscience Formation by Previous Religious Education

| Previous Religious Education | Conscious Formation | | | | | | | |
| | Chrch Tch | | Listn-Me | | No Auth | | Total | |
| | No. | % | No. | % | No. | % | No. | % |
|---|---|---|---|---|---|---|---|---|
| Cathschl | 43 | 12.6 | 265 | 77.7 | 33 | 9.7 | 341 | 100.0 |
| CCD | 32 | 10.5 | 247 | 81.0 | 26 | 8.5 | 305 | 100.0 |
| None | 8 | 5.8 | 104 | 74.8 | 27 | 19.4 | 139 | 100.0 |

p = 0.0000

## Table 20
### Conscience Formation by Importance of Religion

| Importance of Religion | Conscious Formation | | | | | | | |
| | Chrch Tch | | Listn-Me | | No Auth | | Total | |
| | No. | % | No. | % | No. | % | No. | % |
|---|---|---|---|---|---|---|---|---|
| Very | 68 | 22.4 | 228 | 75.2 | 7 | 2.3 | 303 | 100.0 |
| Fairly | 20 | 5.4 | 326 | 87.9 | 25 | 6.7 | 371 | 100.0 |
| Unimp. | — | — | 75 | 57.3 | 56 | 42.7 | 131 | 100.0 |

p = 0.0000

**Table 21**

**Conscience Formation by Religious Conviction**

| Religious Conviction | Conscious Formation | | | | | | | |
| | Chrch Tch | | Listn-Me | | No Auth | | Total | |
| | No. | % | No. | % | No. | % | No. | % |
|---|---|---|---|---|---|---|---|---|
| Very | 56 | 26.5 | 154 | 73.0 | 1 | .5 | 211 | 100.0 |
| Fairly | 31 | 8.1 | 333 | 87.4 | 17 | 4.5 | 381 | 100.0 |
| DK | 1 | 3.1 | 22 | 68.8 | 9 | 28.1 | 32 | 100.0 |
| Not Too | — | — | 120 | 66.3 | 61 | 33.7 | 181 | 100.0 |

p = 0.0000

**Table 22**

**Conscience Formation by Credibility of Teachings**

| Credibility | Conscious Formation | | | | | | | |
| | Chrch Tch | | Listn-Me | | No Auth | | Total | |
| | No. | % | No. | % | No. | % | No. | % |
|---|---|---|---|---|---|---|---|---|
| More | 72 | 13.7 | 436 | 83.0 | 17 | 3.2 | 525 | 100.0 |
| DK | 11 | 6.0 | 134 | 73.2 | 38 | 20.8 | 183 | 100.0 |
| Less | 5 | 5.1 | 60 | 61.2 | 33 | 33.7 | 98 | 100.0 |

p = 0.0000

**Table 23**

**"Premarital Sex is Immoral" by Sex**

| Gender | "Premarital Sex is Immoral" | | | | | | | | | |
| | Agree | | DK | | Disagree | | Str Disag | | Total | |
| | No. | % | No. | % | No. | % | No. | % | No. | % |
|---|---|---|---|---|---|---|---|---|---|---|
| Male | 265 | 32.0 | 105 | 12.4 | 263 | 31.8 | 197 | 23.8 | 828 | 100.0 |
| Female | 356 | 37.4 | 139 | 14.6 | 261 | 27.4 | 195 | 20.5 | 951 | 100.0 |

p = 0.02

## Table 24
### "Premarital Sex is Immoral" by Grade Point Average

| Grade Point Average | "Premarital Sex is Immoral" | | | | | | | | | |
| | Agree | | DK | | Disagree | | Str Disag | | Total | |
| | No. | % | No. | % | No. | % | No. | % | No. | % |
|---|---|---|---|---|---|---|---|---|---|---|
| 3.5+ | 202 | 42.8 | 57 | 12.1 | 138 | 29.2 | 75 | 15.9 | 472 | 100.0 |
| 3.0–3.4 | 255 | 36.7 | 98 | 14.1 | 196 | 28.2 | 145 | 20.9 | 694 | 100.0 |
| 2.5–2.9 | 137 | 27.5 | 69 | 13.8 | 162 | 32.5 | 131 | 26.3 | 499 | 100.0 |
| Below 2.5 | 24 | 22.0 | 17 | 15.6 | 27 | 4.8 | 41 | 37.6 | 109 | 100.0 |

p = 0.0000

## Table 25
### "Premarital Sex is Immoral" by Year Grouping

| Year Grouping | "Premarital Sex is Immoral" | | | | | | | | | |
| | Agree | | DK | | Disagree | | Str Disag | | Total | |
| | No. | % | No. | % | No. | % | No. | % | No. | % |
|---|---|---|---|---|---|---|---|---|---|---|
| Before 1983 | 382 | 39.5 | 101 | 10.4 | 263 | 27.2 | 222 | 22.9 | 968 | 100.0 |
| After 1983 | 239 | 29.5 | 141 | 17.4 | 261 | 32.2 | 170 | 21.0 | 811 | 100.0 |

p = 0.0000

## Table 26
### "Premarital Sex is Immoral" by Mother's Occupation

| Mother's Occupation | "Premarital Sex is Immoral" | | | | | | | | | |
| | Agree | | DK | | Disagree | | Str Disag | | Total | |
| | No. | % | No. | % | No. | % | No. | % | No. | % |
|---|---|---|---|---|---|---|---|---|---|---|
| Housewife | 227 | 40.1 | 82 | 14.5 | 141 | 24.9 | 116 | 20.5 | 566 | 100.0 |
| W Col. | 174 | 32.5 | 71 | 13.3 | 177 | 33.1 | 113 | 21.1 | 535 | 100.0 |
| Own/Mgr. | 52 | 32.9 | 16 | 10.1 | 43 | 27.2 | 47 | 29.7 | 158 | 100.0 |
| Prof. | 155 | 32.4 | 67 | 14.0 | 156 | 32.6 | 101 | 21.1 | 479 | 100.0 |

p = 0.01

**Table 27**

**"Premarital Sex is Immoral" by Importance of Ethnicity**

| Importance of Ethnic Background | "Premarital Sex is Immoral" | | | | | | | | | |
|---|---|---|---|---|---|---|---|---|---|---|
| | Agree | | DK | | Disagree | | Str Disag | | Total | |
| | No. | % | No. | % | No. | % | No. | % | No. | % |
| V. Imp. | 102 | 38.6 | 73 | 15.5 | 124 | 26.3 | 93 | 19.7 | 472 | 100.0 |
| Somewhat | 229 | 36.5 | 85 | 13.5 | 189 | 30.1 | 125 | 19.9 | 628 | 100.0 |
| Not Imp. | 207 | 31.0 | 81 | 12.1 | 207 | 31.0 | 172 | 25.8 | 667 | 100.0 |

p = 0.0121

**Table 28**

**"Premarital Sex is Immoral" by Credibility of Teaching**

| Credibility of Church Teaching | "Premarital Sex is Immoral" | | | | | | | | | |
|---|---|---|---|---|---|---|---|---|---|---|
| | Agree | | DK | | Disagree | | Str Disag | | Total | |
| | No. | % | No. | % | No. | % | No. | % | No. | % |
| More | 463 | 40.5 | 163 | 14.3 | 331 | 29.0 | 186 | 16.3 | 1143 | 100.0 |
| DK | 81 | 23.4 | 55 | 15.9 | 105 | 30.3 | 105 | 30.3 | 346 | 100.0 |
| Less | 30 | 21.9 | 11 | 8.0 | 34 | 24.8 | 62 | 45.3 | 137 | 100.0 |

p = 0.0000

**Table 29**

**"Premarital Sex is Immoral" by Importance of Religion**

| Importance of Religion | "Premarital Sex is Immoral" | | | | | | | | | |
|---|---|---|---|---|---|---|---|---|---|---|
| | Agree | | DK | | Disagree | | Str Disag | | Total | |
| | No. | % | No. | % | No. | % | No. | % | No. | % |
| V Imp. | 368 | 49.5 | 105 | 14.1 | 169 | 22.7 | 101 | 13.6 | 743 | 100.0 |
| Fairly | 231 | 27.4 | 116 | 13.8 | 296 | 35.1 | 200 | 23.7 | 843 | 100.0 |
| Unimp. | 21 | 11.2 | 18 | 9.6 | 59 | 31.4 | 90 | 47.9 | 188 | 100.0 |
| Totals | 620 | | 239 | | 524 | | 391 | | 1774 | |

p = 0.0000

**Table 30**

**"Premarital Sex is Immoral" by Religious Conviction**

| Degree of Religious Conviction | "Premarital Sex is Immoral" | | | | | | | | | |
|---|---|---|---|---|---|---|---|---|---|---|
| | Agree | | DK | | Disagree | | Str Disag | | Total | |
| | No. | % | No. | % | No. | % | No. | % | No. | % |
| Very | 258 | 51.9 | 55 | 11.1 | 113 | 22.7 | 71 | 14.3 | 497 | 100.0 |
| Fairly | 317 | 33.7 | 138 | 14.7 | 305 | 32.4 | 180 | 19.1 | 940 | 100.0 |
| DK | 5 | 15.6 | 9 | 28.1 | 6 | 18.8 | 12 | 37.5 | 32 | 100.0 |
| Not Too | 40 | 13.1 | 37 | 12.1 | 100 | 32.8 | 128 | 42.0 | 305 | 100.0 |
| Totals | 620 | | 239 | | 524 | | 391 | | 1774 | |

$p = 0.0000$

**Table 31**

**"Premarital Sex is Immoral" by Previous Religious Education**

| Previous Religious Education | "Premarital Sex is Immoral" | | | | | | | | | |
|---|---|---|---|---|---|---|---|---|---|---|
| | Agree | | DK | | Disagree | | Str Disag | | Total | |
| | No. | % | No. | % | No. | % | No. | % | No. | % |
| Cathschl | 304 | 36.1 | 116 | 13.8 | 250 | 29.7 | 172 | 20.4 | 842 | 100.0 |
| CCD | 236 | 38.5 | 79 | 12.9 | 176 | 28.7 | 122 | 19.9 | 613 | 100.0 |
| None | 68 | 23.5 | 39 | 13.5 | 96 | 33.2 | 86 | 29.8 | 289 | 100.0 |
| Totals | 608 | | 234 | | 522 | | 380 | | 1744 | |

$p = 0.0003$

**Table 32**

**"Premarital Sex is Immoral" by Religious Attendance**

| Religious Attendance | "Premarital Sex is Immoral" | | | | | | | | | |
|---|---|---|---|---|---|---|---|---|---|---|
| | Agree | | DK | | Disagree | | Str Disag | | Total | |
| | No. | % | No. | % | No. | % | No. | % | No. | % |
| Weekly | 511 | 42.4 | 173 | 14.4 | 338 | 28.0 | 183 | 15.2 | 1205 | 100.0 |
| 2–3 Mo. | 70 | 22.2 | 39 | 12.4 | 105 | 33.3 | 101 | 32.1 | 315 | 100.0 |
| Few–Year | 37 | 14.9 | 25 | 10.1 | 80 | 32.2 | 106 | 42.7 | 248 | 100.0 |
| Totals | 718 | | 237 | | 523 | | 390 | | 1768 | |

$p = 0.0000$

**Table 33**

**"Premarital Sex is Immoral" by Religious Group Membership**

| Membership in Religious Group | "Premarital Sex is Immoral" | | | | | | | | | |
|---|---|---|---|---|---|---|---|---|---|---|
| | Agree | | DK | | Disagree | | Str Disag | | Total | |
| | No. | % | No. | % | No. | % | No. | % | No. | % |
| None | 453 | 31.8 | 187 | 13.1 | 441 | 30.9 | 345 | 24.2 | 1426 | 100.0 |
| Belong | 162 | 48.9 | 49 | 14.8 | 77 | 23.3 | 43 | 13.0 | 331 | 100.0 |
| Totals | 615 | | 236 | | 518 | | 388 | | 1757 | |

p = 0.0000

**Table 34**

**"Premarital Sex is Immoral" by Program Rating**

| Rating of Theology Program | "Premarital Sex is Immoral" | | | | | | | | | |
|---|---|---|---|---|---|---|---|---|---|---|
| | Agree | | DK | | Disagree | | Str Disag | | Total | |
| | No. | % | No. | % | No. | % | No. | % | No. | % |
| Excellent | 219 | 41.6 | 70 | 13.3 | 158 | 30.0 | 80 | 15.2 | 527 | 100.0 |
| Good | 300 | 36.8 | 116 | 14.2 | 243 | 29.8 | 157 | 19.2 | 816 | 100.0 |
| Fair–Poor | 101 | 24.0 | 50 | 11.9 | 122 | 29.0 | 148 | 35.2 | 421 | 100.0 |
| Totals | 620 | | 236 | | 523 | | 385 | | 1764 | |

p = 0.0000

**Table 35**

**More Sexual Freedom a Good Thing? By Program Credibility**

| Theology Makes Teaching Credible? | More Sexual Freedom a Good Thing? | | | | | | | | | |
|---|---|---|---|---|---|---|---|---|---|---|
| | Agree | | DK | | Disagree | | Str Disag | | Total | |
| | No. | % | No. | % | No. | % | No. | % | No. | % |
| More | 351 | 30.8 | 255 | 22.4 | 377 | 33.1 | 155 | 13.6 | 1138 | 100.0 |
| DK | 143 | 41.4 | 74 | 21.4 | 98 | 28.4 | 30 | 8.7 | 345 | 100.0 |
| Less | 66 | 47.8 | 28 | 20.3 | 28 | 20.3 | 16 | 11.6 | 138 | 100.0 |
| Totals | 561 | | 357 | | 503 | | 201 | | 1621 | |

p = 0.0001

## Table 36

### More Sexual Freedom a Good Thing? By Program Rating

| Rating of Theology Program | More Sexual Freedom a Good Thing? | | | | | | | | | |
|---|---|---|---|---|---|---|---|---|---|---|
| | Agree | | DK | | Disagree | | Str Disag | | Total | |
| | No. | % | No. | % | No. | % | No. | % | No. | % |
| Excellent | 164 | 31.2 | 126 | 24.0 | 165 | 31.4 | 71 | 13.5 | 526 | 100.0 |
| Good | 287 | 35.2 | 162 | 19.9 | 265 | 32.5 | 101 | 12.4 | 815 | 100.0 |
| Fair–Poor | 162 | 38.5 | 103 | 24.5 | 114 | 27.1 | 42 | 10.0 | 421 | 100.0 |
| Totals | 613 | | 391 | | 544 | | 214 | | 1762 | |

$p = 0.05$

## Table 37

### More Sexual Freedom a Good Thing? By Parents' Political Views

| Parents' Political Views | Is Sexual Freedom a Good Thing? | | | | | | | | | |
|---|---|---|---|---|---|---|---|---|---|---|
| | Agree | | DK | | Disagree | | Str Disag | | Total | |
| | No. | % | No. | % | No. | % | No. | % | No. | % |
| Conserv. | 196 | 32.6 | 111 | 18.4 | 194 | 32.2 | 101 | 16.8 | 602 | 100.0 |
| Middle | 212 | 35.6 | 147 | 24.7 | 175 | 29.4 | 61 | 10.3 | 595 | 100.0 |
| Liberal | 152 | 35.8 | 95 | 22.4 | 139 | 32.8 | 38 | 9.0 | 424 | 100.0 |
| Totals | 560 | | 353 | | 508 | | 200 | | 1621 | |

$p = 0.0007$

## Table 38

### Is Sexual Freedom a Good Thing? By Male–Female

| Gender | Is Sexual Freedom a Good Thing? | | | | | | | | | |
|---|---|---|---|---|---|---|---|---|---|---|
| | Agree | | DK | | Disagree | | Str Disag | | Total | |
| | No. | % | No. | % | No. | % | No. | % | No. | % |
| Male | 373 | 45.1 | 171 | 20.7 | 212 | 25.6 | 71 | 8.6 | 827 | 100.0 |
| Female | 246 | 25.9 | 223 | 23.4 | 338 | 35.5 | 144 | 15.1 | 951 | 100.0 |
| Totals | 619 | | 394 | | 550 | | 215 | | 1778 | |

$p = 0.0000$

## Table 39

### Is Sexual Freedom a Good Thing? By Grade Point Average

| Grade Point Average | Is Sexual Freedom a Good Thing? | | | | | | | | | |
|---|---|---|---|---|---|---|---|---|---|---|
| | Agree | | DK | | Disagree | | Str Disag | | Total | |
| | No. | % | No. | % | No. | % | No. | % | No. | % |
| 3.5 + | 126 | 26.8 | 94 | 20.0 | 167 | 35.5 | 83 | 17.7 | 470 | 100.0 |
| 3.0–3.4 | 230 | 33.2 | 163 | 23.5 | 213 | 30.7 | 87 | 12.6 | 693 | 100.0 |
| 2.5–2.9 | 207 | 41.2 | 118 | 23.5 | 137 | 27.3 | 40 | 8.0 | 502 | 100.0 |
| Below 2.5 | 52 | 48.1 | 19 | 17.6 | 32 | 29.6 | 5 | 4.6 | 108 | 100.0 |
| Totals | 615 | | 394 | | 549 | | 215 | | 1773 | |

$p = 0.0000$

## Table 40

### Is Sexual Freedom a Good Thing? By Mothers Occupation

| Mother's Occupation | Is Sexual Freedom a Good Thing? | | | | | | | | | |
|---|---|---|---|---|---|---|---|---|---|---|
| | Agree | | DK | | Disagree | | Str Disag | | Total | |
| | No. | % | No. | % | No. | % | No. | % | No. | % |
| Housewife | 186 | 33.0 | 131 | 23.3 | 155 | 27.5 | 91 | 16.2 | 563 | 100.0 |
| W. Col. | 185 | 34.5 | 113 | 21.0 | 184 | 34.3 | 55 | 10.2 | 537 | 100.0 |
| Own/Mgr. | 67 | 42.7 | 32 | 20.4 | 44 | 28.0 | 14 | 8.9 | 157 | 100.0 |
| Prof. | 168 | 35.0 | 109 | 22.7 | 156 | 32.5 | 47 | 9.8 | 480 | 100.0 |
| Totals | 606 | | 385 | | 539 | | 207 | | 1737 | |

$p = 0.0094$

## Table 41

### More Sexual Freedom a Good Thing? By Importance of Religion

| Importance of Religion | More Sexual Freedom a Good Thing? | | | | | | | | | |
|---|---|---|---|---|---|---|---|---|---|---|
| | Agree | | DK | | Disagree | | Str Disag | | Total | |
| | No. | % | No. | % | No. | % | No. | % | No. | % |
| V. Imp. | 181 | 24.4 | 147 | 19.8 | 259 | 35.0 | 154 | 20.8 | 741 | 100.0 |
| Fairly | 334 | 39.6 | 200 | 23.7 | 254 | 30.1 | 55 | 6.5 | 843 | 100.0 |
| Unimp. | 101 | 53.7 | 45 | 23.9 | 37 | 19.7 | 5 | 2.7 | 188 | 100.0 |
| Totals | 616 | | 392 | | 550 | | 214 | | 1772 | |

$p = 0.0000$

**Table 42**

**More Sexual Freedom a Good Thing? By Religious Conviction**

| Degree of Religion Conviction | More Sexual Freedom a Good Thing? | | | | | | | | | |
|---|---|---|---|---|---|---|---|---|---|---|
| | Agree | | DK | | Disagree | | Str Disag | | Total | |
| | No. | % | No. | % | No. | % | No. | % | No. | % |
| Very | 130 | 26.2 | 94 | 18.9 | 162 | 32.6 | 111 | 22.3 | 497 | 100.0 |
| Fairly | 324 | 34.6 | 218 | 23.3 | 305 | 32.6 | 90 | 9.6 | 937 | 100.0 |
| DK | 13 | 40.6 | 7 | 21.9 | 9 | 28.1 | 3 | 9.4 | 32 | 100.0 |
| Not Too | 149 | 48.7 | 73 | 23.9 | 74 | 24.2 | 10 | 3.3 | 306 | 100.0 |
| Totals | 516 | | 392 | | 550 | | 214 | | 1772 | |

$p = 0.0000$

**Table 43**

**More Sexual Freedom a Good Thing? By Religious Group Membership**

| Membership in Religious Group | More Sexual Freedom a Good Thing? | | | | | | | | | |
|---|---|---|---|---|---|---|---|---|---|---|
| | Agree | | DK | | Disagree | | Str Disag | | Total | |
| | No. | % | No. | % | No. | % | No. | % | No. | % |
| None | 527 | 37.0 | 323 | 22.7 | 434 | 30.5 | 140 | 9.8 | 1424 | 100.0 |
| Belong | 81 | 24.4 | 67 | 20.2 | 114 | 34.5 | 70 | 21.1 | 332 | 100.0 |
| Total | 608 | | 390 | | 548 | | 210 | | 1756 | |

$p = 0.0000$

**Table 44**

**More Sexual Freedom a Good Thing? By Religious Attendance**

| Religious Attendance | More Sexual Freedom a Good Thing? | | | | | | | | | |
| | Agree | | DK | | Disagree | | Str Disag | | Total | |
| | No. | % | No. | % | No. | % | No. | % | No. | % |
| Weekly | 346 | 28.7 | 274 | 22.8 | 400 | 33.2 | 184 | 15.3 | 1204 | 100.0 |
| 2–3 Mo. | 151 | 48.1 | 57 | 18.2 | 86 | 27.4 | 20 | 6.4 | 314 | 100.0 |
| Few–Year | 118 | 47.4 | 61 | 24.5 | 62 | 24.9 | 8 | 3.2 | 249 | 100.0 |
| Totals | 615 | | 392 | | 548 | | 212 | | 1767 | |

$p = 0.0000$

**Table 45**

**More Sexual Freedom a Good Thing? By Previous Religious Education**

| Previous Religious Education | More Sexual Freedom a Good Thing? | | | | | | | | | |
| | Agree | | DK | | Disagree | | Str Disag | | Total | |
| | No. | % | No. | % | No. | % | No. | % | No. | % |
| Cathschl | 290 | 34.5 | 196 | 23.3 | 252 | 30.0 | 103 | 12.2 | 841 | 100.0 |
| CCD | 185 | 30.2 | 128 | 20.9 | 213 | 34.8 | 86 | 14.1 | 612 | 100.0 |
| None | 126 | 43.6 | 63 | 21.8 | 78 | 27.0 | 22 | 7.6 | 289 | 100.0 |
| Totals | 601 | | 387 | | 543 | | 211 | | 1742 | |

$p = 0.0010$

### Table 46
**Abortion Acceptable if Fetus Deformed? By Program Credibility**

| Theology Makes Teachings Credible | More Sexual Freedom a Good Thing? | | | | | | | | | | | |
|---|---|---|---|---|---|---|---|---|---|---|---|---|
| | St Agree | | Agree | | DK | | Disagree | | Str Disag | | Total | |
| | No. | % | No. | % | No. | % | No. | % | No. | % | No. | % |
| More | 97 | 8.6 | 172 | 15.3 | 109 | 9.7 | 324 | 28.8 | 424 | 37.7 | 1124 | 100.0 |
| DK | 52 | 15.2 | 66 | 19.3 | 33 | 9.6 | 93 | 27.2 | 98 | 28.7 | 342 | 100.0 |
| Less | 34 | 24.8 | 24 | 17.5 | 10 | 7.3 | 30 | 21.9 | 39 | 28.5 | 137 | 100.0 |
| Totals | 183 | | 262 | | 152 | | 447 | | 561 | | 1605 | |

p = 0.0000

### Table 47
**Abortion Acceptable if Fetus Deformed? By Program Rating**

| Rating of Theology Program | More Sexual Freedom a Good Thing? | | | | | | | | | | | |
|---|---|---|---|---|---|---|---|---|---|---|---|---|
| | St Agree | | Agree | | DK | | Disagree | | Str Disag | | Total | |
| | No. | % | No. | % | No. | % | No. | % | No. | % | No. | % |
| Excellent | 54 | 10.4 | 60 | 11.5 | 57 | 10.9 | 149 | 28.6 | 201 | 38.6 | 521 | 100.0 |
| Good | 94 | 11.6 | 145 | 18.0 | 65 | 8.1 | 237 | 29.4 | 266 | 33.0 | 807 | 100.0 |
| Fair–Poor | 51 | 12.3 | 84 | 20.2 | 44 | 10.6 | 104 | 25.1 | 132 | 31.8 | 415 | 100.0 |
| Totals | 199 | | 289 | | 166 | | 490 | | 599 | | 1743 | |

p = 0.0042

## Table 48
### Abortion Acceptable if Fetus Deformed? By Grade Point Average

| Grade Point Average | St Agree | | Agree | | DK | | Disagree | | Str Disag | | Total | |
|---|---|---|---|---|---|---|---|---|---|---|---|---|
| | No. | % | No. | % | No. | % | No. | % | No. | % | No. | % |
| 3.5+ | 38 | 8.2 | 69 | 14.9 | 44 | 9.5 | 126 | 27.2 | 186 | 40.2 | 463 | 100.0 |
| 3.0–3.4 | 82 | 12.0 | 116 | 16.9 | 62 | 9.1 | 185 | 27.0 | 240 | 35.0 | 685 | 100.0 |
| 2.5–2.9 | 61 | 12.2 | 93 | 18.7 | 53 | 10.6 | 147 | 29.5 | 144 | 28.9 | 498 | 100.0 |
| Below 2.5 | 18 | 16.7 | 18 | 16.7 | 9 | 8.3 | 35 | 32.4 | 28 | 25.9 | 108 | 100.0 |
| Totals | 199 | | 296 | | 168 | | 493 | | 598 | | 1754 | |

*Abortion Acceptable if Fetus Deformed?*

p = 0.03

## Table 49
### Abortion Acceptable if Fetus Deformed? By Male-Female

| Gender | St Agree | | Agree | | DK | | Disagree | | Str Disag | | Total | |
|---|---|---|---|---|---|---|---|---|---|---|---|---|
| | No. | % | No. | % | No. | % | No. | % | No. | % | No. | % |
| Male | 91 | 11.0 | 145 | 17.4 | 69 | 8.4 | 261 | 31.7 | 260 | 31.6 | 824 | 100.0 |
| Female | 109 | 11.7 | 153 | 16.4 | 100 | 10.7 | 233 | 24.9 | 340 | 36.4 | 935 | 100.0 |
| Totals | 200 | | 296 | | 169 | | 494 | | 600 | | 1759 | |

*Abortion Acceptable if Fetus Deformed?*

p = 0.01

**Table 50**

**Abortion Acceptable if Fetus Deformed? By Mother's Occupation**

| Mother's Occupation | Abortion Acceptable if Fetus Deformed? | | | | | | | | | | | |
| | St Agree | | Agree | | DK | | Disagree | | Str Disag | | Total | |
| | No. | % | No. | % | No. | % | No. | % | No. | % | No. | % |
|---|---|---|---|---|---|---|---|---|---|---|---|---|
| Housewife | 66 | 11.8 | 72 | 12.9 | 59 | 10.5 | 146 | 26.1 | 217 | 38.7 | 560 | 100.0 |
| W. Col. | 55 | 10.4 | 92 | 17.4 | 51 | 9.6 | 154 | 29.1 | 177 | 33.5 | 529 | 100.0 |
| Own/Mgr. | 25 | 15.9 | 27 | 17.2 | 12 | 7.6 | 49 | 31.2 | 44 | 28.0 | 157 | 100.0 |
| Prof. | 49 | 10.4 | 94 | 19.9 | 44 | 9.3 | 138 | 29.2 | 148 | 31.3 | 473 | 100.0 |
| Totals | 195 | | 285 | | 166 | | 487 | | 586 | | 1719 | |

p = 0.0486

**Table 51**

**Abortion Acceptable if Fetus Deformed? By Year**

| Year | Abortion Acceptable if Fetus Deformed? | | | | | | | | | | | |
| | St Agree | | Agree | | DK | | Disagree | | Str Disag | | Total | |
| | No. | % | No. | % | No. | % | No. | % | No. | % | No. | % |
|---|---|---|---|---|---|---|---|---|---|---|---|---|
| Before 1983 | 91 | 9.6 | 148 | 15.6 | 74 | 7.8 | 260 | 27.5 | 374 | 39.5 | 947 | 100.0 |
| After 1983 | 109 | 13.4 | 148 | 18.2 | 95 | 11.7 | 234 | 28.8 | 226 | 27.8 | 812 | 100.0 |
| Totals | 200 | | 296 | | 169 | | 504 | | 600 | | 1759 | |

p = 0.0000

## Table 52
## Abortion Acceptable if Fetus Deformed? By Importance of Religion

| Importance of Religion | Abortion Acceptable if Fetus Deformed | | | | | | | | | | | |
|---|---|---|---|---|---|---|---|---|---|---|---|---|
| | St Agree | | Agree | | DK | | Disagree | | Str Disag | | Total | |
| | No. | % | No. | % | No. | % | No. | % | No. | % | No. | % |
| V. Imp. | 49 | 6.7 | 76 | 10.4 | 68 | 9.3 | 201 | 27.5 | 337 | 46.1 | 731 | 100.0 |
| Fairly | 105 | 12.6 | 165 | 19.8 | 82 | 9.8 | 250 | 29.9 | 233 | 27.9 | 835 | 100.0 |
| Unimp. | 46 | 24.6 | 54 | 28.9 | 18 | 9.6 | 40 | 21.4 | 29 | 15.5 | 187 | 100.0 |
| Totals | 200 | | 295 | | 168 | | 491 | | 599 | | 1753 | |

p = 0.0000

## Table 53
## Is Abortion Acceptable if Fetus Deformed? By Religious Conviction

| Degree of Religious Conviction | Abortion Acceptable if Fetus Deformed | | | | | | | | | | | |
|---|---|---|---|---|---|---|---|---|---|---|---|---|
| | St Agree | | Agree | | DK | | Disagree | | Str Disag | | Total | |
| | No. | % | No. | % | No. | % | No. | % | No. | % | No. | % |
| Very | 40 | 8.1 | 55 | 11.2 | 43 | 8.8 | 119 | 24.2 | 234 | 47.7 | 491 | 100.0 |
| Fairly | 91 | 9.8 | 152 | 16.4 | 93 | 10.1 | 287 | 31.9 | 302 | 32.6 | 925 | 100.0 |
| DK | 7 | 21.9 | 10 | 31.3 | 7 | 21.9 | 5 | 15.6 | 3 | 9.4 | 32 | 100.0 |
| Not Too | 62 | 20.3 | 78 | 25.6 | 25 | 8.2 | 80 | 26.2 | 60 | 19.7 | 305 | 100.0 |
| Totals | 200 | | 295 | | 168 | | 491 | | 599 | | 1753 | |

p = 0.0000

## Table 54

### Is Abortion Acceptable if Fetus Deformed? By Previous Religious Education

| Previous Religious Education | Abortion Acceptable if Fetus Deformed | | | | | | | | | | | |
|---|---|---|---|---|---|---|---|---|---|---|---|---|
| | St Agree | | Agree | | DK | | Disagree | | Str Disag | | Total | |
| | No. | % | No. | % | No. | % | No. | % | No. | % | No. | % |
| Cathschl | 84 | 10.1 | 132 | 15.9 | 81 | 9.8 | 221 | 26.6 | 312 | 37.6 | 830 | 100.0 |
| CCD | 58 | 9.5 | 96 | 15.8 | 57 | 9.4 | 183 | 30.1 | 214 | 35.2 | 608 | 100.0 |
| None | 53 | 18.5 | 66 | 23.1 | 25 | 8.7 | 78 | 27.3 | 64 | 22.4 | 286 | 100.0 |
| Totals | 195 | | 294 | | 163 | | 482 | | 590 | | 1724 | |

p = 0.0000

## Table 55

### Is Abortion Acceptable if Fetus Deformed? By Church Attendance

| Religious Attendance | Abortion Acceptable if Fetus Deformed | | | | | | | | | | | |
|---|---|---|---|---|---|---|---|---|---|---|---|---|
| | St Agree | | Agree | | DK | | Disagree | | Str Disag | | Total | |
| | No. | % | No. | % | No. | % | No. | % | No. | % | No. | % |
| Weekly | 92 | 7.7 | 151 | 12.7 | 109 | 9.2 | 351 | 29.5 | 485 | 40.8 | 1186 | 100.0 |
| 2–3 Mo. | 49 | 15.7 | 74 | 23.6 | 31 | 9.9 | 90 | 28.8 | 69 | 22.0 | 313 | 100.0 |
| Few–Year | 58 | 23.5 | 69 | 27.9 | 27 | 10.9 | 49 | 19.8 | 44 | 17.8 | 247 | 100.0 |
| Totals | 199 | | 294 | | 167 | | 490 | | 598 | | 1748 | |

p = 0.0000

**Table 56**

**Is Abortion Acceptable if Fetus Deformed? By Religious Group Membership**

| Membership in Religious Group | Abortion Acceptable if Fetus Deformed | | | | | | | | | | | | | |
| | St Agree | | Agree | | DK | | Disagree | | Str Disag | | Total | |
| | No. | % | No. | % | No. | % | No. | % | No. | % | No. | % |
| None | 180 | 12.8 | 251 | 17.9 | 138 | 9.8 | 383 | 27.2 | 454 | 32.3 | 1406 | 100.0 |
| Belong | 20 | 6.0 | 39 | 11.8 | 28 | 8.5 | 104 | 31.4 | 140 | 42.3 | 331 | 100.0 |
| Totals | 200 | | 290 | | 166 | | 487 | | 594 | | 1737 | |

p = 0.0000

**Table 57**

**Future Participation in Parish by Religious Group Membership**

| Religious Group | Future Participation in Parish | | | | | | | | | |
| | Active | | Little | | DK | | Nothing | | Total | |
| | No. | % | No. | % | No. | % | No. | % | No. | % |
| None | 234 | 16.4 | 627 | 44.0 | 398 | 27.9 | 166 | 11.6 | 1425 | 100.0 |
| Belong | 185 | 55.4 | 79 | 23.7 | 37 | 11.1 | 33 | 9.9 | 334 | 100.0 |

p = 0.0000

**Table 58**

**Future Participation in Parish by Program Rating**

| Rate Theology Program | Future Participation in Parish | | | | | | | | | |
| | Active | | Little | | DK | | Nothing | | Total | |
| | No. | % | No. | % | No. | % | No. | % | No. | % |
| Excellent | 170 | 32.3 | 197 | 37.4 | 101 | 19.2 | 59 | 11.2 | 527 | 100.0 |
| Good | 188 | 23.0 | 343 | 42.0 | 187 | 22.9 | 99 | 12.1 | 817 | 100.0 |
| Fair–Poor | 68 | 16.2 | 171 | 40.6 | 140 | 33.3 | 42 | 10.0 | 421 | 100.0 |

p = 0.0000

**Table 59**

**Future Participation in Parish by Importance of Religion**

| Importance of Religion | Future Participation in Parish | | | | | | | | | |
| | Active | | Little | | DK | | Nothing | | Total | |
| | No. | % | No. | % | No. | % | No. | % | No. | % |
| V. Imp. | 318 | 42.7 | 258 | 34.6 | 113 | 15.2 | 56 | 7.5 | 745 | 100.0 |
| Fairly | 109 | 12.9 | 422 | 50.0 | 207 | 24.5 | 106 | 12.6 | 844 | 100.0 |
| Unimp. | | | 34 | 18.2 | 114 | 61.0 | 39 | 20.9 | 187 | 100.0 |

p = 0.0000

**Table 60**

**Future Participation in Parish by Religious Conviction**

| Religious Conviction | Future Participation in Parish | | | | | | | | | |
|---|---|---|---|---|---|---|---|---|---|---|
| | Active | | Little | | DK | | Nothing | | Total | |
| | No. | % | No. | % | No. | % | No. | % | No. | % |
| Very | 226 | 45.5 | 174 | 35.0 | 61 | 12.3 | 36 | 7.2 | 497 | 100.0 |
| Fairly | 187 | 19.9 | 440 | 46.7 | 218 | 23.1 | 97 | 10.3 | 942 | 100.0 |
| DK | 3 | 9.4 | 8 | 25.0 | 3 | 9.4 | 18 | 56.3 | 32 | 100.0 |
| Not Too | 11 | 3.6 | 92 | 30.2 | 152 | 49.8 | 50 | 16.4 | 305 | 100.0 |

p = 0.0000

**Table 61**

**Future Participation in Parish by Program Credibility**

| Theology Makes Teaching Credible? | Future Participation in Parish | | | | | | | | | |
|---|---|---|---|---|---|---|---|---|---|---|
| | Active | | Little | | DK | | Nothing | | Total | |
| | No. | % | No. | % | No. | % | No. | % | No. | % |
| More | 322 | 28.2 | 483 | 42.3 | 218 | 19.1 | 119 | 10.4 | 1142 | 100.0 |
| DK | 42 | 12.2 | 133 | 38.8 | 118 | 34.4 | 50 | 14.6 | 343 | 100.0 |
| Less | 18 | 13.0 | 38 | 27.5 | 49 | 35.5 | 33 | 23.9 | 138 | 100.0 |

p = 0.0000

**Table 62**

**Future Participation in Parish by GPA**

| GPA | Future Participation in Parish | | | | | | | | | |
|---|---|---|---|---|---|---|---|---|---|---|
| | Active | | Little | | DK | | Nothing | | Total | |
| | No. | % | No. | % | No. | % | No. | % | No. | % |
| 3.5+ | 143 | 30.4 | 160 | 34.0 | 119 | 25.3 | 49 | 10.4 | 471 | 100.0 |
| 3.0–3.4 | 151 | 21.8 | 302 | 43.5 | 152 | 21.9 | 89 | 12.8 | 694 | 100.0 |
| 2.5–2.9 | 115 | 22.9 | 208 | 41.4 | 128 | 25.5 | 51 | 10.2 | 502 | 100.0 |
| Below 2.5 | 18 | 16.8 | 42 | 39.3 | 35 | 32.7 | 12 | 11.2 | 107 | 100.0 |

p = 0.002

**Table 63**

**Future Participation in Parish by Sex**

| | Future Participation in Parish | | | | | | | | | |
|---|---|---|---|---|---|---|---|---|---|---|
| | Active | | Little | | DK | | Nothing | | Total | |
| Gender | No. | % | No. | % | No. | % | No. | % | No. | % |
| Male | 188 | 22.7 | 317 | 38.3 | 239 | 28.9 | 84 | 10.1 | 828 | 100.0 |
| Female | 239 | 25.1 | 397 | 41.7 | 197 | 20.7 | 118 | 12.4 | 951 | 100.0 |

p = 0.0009

**Table 64**

**Future Participation in Parish by Importance of Ethnicity**

| | Future Participation in Parish | | | | | | | | | |
|---|---|---|---|---|---|---|---|---|---|---|
| | Active | | Little | | DK | | Nothing | | Total | |
| Importance | No. | % | No. | % | No. | % | No. | % | No. | % |
| V. Imp. | 135 | 28.6 | 193 | 40.9 | 104 | 22.0 | 40 | 8.5 | 472 | 100.0 |
| Somewhat | 148 | 23.6 | 263 | 41.9 | 147 | 23.4 | 70 | 11.1 | 628 | 100.0 |
| Not Imp. | 143 | 21.4 | 255 | 38.2 | 182 | 27.3 | 87 | 13.0 | 667 | 100.0 |

p = 0.0143

**Table 65**

**Future Participation in Parish by Father's Occupation**

| | Future Participation in Parish | | | | | | | | | |
|---|---|---|---|---|---|---|---|---|---|---|
| Father's | Active | | Little | | DK | | Nothing | | Total | |
| Occupation | No. | % | No. | % | No. | % | No. | % | No. | % |
| Blue Col. | 28 | 23.7 | 46 | 39.0 | 36 | 30.5 | 8 | 6.8 | 118 | 100.0 |
| White Col. | 89 | 27.1 | 141 | 43.0 | 65 | 19.8 | 33 | 10.1 | 328 | 100.0 |
| Own–Mgr. | 77 | 23.1 | 134 | 40.2 | 88 | 26.4 | 34 | 10.2 | 333 | 100.0 |
| Lower Prof. | 115 | 25.8 | 194 | 43.5 | 92 | 20.6 | 45 | 10.1 | 446 | 100.0 |
| Upper Prof. | 100 | 22.5 | 151 | 34.9 | 123 | 27.7 | 70 | 15.8 | 444 | 100.0 |

p = 0/0034

**Table 66**

**Future Participation in Parish by Religious Education**

| Previous Religous Education | Future Participation in Parish | | | | | | | | | |
|---|---|---|---|---|---|---|---|---|---|---|
| | Active | | Little | | DK | | Nothing | | Total | |
| | No. | % | No. | % | No. | % | No. | % | No. | % |
| Cathschl | 211 | 25.0 | 350 | 41.5 | 202 | 24.0 | 80 | 9.5 | 843 | 100.0 |
| CCD | 170 | 27.8 | 239 | 39.1 | 127 | 20.8 | 76 | 12.4 | 612 | 100.0 |
| None | 41 | 14.2 | 108 | 37.4 | 101 | 34.9 | 39 | 13.5 | 289 | 100.0 |

$p = 0.0000$

**Table 67**

**Future Participation in Parish by Religious Attendance**

| Religious Attendance | Future Participation in Parish | | | | | | | | | |
|---|---|---|---|---|---|---|---|---|---|---|
| | Active | | Little | | DK | | Nothing | | Total | |
| | No. | % | No. | % | No. | % | No. | % | No. | % |
| Weekly | 384 | 31.8 | 504 | 41.8 | 216 | 17.9 | 103 | 8.5 | 1207 | 100.0 |
| 2–3 Mo. | 30 | 9.5 | 147 | 46.7 | 95 | 30.2 | 43 | 13.7 | 315 | 100.0 |
| Few–Year | 11 | 4.4 | 61 | 24.6 | 122 | 49.2 | 54 | 21.8 | 248 | 100.0 |

$p = 0.0000$

# Notes

## Introduction

1. Max Weber, *Economy and Society,* vol. 1. Edited by Guenther Roth and Claus Wittich (Berkeley: University of California Press, 1978), p. 215.

2. Max Weber, "The Social Psychology of the World Religions." In H. H. Gerth and C. Wright Mills, eds., *From Max Weber: Essays in Sociology* (New York: Oxford University Press, 1958), p. 299.

3. Ibid.

4. Ibid.

5. Edward Shils, *Tradition* (Chicago: University of Chicago Press, 1981), p. 291.

6. Robert N. Bellah, Richard Madsen, William M. Sullivan, Ann Swidler, and Steven M. Tipton, *Habits of the Heart: Individualism and Commitment in American Life* (Berkeley: University of California Press, 1985), pp. 281–282.

7. Ibid., p. 221.

8. Phillip Hammond, "Religion and the Persistence of Identity," *Journal for the Scientific Study of Religion,* 27 (March, 1988), p. 2.

9. Ibid., p. 3.

10. Ibid., p. 5.

11. Ibid., p. 5.

12. Edward Shils, *Tradition,* p. 44.

13. Andrew M. Greeley, *American Catholics Since the Council: An Unauthorized Report* (Chicago: Thomas More, 1985).

14. Richard P. McBrien, *Catholicism* (Minneapolis: Winston, 1981).

15. John Seidler and Katherine Meyer, *Conflict and Change in the Catholic Church* (New Brunswick: Rutgers University Press, 1989).

16. Patrick H. McNamara, "Conservative Christian Families and Their Moral World: Some Reflections for Sociologists," *Sociological Analysis* 46, 2 (Summer, 1985), p. 96.

17. Dean R. Hoge, "Interpreting Change in American Catholicism: The River and the Floodgate," *Review of Religious Research* 27, 4 (June, 1986), p. 294.

18. Jay P. Dolan, *The American Catholic Experience: A History from Colonial Times to the Present* (New York: Doubleday, 1985).

19. John Deedy, *American Catholicism: Now Where* (New York: Plenum, 1987).

20. Dolan, *The American Catholic Experience,* p. 428.

### *Chapter 1. From Ghetto to Suburbs*

1. Anthony Giddens, *The Constitution of Society* (Berkeley: University of California Press, 1984), pp. 362–363.

2. Mary Gordon, *The Company of Women* (New York: Random House, 1980), p. 17.

3. Ibid., p. 33.

4. Ibid., p. 46.

5. James T. Farrell, *Studs Lonigan* (New York: Random House, 1938), pp. 197–198.

6. Mary McCarthy, *Memories of a Catholic Girlhood* (New York: Harcourt, 1946), pp. 120–121.

7. Harvey Cox, *Seduction of the Spirit* (New York: Simon and Schuster, 1973), p. 50.

8. John Cogley, *Catholic America* (New York: Dial, 1973), p. 180.

9. Ibid.

10. Gary Wills, *Bare Ruined Choirs* (New York: Doubleday, 1973), pp. 15–16.

11. John R. Powers, *The Last Catholic in America* (New York: Popular Library), p. 96.

12. Joseph Fichter, S.J. *Social Relations in the Urban Parish* (Chicago: University of Chicago Press, 1954), p. 59.

13. Ibid.

14. Ibid., p. 66.

15. Ibid., p. 119.

16. Ibid., p. 213.

17. Joseph Fichter, S.J. *Parochial School: A Sociological Study.* (Notre Dame: University of Notre Dame Press, 1958), p. 439.

18. Ibid., p. 452.

19. Ibid., p. 451.

20. Will Herberg, *Protestant-Catholic-Jew: An Essay in Religious Sociology* (Garden City: Doubleday, 1955), p. 150.

21. Ibid., p. 164.

22. Ibid., p. 175.

23. Ibid., p. 287.

24. Ibid., p. 285.

25. Gerhard Lenski, *The Religious Factor: A Sociological Study of Religion's Impact on Politics, Economics, and Family Life* (Garden City, N.Y.: Doubleday, 1961), pp. 8–10.

26. Ibid., pp. 312–326.

27. Ibid., p. 327.

28. Ibid., p. 328.

29. Ibid.

30. Ibid., p. 329.

31. Andrew M. Greeley, *Religion and Career: A Study of College Graduates* (New York: Sheed and Ward, 1963), pp. 99–109.

32. Ibid., p. 138.

33. Jay P. Dolan, *The American Catholic Experience* (Garden City, N.Y.: Doubleday, 1985), p. 221.

34. Ibid., p. 225.

35. Ibid., p. 228.

36. Ibid., p. 231.

37. Ibid., p. 233.

38. Walter Lippman, *A Preface to Morals.* Quoted in William M. Halsey, *The Survival of American Innocence: Catholicism in an Era of Disillusionment, 1920–1940* (Notre Dame: Notre Dame Press, 1980), p. 164.

39. Halsey, *The Survival of American Innocence*, p. 167.

40. Ibid., p. 169.

41. Rembert G. Weakland, "The Church in Worldly Affairs: Tensions Between Laity and Clergy," *America*, October 18, 1986, p. 201.

42. My exposition of Giddens's ideas are from *The Constitution of Society*, op.

cit., and *Central Problems of Social Theory: Action, Structure and Contradiction in Social Analysis* (Berkeley: University of California Press, 1979).

43. Robert K. Merton, *Social Theory and Social Structure,* rev. ed. (Glencoe, Illinois: Free Press, 1964), pp. 64–65.

44. William McSweeney, S.J., *Roman Catholicism: The Search for Relevance* (New York: St. Martin's, 1980), p. 138.

45. Ibid., p. 138.

46. Ibid., p. 139.

47. Ibid., p. 140.

48. See, for example, the formulation in the document, *Lumen Gentium:* "All men are called to belong to the new People of God . . . a unity which is a harbinger of the universal peace it promotes" (paragraph 13). In Walter M. Abbott, S.J., ed., *The Documents of Vatican II* (New York: America Press, 1966), pp. 30 and 32.

49. Giddens, *The Constitution of Society,* p. 200.

50. Ibid.

51. Ibid.

52. McSweeney, *Roman Catholicism,* pp. 191–192.

53. Giddens, *The Constitution of Society,* p. 375.


## *Chapter 2. "According to My Conscience"*

1. It is important to remember that for a year preceding issuance of the "birth control" letter, expectations had run high among American Catholics. By this date (1967), over half of married couples were using some form of artificial contraception. The report of the commission appointed by the Pope to study the question and make recommendations was leaked to the press and reprinted in its entirety in *The National Catholic Reporter.* The report recommended that the decision on which birth control method was used be left to the choice of the individual couple. This event understandably raised the hopes of many Catholics that a change in church teaching was in the offing. When, a year later, this was emphatically not the case, the outcry was heard loudest among some members of the clergy—or at least their dissent received more publicity. Some bishops tried to soft-pedal the dissent in their own comments on the Pope's letter. Dolan in *The American Catholic Experience* offers the following portrayal of the encyclical's aftermath:

> Theologians and clergy held news conferences, signed petitions, and publicly dissented from the papal teaching. In Washington, D.C., the dissent became especially bitter when the archbishop, Patrick A. O'Boyle, disciplined fifty-one priests who refused in conscience to accept the encyclical's teaching. Cut off from exercising their ministry until they recanted, many of the fifty-one—twenty-five at least—eventually left the priesthood. (p. 430)

2. A few years later, sociologists Andrew Greeley, William McCready, and Kathleen McCourt examined the encyclical's impact upon current American Catholic belief and practice. In *Catholics Schools in a Declining Church* (Kansas City, Mo: Sheed and Ward, 1976), they featured a 1973 survey showing that the decline in Mass attendance recorded since 1968 affected principally Catholics in their thirties and forties (See William C. McCready and Andrew M. Greeley, "The End of American Catholicism?" *America*, October 28, 1972, pp. 334–338). Those coming of age in the 1960s—the so-called Vietnam generation—were no less religious in practice than their elders (*Catholic Schools in a Declining Church*, p. 303). But in the most publicized of the study's findings, the authors discovered that the decline phenomenon for both cohorts was linked *not* to the Second Vatican Council itself and the changes it had brought about but rather to issuance in 1968 of the papal encyclical letter *Humanae Vitae*. The authors' comments mince no words,

> The belated papal decision disapproving this method of family limitation was ineffective both in preventing the use of the pill and in inhibiting any major change in the sexual attitudes of American Catholics. It also apparently seriously impaired the credibility and authority of the papacy, leading to an increase in apostasy in the years immediately after the encyclical. (p. 304)

In fact, "the apostasy rate has doubled, approaching almost 30 percent among the college-educated young" (p. 303).

3. Dolan, *The American Catholic Experience*, p. 436.

4. Ibid., pp. 436–437.

5. Andrew M. Greeley, *The American Catholic* (New York: Basic Books, 1977), p. 272.

6. Ibid.

7. Greeley, *Crisis in the Church* (Chicago: Thomas More, 1979), p. 260.

8. Ibid., p. 13. Greeley also analyzes data from previous surveys together with data on American Catholics from the National Opinion Research Center's (NORC) annual General Social Survey of the American adult population through 1977. In addition, the book reports on a *Chicago Tribune* study in 1977 of Roman Catholics in the Archdiocese of Chicago. The national data pointed to the central importance of the family in accounting for religiousness of adult respondents,

> It is the family of procreation, the family in which one participates as a husband and wife, that really matters. In most cases that family accounts for more of the variance in religious behavior than all the other variables put together. Perhaps the most effective proof of the importance of the family in American religiousness is the fact that the vast majority of the religious disidentifiers are those who entered religious mixed marriages—apparently with someone more strongly committed to his/her denomination. Marriage and religion seem linked inseparably. (*Crisis in the Church*, p. 255)

Greeley suggested that evangelization efforts then being sponsored by a national committee of the American bishops thus focus not on the individual person as such but take into account the impact of family relationships on how one practices his or her religion.

9. Joan Fee, Andrew M. Greeley, William C. McCready, and Teresa Sullivan, *Young Catholics* (New York: Sadlier, 1981), p. 230. Some "upbeat" findings appear in the study, compared to the negative cast of previous research: despite unorthodox doctrinal and ethical beliefs, the "religious imagination" of young Catholics, as indicated by those favoring "warm" as opposed to "stern" images of God, Jesus, and the Blessed Virgin Mary, is "a more important force for the continuation of personal prayer, social commitment, world view, and marital adjustment, than is doctrinal orthodoxy." Important positive influences on religious behavior of young Catholics are the quality of the sermons they hear, and whether or not they are in contact with sympathetic priests. If married, young Catholics find these two factors second only to religion of spouse as an important factor in their religious lives.

10. Ibid.

11. Andrew M. Greeley, *American Catholics Since the Council: An Unauthorized Report* (Chicago; Thomas More, 1985), p. 223; *Religious Change in America* (Cambridge: Harvard University Press, 1989).

12. George Gallup and James Castelli, *The American Catholic People: Their Beliefs, Practices, and Values* (Garden City: Doubleday, 1987). An opening demographic profile shows Catholics in the mid-1980s to be a young population, e.g., 35 percent of Catholic are over fifty years of age compared to 41 percent of Protestants. One Catholic out of five belongs to a minority group. Hispanics, for example, make up 16 percent of American Catholics (more than eleven million persons) (p. 3). In terms of married status, "the percentage of Catholics who are married has dropped since 1976, while the percentage that are single, separated, or divorced has increased. . . . One Catholic teenager in four says that his or her natural parents have been divorced, the same rate found in the general population;" and the proportion of Catholics "currently divorced doubled . . . between 1976 and 1985" (p. 6).

13. William D'Antonio, James Davidson, Dean Hoge, and Ruth Wallace, *The American Catholic Laity in a Changing Church* (Kansas City, Mo: Sheed and Ward, 1989).

14. Gallup and Castelli, *The American Catholic People*, p. 56.

15. Ibid., p. 50.

16. Ibid., p. 147.

17. Ibid., p. 148.

18. Ibid., p. 190.

19. *American Catholic Laity*, p. 47.

20. Ibid., pp. 88–89.

21. Ibid., p. 188.

22. *The American Catholic People,* p. 13.

23. Ibid., p. 9.

24. Ibid., p. 65.

25. Ibid., p. 14.

26. Ibid., p. 15.

27. Ibid., pp. 24–25.

28. John Deedy, *American Catholicism: And Now Where?* (New York: Plenum, 1987), pp. 72–73.

29. "Emerging Trends," September, 1987 (Princeton, N.J.: Princeton Religious Research Center), p. 2.

30. John Deedy, *American Catholicism,* p. 74.

31. David C. Leege, "Catholic Parishes in the 1980s," *Church* 17 (Summer, 1985), p. 21.

32. Gallup and Castelli, *The American Catholic People,* p. 182.

33. Perceptive observers such as Lutheran theologian John Neuhaus note the similarity of selective Catholicism to the "experiential-expressive" understanding characterizing liberal Protestantism. "In this view, Church, ministry, tradition, liturgy, and doctrine are all symbolic resources to be selectively employed in order to express the authentic experience of the autonomous individual." Neuhaus, *The Catholic Moment: The Paradox of the Church in the Postmodern World* (San Francisco: Harper and Row, 1987), p. 280.

34. David J. O'Brien and Thomas A. Shannon, "Roman Catholic Social Theology," in O'Brien and Shannon, eds., *Renewing the Earth: Catholic Documents on Peace, Justice, and Liberation* (Garden City, N.Y.: Doubleday, 1977), p. 38.

35. See John P. Langan, S.J., "The Bishops and the Bottom Line," *Commonweal,* November 2–16, 1984, pp. 586–592.

36. Thomas M. Gannon, S.J., "Introduction," In Thomas M. Gannon, S.J., ed., *The Catholic Challenge to the American Economy. Reflections on the U.S. Bishops' Pastoral Letter on Catholic Social Teaching and the U.S. Economy* (New York: Macmillan, 1987), p. 5.

37. U.S. Catholic Bishops, *Economic Justice for All.* Pastoral Letter on Catholic Social Teaching and the U.S. Economy (Washington, D.C.: National Conference of Catholic Bishops, 1986), p. XII, paragraph 20.

38. Ibid., p. XIII, paragraph 22.

39. The assimilation picture in the mid-1980s showed continuing advancement of Catholics along lines drawn by Fichter and Herberg three decades ago. Andrew

Greeley, periodically reviewing Catholic mobility data, has been joined in the 1970s and 1980s by other sociologists and historians equally interested in charting Catholic mobility trails. The focus has been mainly upon descendants of European immigrants; it is conceded that Catholics of Spanish-origin, who currently comprise 16 percent of all American Catholics, have not yet achieved parity, due largely to their sizable representation among more recently arrived immigrants to the United States.

Researchers look at both *cultural* and *structural* assimilation. Cultural assimilation involves the extent to which ethnic group members have taken on the cultural traits of the host society. Thus, Olson points to "the disappearance of the immigrant church and the emergence of an assimilated religious community," including learning English and accommodation to the standardization of Catholic religious education and worship imposed by Irish-American bishops during the first half of this century (cf. James S. Olson, *Catholic Immigrants in America*. Chicago: Nelson-Hall, 1970, p. 220). However, structural assimilation, the entrance of a group into intimate relationships with members of the host society, has received the most attention, with its implication of disappearing ethnic boundaries. A "direct" indicator of structural assimilation is the marriage rate to those outside the ethnic or religious group. But educational and occupational mobility are also chief indicators in their own right of "parity" with members of the host society in terms of access to middle- and upper-middle-class status, regardless of intermarriage rates.

In the 1970s, sociologist Richard Alba, relying on NORC General Social Survey data from the mid-1970s, zeroed in on the four largest European-ancestry Catholic groups: German, Irish, Italian, and Polish. Ethnic intermarriage had been going on for a long time. "Among those who were 30 years old or younger in 1963 . . . 82, 74, 65, and 69 percent of Irish, German, Polish and Italian Catholics, respectively, had intermarried." But marriage to non-Catholics was also considerable. "Over 40 percent of Catholics born after World War II have married individuals not raised as Catholics, with the vast majority of these marriages to persons raised as Protestants." Educationally, post–World War II younger Catholics of these four groups had caught up with British Protestants in terms of college attendance (though Germans, as the least urbanized of the four groups, fell slightly behind the other three). (Cf. Richard Alba, "The Twilight of Ethnicity Among American Catholics of European Ancestry," pp. 420–428 in R. Yetman, ed., *Majority and Minority: The Dynamics of Race and Ethnicity in American Society,* 4th ed. Boston: Allyn and Bacon, 1985, pp. 423–426).

By the 1980s, assimilation trends were even more striking. Andrew Greeley summarizes: "Catholics who are maturing in the 1980s are half-again as likely to attend college as white Protestants in the same age cohort." They are no less likely to choose managerial and professional careers. In terms of personal income, the catch-up is also evident, especially for those under forty. Irish, Italian, and Polish Catholics, taken as a group, are the most affluent non-Jewish religious group in America. Greeley's conclusion in *American Catholics Since the Council:*

The transformation from immigrant to professional upper-middle-class for non-Hispanic Catholics has been achieved almost completely in the last twenty years—an enormous transformation. All the indicators are that the pace and the scope of this transformation will continue and accelerate in the remaining years of the century. (p. 27).

40. *Economic Justice for All,* paragraphs 328 and 334, pp. 164–165; 167–168 (emphasis added).

41. James R. Kelly, "Catholicism and Modern Memory: Some Sociological Reflections on the Symbolic Foundations of the Rhetorical Force of the Pastoral Letter, 'The Challenge of Peace,' " *Sociological Analysis,* 42, 2 (Summer, 1984), p. 140.

42. Greeley, *American Catholics Since the Council,* p. 223.

43. Ibid., p. 94.

44. Ibid., p. 99.

45. *American Catholic Laity,* chapter 8, "The Pastoral Letters on Peace and the Economy," pp. 166–181.

46. A frequently cited study relating socioeconomic status to religious beliefs and outlooks is somewhat dated, but it indicates that among church members in the American population, *lower* SES members exhibit greater commitment to religious beliefs than *upper* SES persons. Upper-class membership accompanies *less* commitment to orthodox beliefs along with a lower importance assigned to loving one's neighbor and doing good for others. These findings held for Catholics as well as Protestants of liberal, moderate, and conservative beliefs. Obviously, these controls are important in research on religious beliefs and practices (Rodney Stark, "The Economics of Piety: Religious Commitment and Social Class," pp. 483–503, in G. W. Thielbar and S. D. Feldman, eds., *Issues in Social Inequality.* [Boston: Little, Brown, 1972]. See also Michael Argyle and Benjamin Beit-Hallahmi, *The Social Psychology of Religion* [London: Routledge and Kegan Paul, 1975]). These and other studies concur that education is negatively related to most indicators of religiosity, except for attendance at church services. Those with higher levels of education apparently attend no less regularly than others.

47. Greeley, *American Catholics Since the Council,* p. 78.

48. Gallup and Castelli, *The American Catholic People,* chapter 13, "Teenage Catholics," pp. 149–161.

### Chapter 3. Social Class and Social Viewpoints

1. Gallup and Castelli, *The American Catholic People,* p. 161.

2. Fayette Veverke, "The Ambiguity of Catholic Educational Separatism," *Religious Education* 80, 1 (1985), p. 98.

3. Dolan, *The American Catholic Experience,* p. 399.

4. Ibid., p. 442.

5. "Four DC Catholic Schools Close." *The National Catholic Reporter,* February 2, 1989, p. 6.

6. Joan Fee, et al., *Young Catholics,* chapter 6.

7. Joseph H. Fichter, S.J., *One-Man Research: Reminiscences of a Catholic Sociologist* (New York: John Wiley, 1973), p. 221.

8. Ibid., p. 222.

9. Ibid., p. 223.

10. Andrew M. Greeley, *Catholic High Schools and Minority Students* (New Brunswick, N.J.: Transaction, 1982).

11. National Catholic Educational Association, *The Catholic High School: A National Portrait* (Washington, D.C.: National Catholic Educational Association, 1985)., p. 45.

12. National Catholic Educational Association, *Effective Catholic Schools: An Exploration.* Executive Summary (Washington, D.C.: National Catholic Educational Association, 1985), p. 13.

13. Ibid., p. 91.

14. Leslie A. Darnieder, *Religiosity of Catholic High School Seniors* (Milwaukee: Archdiocese of Milwaukee, 1982), p. 128.

15. Ibid., pp. 121–122.

16. Ibid., pp. 29–30; 125.

17. Ibid., Appendix, pp. 36–43.

18. E. Nancy McAuley and Moira Mathieson, *Faith Without Form: Beliefs of Catholic Youth* (Kansas City, Mo: Sheed and Ward, 1986), p. 6.

19. Ibid., pp. 156–157.

20. Ibid., p. 55.

21. Ibid., pp. 55–56.

22. Ibid., p. 80.

23. Ibid., p. 82.

24. Ibid., p. 83.

25. James R. Kluegel and Eliot R. Smith, *Beliefs about Inequality: Americans' Views of What Is and What Ought To Be* (New York: Aldine de Gruyter, 1986), p. 255.

26. Ibid., p. 256.

27. Ibid., p. 258.

28. Mary R. Jackman and Robert W. Jackman, *Class Awareness in the United States*. (Berkeley: University of California Press, 1983), p. 210.

29. David O. Moberg and Dean R. Hoge, "Catholic College Students' Religious and Moral Attitudes, 1961 to 1982: Effects of the Sixties and Seventies," *Review of Religious Research*, 28, 2 (December, 1986), pp. 115–116.

30. Given the large numbers of fathers reported in categories generally referred to as professional-technical-managerial, the following breakdown of the two-digit occupational code was devised. Fathers reported as business owners or as business or agency managers, supervisors, or executives were included in codes 50 through 55. Digits 56 through 66 designated "lower professional," included elementary through high school teachers, military officers, and various technical occupations, e.g., in electronics and medical technology. "Higher professional" embraced engineers, doctors, lawyers, professors, architects, and so on. Just how skewed toward higher SES the fathers of St. Martin's seniors are is easily gauged by comparison with the 1984 data on Catholics presented in Gallup and Castelli. Nationally, 30 percent of all Catholics were in the "business or professional" categories, as compared with *72 percent* of St. Martin's fathers in these combined categories in 1984 (Gallup and Castelli, p. 5). In terms of educational attainment (asked only from 1983 on), 17 percent of all Catholics nationally in 1984 were college graduates. *Sixty-four percent* of St. Martin's fathers held college degrees that year; in fact, 40 percent had earned a graduate degree (master's or Ph.D.).

31. Data are summarized from Robert O. Gonzalez and Michael LaVelle, *The Hispanic Catholic in the U.S.: A Sociocultural and Religious Profile* (New York: Northeast Catholic Pastoral Center for Hispanics, 1985), pp. 175–188.

32. Mother's occupational and educational attainment exhibit the same pattern. The proportion of housewives among seniors' mothers began to decline in 1980. By 1987 only a quarter of all seniors state their mothers as housewives compared to 45 percent a decade earlier. On the other end of the spectrum, almost a third of the seniors in 1989 reported a professional occupation for their mothers, compared to 19 percent in 1977. Considering mothers' educational attainments, an upward trend again appears: college graduate and graduate-degree holders comprised 39 percent of all mothers in 1983; by 1989 this combined category had risen to 42 percent.

33. Corresponding gaps occur between the two groups in the "some high school" and "high school graduate" categories. Mothers' occupations show that on the average, Hispanic mothers are about 10 percent less likely through the years to be in the professional category. Housewives have been a diminishing category for both groups, with percentages virtually identical since 1983.

34. Gallup and Castelli, *The American Catholic People*, p. 51.

35. Ibid.

36. *Economic Justice for All*, paragraph 360, pp. 179–180.

37. D'Antonio et al., *American Catholic Laity,* p. 147.

38. Ann Swidler, "Culture in Action: Symbols and Strategies," *The American Sociological Review,* 51 (April, 1986), p. 284.

39. Ibid.

## Chapter 4. *"Selling More Than Telling"*

1. Louise Bernikow, *Alone in America* (New York: Harper & Row, 1986), p. 5.

2. Gary Schwartz, *Beyond Conformity or Rebellion: Youth and Authority in America* (Chicago: University of Chicago Press, 1987), p. 28.

3. Ibid., p. 29.

4. Ibid., p. 30, n. 22.

5. Ibid., p. 236.

6. Ibid., p. 172.

7. Ibid., p. 180.

8. Ibid., p. 248.

9. *The Declaration on Religious Freedom,* paragraph 2, in Walter A. Abbott, S.J., *The Documents of Vatican II* (New York: Guild Press, 1966), p. 672.

10. Ibid., p. 679, n. 5.

11. W. Clark Roof and William McKinney, *American Mainline Religion: Its Changing Shape and Future* (New Brunswick: Rutgers University Press, 1987), p. 56.

12. Daniel Yankelovich, *New Rules: Searching for Self-Fulfillment in a World Turned Upside-Down* (New York: Bantam, 1981).

13. Roof and McKinney, *American Mainline Religion,* p. 56.

14. McAuley and Mathieson, *Faith Without Form,* pp. 80–83.

15. Schwartz, *Beyond Conformity or Rebellion,* p. 175.

16. Peter McLaren, *Schooling as Ritual Performance: Towards a Political Economy of Educational Symbols and Gestures* (London: Routledge and Kegan Paul, 1986), p. 132.

17. Ibid., pp. 139–140.

18. Ibid., p. 185.

19. Ibid.. p. 248.

20. Nancy Lesko, *Symbolizing Society: Stories, Rites, and Structure in a Catholic High School* (New York: Falmer Press, 1988), p. 111.

21. Schwartz, *Beyond Conformity or Rebellion*, p. 250.

22. Ibid., p. 175.

### Chapter 5. *"People Nowadays Put Religion on the Back Burner"*

1. Joan Fee, et al., *Young Catholics*, o. 91.

2. Gallup and Castelli, *The American Catholic People*, pp. 28–30.

3. Daniel P. Mueller and Philip W. Cooper, "Religious Interest and Involvement of Young Adults: A Research Note," *Review of Religious Research*, 27 (March, 1986), p. 251.

4. James W. Fowler, *Stages of Faith: The Psychology of Human Development and the Quest for Meaning* (San Francisco: Harper and Row, 1981).

5. Sharon Parks, *The Critical Years: The Young Adult Search for a Faith to Live By* (San Francisco: Harper and Row, 1986).

6. Joan Fee, et al., *Young Catholics*, p. 115.

7. Gallup and Castelli, *The American Catholic People*, p. 51.

8. Dean R. Hoge, *Converts, Dropouts, Returnees: A Study of Religious Change Among Catholics* (New York: Pilgrim Press, 1981), pp. 95–129. Hoge's types include, besides family-tension dropouts, those dropping out because of weariness, lifestyle conflicts with Church teaching, spiritual needs not met by the Church, and dislike for the changes in Mass and other features of the liturgy and parish life brought about by Vatican II.

### Conclusion

1. Anthony Giddens, *Central Problems*, p. 83.

2. Ibid., p. 86.

3. Schwartz, *Beyond Conformity or Rebellion*, p. 174.

4. Bellah, et al., *Habits of the Heart*, p. 285.

5. Robert N. Bellah, "Resurrecting the Common Good: The Economics Pastoral a Year Later," *Commonweal*, December 18, 1987, p. 737.

6. Bellah, et al., *Habits of the Heart*, p. 286.

7. Eugene Kennedy, *The Now and Future Church* (Garden City, N.Y.: Doubleday, 1984), p. 160.

8. James W. Sanders, *The Education of an Urban Minority: Catholics in Chicago, 1833–1965* (New York: Oxford University Press, 1977), p. 230.

9. Dean Hoge, "Interpreting Change in American Catholicism," p. 293.

10. Ibid., p. 294.

11. Ibid., p. 296.

12. Ibid., p. 297.

13. *Economic Justice for All,* paragraph 341.

# Bibliography

Abbott, Walter A. 1966. *The Documents of Vatican II*. New York: Guild Press.

Alba, Richard D. 1985. *Italian Americans: Into the Twilight of Ethnicity*. Englewood Cliffs: Prentice-Hall.

Archdeacon, Thomas J. 1983. *Becoming American: An Ethnic History*. New York: Free Press.

Argyle, Michael, and Benjamin Beit-Hallahmi. 1975. *The Social Psychology of Religion*. London: Routledge and Kegan Paul.

Bellah, Robert N. 1987. "Resurrecting the Common Good: The Economics Pastoral a Year Later." *Commonweal*, December 18.

Bellah, Robert N., Richard Madsen, William M. Sullivan, Ann Swidler, and Steven M. Tipton. 1985. *Habits of the Heart: Individualism and Commitment in American Life*. Berkeley: University of California Press.

Cogley, John. 1973. *Catholic America*. New York: Dial.

Cox, Harvey. 1973. *Seduction of the Spirit*. New York: Simon and Schuster.

D'Antonio, William, James Davidson, Dean Hoge, and Ruth Wallace. 1989. *American Catholic Laity in a Changing Church*. Kansas City, Mo.: Sheed and Ward.

Darnieder, Leslie A. 1982. *Religiosity of Catholic High School Seniors*. Milwaukee: Archdiocese of Milwaukee.

Deedy, John. 1987. *American Catholicism: Now Where?* New York: Plenum.

Dolan, Jay P. 1985. *The American Catholic Experience: A History from Colonial Times to the Present*. New York: Doubleday.

Elizondo, Virgilio. 1987. "The Mexican American Religious Education Experience." In Charles R. Foster, ed., *Ethnicity in the Education of the Church*. Nashville: Scarrit Press, pp. 75–89.

Farrell, James T. 1938. *Studs Lonigan.* New York: Random House.

Fee, Joan, Andrew M. Greeley, William C. McCready, and Teresa Sullivan. 1981. *Young Catholics.* New York: Sadlier.

Fichter, Joseph H. 1973. *One-Man Research: Reminiscences of a Catholic Sociologist.* New York: John Wiley and Sons.

_____. 1958. *Parochial School: A Sociological Study.* Notre Dame: Notre Dame University Press.

_____. 1951. *Southern Parish: Dynamics of a City Church.* Chicago: University of Chicago Press.

Fowler, James W. 1981. *Stages of Faith: The Psychology of Human Development and the Quest for Meaning.* San Francisco: Harper and Row.

Gallup, George, and James Castelli. 1987. *The American Catholic People: Their Beliefs, Practices, and Values.* Garden City, N.Y.: Doubleday.

Gannon, Thomas M., ed. 1987. *The Catholic Challenge to the American Economy: Reflections on the U.S. Bishops' Pastoral Letter on Catholic Social Teaching and the U.S. Economy.* New York: Macmillan.

Giddens, Anthony. 1979. *Central Problems in Social Theory: Action, Structure and Contradiction in Social Analysis.* London: Macmillan.

_____. 1984. *The Constitution of Society: Outline of the Theory of Structuration.* London: Polity Press.

Gordon, Mary. 1980. *The Company of Women.* New York: Random House.

Greeley, Andrew M. 1985. *American Catholics Since the Council: An Unauthorized Report.* Chicago: Thomas More.

_____. 1982. *Catholic High Schools and Minority Students.* New Brunswick, N.J.: Transaction.

_____. 1976. *The Communal Catholic: A Personal Manifesto.* New York: Seabury Press.

_____. 1979. *Crisis in the Church.* Chicago: Thomas More.

_____. 1963. *Religion and Career: A Study of College Graduates.* New York: Sheed and Ward.

————. 1989. *Religious Change in America.* Cambridge: Harvard University Press.

Greeley, Andrew M., William McCready, and Kathleen McCourt. 1976. *Catholic Schools in a Declining Church.* Kansas City: Sheed and Ward.

Gonzalez, Roberto O., and Michael LaVelle. 1985. *The Hispanic Catholic in the U.S.: A Sociocultural and Religious Profile.* New York: Northeast Catholic Pastoral Center for Hispanics.

Halsey, William M. 1980. *The Survival of American Innocence: Catholicism in an Era of Disillusionment.* Notre Dame: Notre Dame Press.

Hammond, Phillip. 1988. "Religion and the Persistence of Identity." *Journal for the Scientific Study of Religion,* 27 (March).

Herberg, Will. 1955. *Protestant-Catholic-Jew: An Essay in American Religious Sociology.* Garden City, N.Y.: Doubleday.

Hoge, Dean R. 1981. *Converts, Dropouts, Returnees: A Study of Religious Change among Catholics.* New York: Pilgrim Press.

————. 1986. "Interpreting Change in Roman Catholicism: The River and the Floodgate." *Review of Religious Research,* 27, 4 (June).

Jackman, Mary R., and Robert W. Jackman. 1983. *Class Awareness in the United States.* Berkeley: University of California Press.

Kelly, James R. 1984. "Catholicism and Modern Memory: Some Sociological Reflections on the Symbolic Foundations of the Rhetorical Force of the Pastoral Letter, 'The Challenge of Peace.'" *Sociological Analysis,* 45, 2 (Summer).

Kennedy, Eugene. 1984. *The Now and Future Church: The Psychology of Being an American Catholic.* Garden City, N.Y.: Doubleday.

Kluegel, James R., and Eliot R. Smith. 1986. *Beliefs about Inequality: Americans' Views of What Is and What Ought to be.* New York: Aldine de Gruyter.

Langan, John P. 1984. "The Bishops and the Bottom Line." *Commonweal,* November 2–16.

Leege, David C. 1985. "Catholic Parishes in the 1980s." *Church,* 17 (Summer).

Lenski, Gerhard. 1961. *The Religious Factor: A Sociological Study of Religion's Impact on Politics, Economics, and Family Life.* Garden City, N.Y.: Doubleday.

Lesko, Nancy. 1988. *Symbolizing Society: Stories, Rites, and Structure in a Catholic High School*. New York: Falmer Press.

McAuley, E. Nancy, and Moira Mathieson. 1986. *Faith Without Form: Beliefs of Catholic Youth*. Kansas City: Sheed and Ward.

McBrien, Richard P. 1981. *Catholicism*. Minneapolis: Winston.

McCarthy, Mary. 1946. *Memories of a Catholic Girlhood*. New York: Harcourt, Brace.

McCready, William C., and Andrew M. Greeley. 1972. "The End of American Catholicism?" *America,* October 28.

McLaren, Peter. 1986. *Schooling as Ritual Performance: Towards a Political Economy of Educational Symbols and Gestures*. London: Routledge and Kegan Paul.

McNamara, Patrick H. 1985. "Conservative Christian Families and Their Moral World: Some Reflections for Sociologists." *Sociological Analysis,* 46, 2 (Summer).

McSweeney, William. 1980. *Roman Catholicism: The Search for Relevance*. New York: St. Martin's Press.

Moberg, David O., and Dean R. Hoge. 1986. "Catholic College Students' Religious and Moral Attitudes, 1961 to 1982: Effects of the Sixties and Seventies." *Review of Religious Research,* 28, 2 (December).

Mueller, Daniel P., and Philip W. Cooper. 1986. "Religious Interest and Involvement of Young Adults: A Research Note." *Review of Religious Research,* 27 (March).

National Catholic Educational Association. 1985. *The Catholic High School: A National Portrait*. Washington, D.C.: National Catholic Educational Association.

———. 1985. *Effective Catholic Schools: An Exploration*. Washington, D.C.: National Catholic Educational Association.

Neuhaus, Richard John. 1987. *The Catholic Moment: The Paradox of the Church in the Postmodern World*. San Francisco: Harper and Row.

Olson, James S. 1987. *Catholic Immigrants in America*. Chicago: Nelson-Hall.

Parks, Sharon. 1986. *The Critical Years: The Young Adult in Search for a Faith to Live By*. San Francisco: Harper and Row.

Parsons, Talcott. 1954. *Essays in Sociological Theory,* rev. ed. New York: Free Press.

————. 1951. *The Social System.* Glencoe, IL: Free Press.

Roof, Clark, and William McKinney. 1987. *American Mainline Religion: Its Changing Shape and Future.* New Brunswick, N.J.: Rutgers University Press.

Sanders, James W. 1977. *The Education of an Urban Minority: Catholics in Chicago, 1833–1965.* New York: Oxford University Press.

Schwartz, Gary. 1987. *Beyond Conformity or Rebellion: Youth and Authority in America.* Chicago: University of Chicago Press.

Seidler, John, and Katherine Meyer. 1989. *Conflict and Change in the Catholic Church.* New Brunswick, N.J.: Rutgers University Press.

Shils, Edward. 1981. *Tradition.* Chicago: University of Chicago Press.

Swidler, Ann. 1986. "Culture in Action: Symbols and Strategies." *The American Sociological Review,* 51 (April).

Veverke, Faye. 1985. "The Ambiguity of Catholic Educational Separatism." *Religious Education,* 80, 1.

Weber, Max. 1978. *Economy and Society,* vol. 1. edited by G. Roth and C. Wittich. Berkeley: University of California Press.

————. 1946. "The Social Psychology of World Religions." In H. H. Gerth and C. Wright Mills, eds., *From Max Weber: Essays in Sociology.* New York: Oxford University Press, pp. 260–305.

Wills, Gary. 1973. *Bare Ruined Choirs.* New York: Doubleday.

Yankelovich, Daniel. 1981. *New Rules: Searching for Self-Fulfillment in a World Turned Upside-Down.* New York: Bantam.

Zeitlin, Irving M. 1968. *Ideology and the Development of Sociological Theory.* Englewood Cliffs: Prentice-Hall.

# Index

# Subject Index

**219**